Courtney Love's MTV . . .

"Kurt Loder was supposed to interview Courtney at the MTV Music Video Awards, but the newscaster was running late. She could see the back of his head, in an area upstage—so she headed up the curving stair to push her way in.

"Alas, Kurt was mid-interview with Madonna.

"Alas, Courtney didn't care—and between apologizing to the off-camera VJ Tabitha Soren for previously calling her 'a thin-lipped Republican bitch,' and explaining to Madonna who she was— 'Hi, Madonna, we've met, remember Maverick [Madonna's label] wanted to sign me?'—she just sat down and barged in.

"'Don't worry,' she confided to Madonna, who was looking at her warily, 'I've never clocked anyone in my life.'

"And then, unknown to the viewing masses, since it was edited from the show, she fell off her chair and stuck her legs straight up, imitating the Wicked Witch of the East.

"So very, very Courtney."

Courtney LOVE:
queen
of
noise

A Most Unauthorized Biography

Melissa Rossi

POCKET BOOKS
New York London Toronto Sydney Tokyo Singapore

An *Original* Publication of POCKET BOOKS

 POCKET BOOKS, a division of Simon & Schuster Inc.
1230 Avenue of the Americas, New York, NY 10020

ISBN: 0-671-00038-1

First Pocket Books printing May 1996

10 9 8 7 6 5 4 3 2 1

POCKET and colophon are registered trademarks of
Simon & Schuster Inc.

Cover photo Bob Gruen/StarFile

Printed in the U.S.A.

Dedicated to Portland, Oregon,
a town filled with characters
every bit as fascinating as Courtney

Acknowledgments

Special thanks to: Jennifer Lobianco, Katherine Dunn, Neal Karlen, Marco Collins, Scott Soderstrom, Craig Hillman, Sue Carswell, Gus Van Sant, Leslie Rae, the British Maggie Simpson, Chuck Walton, Tinuviel, Jeannette Walls, Adam Fisher, Robin Rosemond, Buck Munger, Dave Hite, Peter Davis, Tom Cunneff, Bill Donahue, Mario Lalich, Carl Abramovic, Tina Randolph, B. J. Robbins, Joel Selvin, Luisa Caldwell, Farai Chideya, Stryker McGuire, Steve Hochman, Dave Stern, Anne Pramaggiore, Mark McLaughlin, Hillcrest, Anne Grgich, Tup, Billy Ruane, Bon Vivant Bob, Hank Harrison, a whole bunch of "Deep Throats" who don't want their names mentioned, the *L.A. Times'* library staff, Liberty Studios, Matt Groening and "The Simpsons."

Introduction

The universe has a sense of humor, I'm convinced. It's just a really warped sense of humor. Take, for instance, how this book came about.

I was yammering away on the phone to a literary agent, talking about a novel I'd just finished, saying, "I love writing fiction, it makes me happier than anything in the world, and I never, ever want to write non-fiction again."

Right then—prompted no doubt by my use of the word "never"—Call Waiting clicked in. On the line was Sue Carswell, a savvy-sounding editor from Pocket Books. She said they were interested in having me write a biography of Courtney Love—another way of saying they were interested in seeing me prematurely wrinkle and gray.

With an important proposition like that winging my way, there was but one way for me to respond: "Uh, I'll call you back." And I went back to the other line and yammered some more about my novel and how much I'd come to hate journalism.

But as hard as I tried to forget it, the idea of writing a bio of Courtney kept coming back to the forefront of my feeble mind. After all, I'd tried to write one twice already. Once, three years before, Courtney had suggested I pen a book about her. Back then, in 1992, the response was outright laughter when I pitched it. The editor suggested I just forget about Courtney, because everyone else would. Clearly he was wrong.

In February 1995 I'd been approached to write a book about her again. This time, however, the person who approached me was the first big love of her life: the charming and talented Rozz Rezabek, former Portland rock star and unofficial keeper of the Courtney archives. When he showed up at my door lugging suitcases filled with her numerous love letters to him, her diaries, which she'd left scattered across Portland, his diaries, and his fan letters, which she'd graded, I knew he was serious.

It was obvious why Courtney had been so taken with him. Rozz is a wonderfully entertaining person: he quickly dubbed SoHo, where I then lived, "So-so" and continually rapped a song about Courtney that he'd made up. It went something like, "She used to be my stalker, now I'm her number one fan, gonna hitch my Ford to her star, like Tom did to Roseanne."

However, despite his charisma, which equals Courtney's, problems quickly emerged. For instance, he didn't want the book to mention Courtney's husband, Kurt Cobain. Rozz also refused to listen to her record, *Live Through This,* though from the little he'd heard, he did construct a botched line from the Hole song, "Doll Parts," that he sang over and over: "Someday you will ache from too much cake."

Alas, the book project was ill-fated. I should have seen it coming, since the omens were there right away: my computer blew up the day Rozz and I were to meet an agent; on our way to meet an editor, our cab got in a wreck. And a few days into the book, after talking to Courtney, Rozz left me a note saying he'd gone for the suitcase full of money, though I was welcome to find a suitcase of my own.

I dropped the Courtney project and wrote my really stupid novel instead.

And so when Pocket Books called a few months later, after I'd returned to Seattle, I wasn't quite sure how to respond.

I sought guidance from my friends, and their advice fell

into two categories: those who lived in forty-nine of the United States said, "Go for it." Those who lived in Seattle, or any of the outlying areas of Washington State, said, "Forget it." It was a bad-karma book, I was told; Courtney was spent. No one would buy it. I shouldn't stoop so low. She would kill me.

The answer seemed clear; write the book, and then hightail it out of Seattle.

So I did. But not before first getting an initial okay from her—though she informed me from the start she refused to authorize this. As it turned out, she didn't give me an interview at all, but at least she didn't directly interfere.

From the beginning of this project, one thing became obvious. Courtney is a self-perpetuating myth. The trail she leaves is not a solid line of black or white; it's a shattered mosaic that winds across the world, making it impossible to track down and verify every tale that she's told. In some cases, I simply had to rely on previously published reports about her childhood, particularly as her mother did not want to be interviewed.

In the course of telling her story—a task that involved interviewing people who know her and piecing together information supplied in published articles—some of her myths may have crept through. With Courtney it's hard to gain the full and total truth, with or without her cooperation.

But since Courtney and I have spent some time together and have lived in both Portland and Seattle at the same time, I hope this book provides a context for her life. And since some people were willing to talk about their experiences with her I believe it gives insight as well.

As for my personal feeling about Ms. Love—I like her, a lot, at least every other day. On those days I can clearly see her talent, her genius, how she's risen above many sad circumstances, and how she's healed her many wounds with creativity and humor. On the days in between, I can clearly see her manipulativeness, and how easy it seems for her to use people.

But even on the days when I'm not much of a fan, I still admire her for sticking to dreams and for creating such a remarkable persona that she simply never gets boring. All in all, I find Courtney inspiring.

Is there a moral to her story? I think there are several, including "Don't give up on your dreams." There is an obvious allegory about heroin, which Courtney as well as Kurt likened to the devil, and their lives clearly illustrate the hellishness of that opiate. There's also a message about family planning. While life as we know it is certainly richer with Courtney and her daughter, Frances, on board, it seems pretty obvious that if they had been born at later times, under more stable circumstances, their early childhoods would not have been so unsettled.

A final message that is embedded in this book came to me while I was writing it. One day it struck me that I should have a thesaurus—a thought that I immediately resisted. A thesaurus always strikes me as cheating somehow; and besides, since I was moving, I didn't want to buy any more books. For several hours I debated the thesaurus issue, deciding that I wouldn't buy one—but if I had one, I'd use it. Heading out several hours later, I opened the door of my apartment building—to find a new thesaurus lying on the ground.

The point is, life is magical—a fact we forget in our eight-to-five, four-walled, scientifically explained world. But it's something Courtney never forgets; in a time when anything is possible, she seems capable of manifesting it all.

With that bit of moralizing, I'll sign off, fully Courtneyed out, and go back to writing my stupid little novels.

Underground Who's Who:
An Incomplete and Abbreviated Guide to
Denizens of the Underground

This guide reflects certain VIPs in Courtney's life, and her relationship to them; it does not attempt to cover all of their accomplishments.

Alex Cox. Director of several acclaimed cult films including *Repo Man* and *Sid and Nancy*. Alex cast Courtney in a small role in the latter. He also directed the stinker *Straight to Hell,* a spoof western in which Courtney played a leading role.

Amanda de Cadenet. Actress and former star of the popular British TV show *The Word,* on which Kurt Cobain proclaimed Courtney the "best fuck in the world." Amanda was Courtney's date to the 1995 Academy Awards and was interviewed by Courtney for *Interview* magazine that spring. Shortly after befriending Courtney, Amanda separated from her husband, John Taylor of Duran Duran.

Billy Corgan. Talented lead singer and songwriter for the popular Smashing Pumpkins. He met Courtney when Hole toured the United States in 1990, and was at one point Courtney's boyfriend. He was hated by Courtney's husband, Kurt Cobain, who referred to Billy as "the Pear-Shaped Box." Billy's relationship with Courtney is often hinted at by how she dedicates the Hole song "Violet," which was written for Billy.

Britt Collins. British coauthor of an unauthorized biography of Nirvana begun in 1992 with Victoria Clarke. The book, which the Cobains wanted halted after learning the writers had interviewed Lynn Hirschberg, was a continuing source of tension. The Cobains made numerous threatening calls to the biographers—which the writers released in the form of a tape—and the Cobains were also alleged to have been behind a break-in at the biographers' apartment, which the Cobains denied; the Cobains alleged the biographers were going through their trash. The book, when it was finally turned in to publisher Hyperion, was reportedly followed by a fifty-page fax from the Cobain lawyers listing segments they intended to legally pursue. Publication of the book was canceled, and like her cowriter, Britt seems to have disappeared into the underground. *See also* Victoria Clarke.

Bruce Pavitt. Co-owner of Seattle's premier independent-label Sub Pop, which grew out of Bruce's fanzine *Subterranean Pop* and later music column in the Seattle rock rag *The Rocket.* The label was the first to record Nirvana and made a bundle when the trio was signed to a major label. Time Warner bought 49 percent of the profitable company in the winter of 1994, and Sub Pop generously supported many local projects.

Carolyn Rue. Hole's drummer from 1990 to 1992, when she was fired after a recording session.

Courtney Michelle Harrison Rodriguez Menely Moreland Love-Cobain. Born July 9, 1964, Courtney is a one-word contradiction.

Dave Grohl. Shy and handsome drummer for Nirvana, who as the latecomer to the band often seemed to feel left out. Shortly after Kurt's death, Dave came out from behind the drum set and took over as head of the acclaimed new band, Foo Fighters.

Dean Mathiesen. Former Portland drag queen, club manager, and performance artist, the hilarious scenester was one of the first to see Courtney's potential, even when she was a teenager. After Kurt's death, he dropped a book offer to fly to Courtney's side and become her assistant. He serves as the anchor in Courtney's Seattle's household and works as a DJ at Seattle clubs such as Linda's Tavern.

Drew Barrymore. The tiny blond actress who appeared in E.T. as a child. Met Hole guitarist Eric Erlandson one night when she was puking, and it was pretty much love at first sight, especially after her purse was stolen during one of their first dates and Eric found it. The movie actress who gave David Letterman a topless shake on his show often attends Hole performances.

Eddie Vedder. Lead singer for Seattle band Pearl Jam. Often regarded as Kurt Cobain's rival, Eddie made several efforts to lessen competition between the two lead singers. Canceled Pearl Jam's summer tour after Kurt's death.

Eric Erlandson. Sweet and soft-spoken lead guitar player for Hole. Eric grew up in a religious home in California, where his father was dean of Loyola Marymount College. A former accountant for a major record label, Eric met Courtney when she placed an ad looking for people to start a band. He's among Courtney's most loyal and dedicated friends and is her surrogate brother. He dates actress Drew Barrymore.

Everett True. An influential writer for the British paper *Melody Maker* who broke much of the news about Courtney and Kurt. A barometer for talent, Everett often covers the hippest American bands before the mainstream American press even hears of them.

Frances Bean Cobain. The only child of Courtney and Kurt, born on August 18, 1992. Los Angeles child service authorities forced the Cobains to briefly give her up, to Courtney's half sister, shortly thereafter. The circumstances surrounding her birth traumatized the Cobains, though they regained custody shortly after she was taken away. Frances, a.k.a. the Bean, is a shy and beautiful child who lives most of the year in Seattle, where she often plays on Kurt's drum set in the basement. As a toddler she frequently talked to a tapestry of Jesus hanging on the wall, believing the image in the rug was her deceased father.

Gold Mountain. The management company for both Nirvana and Hole until mid-1995.

Hank Harrison. Courtney's real father, a.k.a. BioDad. Author of seven books on esoteric topics ranging from the Grateful Dead's days in the Haight to the Holy Grail, Hank was the first of the several husbands of Courtney's mother, whom he married in late 1963. After their divorce he lost custody of his firstborn and did not see Courtney from age five until she was a teenager. Hank, who heads a small publishing company, wrote an unauthorized posthumous biography of Kurt. He lives in Palo Alto on a horse ranch and awaits the day when Courtney's limo will pull up in his driveway and he will meet Frances.

Heroin. Dope, black tar, smack. The highly addictive, pain-numbing opiate that is regarded as the champagne of drugs in some music and artistic circles. It almost invariably comes hand in hand with deceit and guilt, and often theft and death.

Ian McCulloch. Head man for 1980's new wave band Echo and the Bunnymen. Ian allegedly rebuffed the young Courtney Love when she was visiting Liverpool. She bragged that in retaliation she swiped his fancy stage jackets, which she reportedly gave to Rozz. She also admitted to swiping Ian's stage poses.

James Moreland. Cross-dressing lead singer for the L.A. punk group Leaving Trains. James was briefly married to Courtney in 1989.

Jennifer Finch. The bass player for L7. She was part of Courtney's first band, Sugar Baby Doll, and she helped to launch Courtney into acting.

Jill Emery. Hole's bass player from 1990 to 1992, when she abruptly quit after a Hole show in L.A.

Jim Rose Circus Sideshow. Eaters of razor blades, light bulbs, and maggots, this troupe of human marvels inadvertently served as matchmakers when they couldn't make it for the first two weeks of the Nine Inch Nails' The Downward Spiral tour. Hole was called in as a temporary replacement. *See also* Trent Reznor.

Jonathan Poneman. The other mastermind of the Seattle label Sub Pop. This reserved entrepreneur also wrote articles about grunge and about the Cobains for *Vogue* and *Spin*.

Julian Cope. The charismatic lead singer for the Teardrop Explodes, a New Wave band based in Liverpool that broke up in 1982, not long after Courtney left town. Although Julian blasted his former acid-dropping pal Courtney in 1992, taking out full-page ads to condemn her, they are said to be on friendly terms now.

Kathleen Hanna. Frontwoman for the riot grrrl band Bikini Kill, Kathleen, a.k.a. Ratface, was a former friend of Kurt's and is credited with inspiring the title of one of Nirvana's biggest hits, "Smells like Teen Spirit." The Olympia resident is an enemy of Courtney's however. She filed assault charges against Courtney in July 1995, when Courtney punched her at Lollapalooza.

Kat Bjelland. Courtney's enemy-friend from Portland and a co-inventor of the so-called Kinderwhore look. With Courtney and Jennifer Finch, she started a band called Sugar

Baby Doll, which broke up in weeks. Kat also formed the Minneapolis-based Babes in Toyland, a band with which Courtney played briefly before being booted.

Kim Gordon. Bassist and singer in the alternative band Sonic Youth. Kim coproduced Hole's first album, *Pretty on the Inside.*

Krist Novoselic. While growing up in the logging town of Aberdeen, Washington, Krist befriended Kurt Cobain and started a band with him that went through a series of names, including Throat Oyster, until they landed on Nirvana. Krist, the bass player, who was one of Kurt's oldest friends, was frustrated by the singer's continuing heroin use and was part of the final intervention in March 1994. Politically active and of Croatian descent, Krist has written about and played for Bosnian relief efforts and censorship causes. He started up a new band, Sweet 75.

Kristen Pfaff. Regarded as one of the best female bass players in the country, Kristen left Minnesota and her band, Janitor Joe, to join Hole after bassist Jill Emery quit. A brooding beauty, Kristen developed a heroin habit in Seattle, and in June 1994, died of an overdose the night before she was to leave town.

Kurt Cobain. Courtney's second husband, the troubled, depressed, and extremely talented head man for the trio Nirvana, whose record *Nevermind* sold ten million copies and revolutionized the music industry, helping to create the new genre known as grunge. Kurt was ultimately made to feel guilty about his success by his anti-corporate peers, and he was plagued by his heroin addiction, which he tried unsuccessfully to kick many times. After escaping a drug rehab center in California, he returned to Seattle in early April 1994 and shot himself on April 6. His suicide triggered copycat suicides across the world. He was, by most accounts, a loving father to his only child, Frances. Although he was usually a pacifist, Kurt's violent streak was roused when he perceived that his family was threatened.

Linda Carroll. Courtney's mother, a.k.a. Linda Risi, Harrison, Rodriguez, Menely. She became a therapist in Oregon best known for convincing fugitive Katherine Ann Power to turn herself in after twenty-three years of dodging authorities for a robbery turned murder. Courtney has said that Linda was "mortified" when the media reported that Courtney was her daughter.

Linda's. A hipster tavern on Seattle's Capitol Hill, where musicians often hang and where the graffiti on the bathroom walls reflect the sentiments of the hour. The bar is co-owned by Sub Pop's Bruce and Jon as well as Linda Derschang, who lent her name to the joint.

Lynn Hirschberg. A talented writer who profiled Courtney for the September 1992 issue of *Vanity Fair*. The Cobains blamed the reporter when they briefly lost custody of their infant after the magazine article appeared. They launched a full frontal attack that included threats of legal action and phone calls threatening to slice up and disembowel the reporter's dog. Lynn, a.k.a. Scapegoat, maintained that her story was correct and that Kurt was still using drugs despite his frequent denials to the press. Articles appearing after Kurt's death seemed to vindicate her and her story concerning him.

Marco Collins. The hip, trend-setting DJ for Seattle radio station KNDD. Marco is one of the DJ's whom national magazines call when they want to know who's hot. He is credited with extending the lifetime of Hole's *Live Through This* into 1995 by playing cuts such as "Violet." When Courtney calls, Marco sometimes puts her on the air live, where she has been known to rattle on for over an hour.

Mark Arm. Lead singer of the Seattle band Mudhoney. He first inspired Courtney to stage-dive, and was among her many musician crushes.

Mary Lou Lord. Massachusetts-based folk singer who briefly dated Kurt prior to his engagement with Courtney. Mary Lou has written several songs about the Cobains and has become another of the females whom Courtney hates. Courtney once chased her down Sunset Boulevard and has frequently attacked her in the press and from the stage. "Mary-Lou Lording" is Courtney's term for giving people she hates free press; the term is based on how she helped make Mary Lou's name well-known by frequently railing about her.

Melissa auf der Maur. A lovely photography student from Canada who was called in to play bass for Hole after bassist Kristen Pfaff's death.

Melissa Rossi. A klutzy, occasionally stuttering dork who unintentionally falls into happening scenes and, sometimes, into umbrella stands. Melissa looks as if she hasn't brushed her hair since around 1963, and she's often accused of having graduated from the Courtney Love School of House-keeping.

Melody Maker. A widely read British music paper, which ran numerous articles about Kurt and Courtney. The first well-read publication to rave about Courtney and her band, Hole.

Milos Forman. Award-winning director of *One Flew Over the Cuckoo's Nest* and *Amadeus.* Forman fought to hire Courtney for a Larry Flynt film he was directing.

Patty Schemel. Stunning, thoughtful red-haired drummer for Hole. Patty was initially considered as drummer for Kurt's band, Nirvana. She's the only member of Hole who was born in Washington, though she moved to L.A. before the grunge craze hit Seattle.

Riot Grrrl. A loosely based network of female artistic types, many of whom live in Olympia, Washington, and Washington, D.C. Linked by fanzines and records, the riot grrrl "movement" spawned many bands in the early 1990s, often made up of members living in different cities. These grrrls hate the media.

Robert Hilburn. Pop writer and editor for the *Los Angeles Times,* whom the Cobains respected and trusted.

Rozz Rezabek-Wright. Lead singer for several bands in the early 1980s, including Theatre of Sheep. This charismatic and talented singer-songwriter was one of Courtney's first loves and is still the keeper of the unofficial Courtney Love Archives, a collection of hundreds of letters and journals. Rozz is said to be working on a book about her, and his talent seems destined to lead him back into music, which he shrugged off in the mid-1980s, leaving Portland and his band, mostly to escape Courtney.

Tom Grant. An L.A.-based private investigator whom Courtney hired to find Kurt in April 1994 after he ran away from a rehab facility. Grant later publicized his opinions about Kurt's death, claiming that Kurt was murdered. He took his theories to the Internet.

Trent Reznor. The dashing rural Pennsylvania-born head of Nine Inch Nails, a popular industrial band. Hole toured briefly with his group, and Courtney developed major thang for Trent.

Thurston Moore. Front man for one of the original alternative bands, Sonic Youth, Moore was influential to both Kurt and Courtney. He's married to Kim Gordon, who co-produced Courtney's first album, *Pretty on the Inside.* When Sonic Youth toured with Hole on Lollapalooza '95, Thurston peppered his on-line diary of the event with many anecdotes about Courtney.

Vanity Fair. The spicy magazine filled with celebrity profiles. *VF* ran two articles about Courtney, the first, in 1992, portrayed her as a drug-using, money-hungry opportunistic grunge mommy; the second, a cover story in June 1995, portrayed her as a misunderstood angel. Strangely enough, both stories were, by and large, accurate portrayals.

Victoria Clarke. Coauthor of an unauthorized book about Nirvana, which was eventually canceled. Victoria was the object of an alleged Courtney assault in the winter of 1992. Charges filed in L.A. were dropped and reportedly settled out of court. *See also* Britt Collins.

CHAPTER 1

So Courtney!
(July 4, 1995)

"FUUUUUUCK YOOOOOU!" THE RASPY WORDS ECHOED through the wind-gouged Columbia Gorge, a sacred Indian site where the mighty northwestern river whips past mounds of gust-twisted rock.

"I haaaaaate this fucking place!"

Courtney Love, lead singer for Hole, widow of Kurt Cobain, perpetual MTV news item and *National Enquirer* poster child, had obviously taken her spot on the stage.

It wasn't just any outdoor stage that Courtney had stumbled onto, beige garters peeking out from beneath her peach-colored baby-doll dress, blond hair mussed, demon diva look in her eyes. This particular stage, perched on a cliff, with the majestic Columbia River valley stretching out behind it and a sea of surging fans in front, was the kickoff site for the music festival Lollapalooza '95. In its fifth year, the musical extravaganza on wheels was the hottest ticket of the summer; with a slew of internationally known performers in tow, the six-week national tour was the equivalent of the Music Olympics, and on opening day the site was swarming with press.

So of course Courtney planned to put on a memorable show. She started with the customary pose—propping her foot on a monitor to maximize crotch-shot opportunities. At least for this occasion she was wearing undies. Baby blue, as the audience would soon find out when she leaned back and bent over. Then again, who knew how long the underwear would stay on. She was known to give it to fans in exchange for such items as Nine Inch Nails hats, which she promptly set on fire.

The thousands who formed a human avalanche running down the hill before her, were there not only to hear Hole, one of the most compelling bands of the nineties, a group that had stayed together in the face of death, drugs, and disaster and whose latest album *Live Through This* had sold over a million copies. Even more, the crowd that pushed toward the stage had gathered to witness the spectacle of Courtney, the fiery head woman whose stage stunts included performing faux fellatio on fans, pelting the audience with radishes, demonstrating the keys to autoeroticism with a guitar, and throwing a hissy fit or twenty-five of them, nightly. Not to mention that she often put on such soul-bearing performances that audience members went home talking about epiphanies.

Hole shows were events that gave fans stories to tell for weeks, if not years. Besides, with the self-destructive rampage she'd been kicking up for months, there was the often voiced possibility that every show might be lead singer Courtney Love's last.

It was more than morbid speculation by some, or wishful thinking by others: only three weeks before, on June 11, 1995, Courtney had nearly died from an overdose of prescription pills. (She later confessed to the *L.A. Times* that it was her second pharmaceutical OD that year; the first was a failed suicide attempt when her love life went sour.) But you sure couldn't tell that she'd had a close brush with death when she stepped on to the doll-covered stage that sultry evening in July as the sky paled behind her and the wind blew back her bleached hair.

For the opening show of Lollapalooza, it was hard to imagine that her red gash of a mouth would ever be closed, that Courtney would ever, could ever, lapse into permanent silence.

As she stood before the thousands gathered in her name, glaring contemptuously at the fans that she'd been trying to conjure up for a decade, Courtney provoked, confronted, and attacked, riling up the masses to do as she ordered.

"I want everybody to yell, 'Fuck you!'" she demanded, her knobby fingers wrapped around a cigarette.

They did, sending a field of verbal assault echoing down the river.

"Now," she commanded, "on the count of three, everyone say, 'Bitch!'"

The masses once again complied.

"Feel better now?" she sassed, a smirk snaking across her plump, lipstick-smeared lips.

Once the singer-audience greetings had been exchanged, Courtney did not disappoint those who had come to hear her one-woman ramble while her chipped green guitar hung from her neck like an albatross. At least during this slurred monologue, unlike some shows, she didn't give the details of her yeast infection or slag off the many rock stars who'd offended her that month. She merely screamed at a woman, demanding that she rip off her top, then flashed her in return. She harassed a few "math boys"—her term for linear thinkers—asking them what they expected, a frat party? Then, sneering, she said, "Can you even name one Sonic Youth song?" She demanded the shirt from only one fan, who was wearing one on which was emblazoned a photo of Courtney's three-year-old child, Frances Bean.

And Hole didn't let down those who had come for the music. Once Courtney finally shut up, and the band started playing, they ripped through their songs, which were broken up by Gregorian chants and whispered confessions. "I am the girl you know can't look you in the eye," Courtney cooed. "I am doll parts," she mewed. "I'm Miss World," she boasted. "I'm overfed," she screamed. "I lie and lie and lie," she confessed. "I want to be the girl with the most cake," she demanded. "Somebody kill me, please," she begged, again via song.

Always larger than life, Courtney was transformed onstage into a mystical presence, channeling both demons and angels, as she dropped to her knees, felt herself up, opened her mouth so wide she could have been giving head to the mike, and loosed a voice filled with seduction and rage, which suddenly softened to that of a scared child only to rise again to a from-the-gut bellowing.

In the 1970s Helen Reddy sang "I am woman, hear me roar." In the 1990s Courtney Love jumped directly to the roaring, complete with its own sexist logic. "When I get what I want," she belted, "I never want it again!"

It was sometimes off-key roaring, but Hole's music could touch the soul, and it was coupled with a dramatic tension that didn't betray Courtney's unseen smirk that she was actually pulling it off.

Although Hole wasn't the headlining act—the avant-punk rock group Sonic Youth was—and though there were a dozen other acts through the day, many of the 18,000 present had come mainly to see Courtney. She was the most compelling, memorable, and archetypal figure to emerge from the underground music scene since her late husband, Kurt Cobain, who had headed Nirvana, the alternative rock band that changed the music of the late twentieth century, much as the Beatles had done thirty years before.

In the year since Nirvana's lead singer died—and Hole's *Live Through This* was voted album of the year by everybody who mattered, including *Spin, Rolling Stone,* and *The Village Voice*—Courtney had proved herself to be more than just the widow Cobain, more than just a blazing talent who led Hole like a war-crying Apache swooping down to assault the crowd with song. Taking full advantage of the microphones dangling before her and the cameras snapping in her trail, Courtney Love drew enough attention to brand her name, image, and antics into the collective consciousness; she forged herself into a media icon, number two only to O.J. in the 1995 troublemaking celebrity department.

Hole was the band, but Courtney was the one-woman myth. She was the high priestess of rock and roll, a performer simultaneously one with headspinner Linda Blair and Glinda the Good. She was the Dark Angel followed by tragedy, the Drama Queen who lived life like a movie, the Black Widow unable to find a new boyfriend, the Wicked Witch of the Northwest who ranted about the Seattle drug scene while admitting to her own occasional heroin use, the media victim forever calling attention to herself. Like a kaleidoscope, Courtney's image was forever transmuting, depending on her mood and the viewer's perspective.

Most people, regardless of what they thought of her in-your-face feminism and her constant bids for attention, were in agreement about one thing: Courtney was a survivor, a veritable phoenix who kept rising out of the ashes, scarcely burned. And wherever she went, whatever she did, she was permanently trailed by the question, "What will she do next?"

Courtney Michelle Harrison Rodriguez Menely Moreland Love-Cobain was born for the stage; she ruled it like a dictator, with such power, venom, and sexual fury that she overshadowed the others in the group: guitarist Eric Erlandson, drummer Patty Schemel, and bassist Melissa Auf der Maur, dubbed by the British press "the Other Three," though "the Silent Three" would have been a more appropriate term, given the way she overpowered them in interviews.

It wasn't fair, but with Courtney nothing was. She suffered from a new kind of attention deficit disorder:

when she didn't have everyone's attention, she did something outrageous to get it. Courtney was the queen bitch, and her presence alone ensured that a Hole show was neither a wooden recitation of tunes that sounded better in the studio nor a rote mouthing of the hits— despite the fact that her set list was often the same, as were her stunts.

Her bellows, rants, and onstage theatrics—telling off band members, laying into audiences, or jumping wide-eyed into the crowd only to complain about her orifices being probed—were as predictable as the ritual dismemberment and tossing of dolls to the audience during "Doll Parts," one of Hole's most popular songs.

That song was, in part, a joke—not only mocking stereotyped images of Barbie Doll good looks but also alluding to *Valley of the Dolls,* the trashy 1960s novel by Jacqueline Susann wherein the dolls are actually pills. And with Courtney there were so many—jokes, that is. The name of the band, for instance, was inspired partly by her mother's warning, "You can't walk around with a big hole inside of yourself," partly by a line from *Medea,* "There's a hole that pierces right through me," and partly by the obvious. She mocked almost everything that had ever hurt her, from the Joni Mitchell song "Clouds," which she'd been forced to sing during car trips as a child and which she purposely mangled on her first album, to cruel names she'd once been called and that she now satirized in songs such as "Pee Girl" and "Retard Girl."

Her retort to media portrayals of her as the Bad Mother Demon was to scream in her songs, "Burn the witch, just bring me back her head" and "I don't do the dishes, I throw them in the crib." Courtney even mocked her notorious slovenliness; she often had a banner hanging behind her onstage, stating in big sparkly letters "Cleanliness is next to godliness."

Courtney was wickedly funny; she was also bigger than the sum of the other parts of the band. She dominated the sometimes raucous, sometimes whispered songs, most of which were generally thought to be her own creations, though the credit always went to Hole.

Predictably, the first Hole performance for Lollapalooza '95 was not without Courtney-audience interaction of the physical sort. Midway through the set, sometime around "Asking for It"—a song written after she'd been attacked after jumping into the crowd—the tossing of bodies into the mosh pit became frenzied; when the women who rode atop the wave of bodies were being grabbed and crushed, Courtney brought the performance to a screeching halt.

"Leave that poor girl alone!" she yelled at the men; one by one, she rescued the women being tossed about by giving them a hand up onto stage, where they lined up as if on *Geraldo,* holding the dolls that were used as props. Courtney then launched into a verbal attack, noting how guys might get banged up in the mosh pit, but the women typically got felt up.

Violence and groping were the unfortunate reality in that area in front of the stage where the audience smashed together and passed its more foolish members overhead. People were frequently hurt, sometimes breaking bones; women were typically mauled. Courtney had learned that firsthand, apparently every time she dived into the crowd, but at this show she didn't tolerate it. At one point, when the mosh pit antics continued, and there was no more room for rescued women on the stage, Courtney simply marched off, leaving the band to guess her next move.

A stagehand ran out and announced her demands. "Courtney's not going to come back unless you make her feel wanted," he told them ominously.

One of the fans led a chant, begging her to return, while Courtney stood backstage smoking and laughing. When the chant grew louder, she finally sauntered back to the mike to finish the set with "Rock Star," her parody of Olympia, Washington, and some of its riot grrrl bands, including the all-girl trio Bikini Kill. The song, filled with fake giggles and simplistic guitar playing, speared the so-called grrrl revolution. "We look the same, we talk the same, we even fuck the same," she sang in the intentionally mistake-filled song.

After an hour of screaming, chanting, taunting, and bellowing, Courtney signed off, climbed onto the back of a security man, and was piggybacked offstage, where little Frances, the result of the whirlwind coupling that was Courtney plus Kurt, was waiting.

Courtney was still the queen. The victor. The show-stealer. She was once again the star, the phoenix rising from the ashes.

The crowd was wild, and many left immediately, not staying for headliners Sonic Youth; the critics were ecstatic as they raced back to write glowing reviews.

Courtney, however, was bummed.

Backstage, lumbering off the burly guard's back, she ran to her manager, crying. When she returned to the side of the stage minutes later, she'd changed into a black slip, a color that matched her mood.

Courtney had been in a bad one since about the time the bus was loaded up and swinging along the highway from Seattle to the Columbia Gorge, the day before the festival opened. And, as always, nobody knew the details of her emotional state better than Hole's lead guitarist, Eric Erlandson. Tall, thin, chalky pale, and soft-spoken, the former record label accountant was more than a guitarist and Courtney's occasional collaborater, a role he's played for the past six years. After a stint as her boyfriend early on in the band's career, he's now Courtney's best friend, her adopted "evil brother," her liaison with lawyers, her adviser, and, since Kurt's death, her surrogate husband. Eric was so dedicated that he even played with the band on the night his father died, because he knew that a *Vanity Fair* writer whom Courtney wanted to impress would be in the audience. Eric was often her whipping boy as well, the target of her vented frustration with the world, whom she sometimes referred to onstage as "the jerk." At shows where her voice was shot, and she dramatically gargled whiskey, she even blamed her throat problems on him, explaining that he'd provoked her to yell at him throughout the day.

On the tour bus that brought Hole to the town of George, Washington, home to the outdoor arena, she was again going off at the person she was prone to call "Eric Barrymore," since he's all but married to actress Drew, who'd trailed along on the tour. And Ms. Barrymore had been relegated to sister-in-law status: though Courtney liked her, she seemed to resent all the adoring press routinely heaped upon the twenty-year-old blonde for appearing on *The Late Show,* where Hole had never played, and for giving David Letterman a topless shake for his birthday. But Drew, after all, was a high-profile colleague, and she *did* have movie connections. All in all, there were pluses to having her hang around.

As the bus roared down forest-lined roads and through mountain passes, Courtney whined, between cigarettes, about not wanting to play this year's tour: it was more fun last year when she'd crashed—butting in on the Smashing Pumpkins' performances, showing up onstage uninvited, guitar in hand, ready to sing. The lineup for Lollapalooza '95, she complained, was "all Sonic Youth–approved, the Sonic Youth butt-kiss nation." Among the other acts—Beck, Sinéad O'Connor, the Jesus Lizard, Pavement, the Mighty Mighty Bosstones, and Cypress Hill—there wasn't one person she wanted to bed. Boring.

Already there'd been talk that none of the musicians wanted to hang out with Courtney, that they were wary she'd been invited along, that few expected her to last the whole six-week tour. Well, screw them. She ranted on and on, even screaming about the hickey Drew had given Eric—clearly visible on his neck. How unprofessional. She snapped at Drew, who sat next to Eric, telling her to save her marks of passion for when the band wasn't on tour. Eric pointed out that the cigarette burn on Courtney's neck that was scabbing over didn't look too great, either, and that shut her up—for a while.

Patty Schemel, the red-haired drummer who had first auditioned for the band on her twenty-fifth birthday, wasn't fazed. Having toured with Hole for nearly two years, she merely took in Courtney's rants without comment, not even bristling when Courtney criticized her drumming onstage. But whenever Hole performed, Patty always wore the pained expression of a child awaiting the parental reaction backstage. Even her mother had asked her to lighten up and smile. But Courtney was demanding; she had fired the last drummer, displeased with her performance at a recording session.

The bandleader might be a pain, but working with her had payoffs: at one point Patty was living at the Cobain residence, and her girlfriend, who'd once been Frances's nanny, was hired as Courtney's tour assistant for the summer.

And as everyone who worked with her knew, whenever Courtney went off on her friends, she typically showed up later with an expensive gift for them. The next day, of course, she'd be ranting that no one gave *her* a present.

Bassist Melissa Auf der Maur, a fair-faced beauty with dark curls cascading down her back, was learning to listen attentively and to shut up—especially about her crushes. Not long before, when Melissa had met musician Jeff Buckley, and the air was zinging with the sparks from their mutual attraction, Courtney had butted right in, demanding his phone number. She used to do that sort of thing all the time in the band's early days, before she coupled with Kurt. Now that Courtney was single again, Melissa's conquests—Courtney said the bassist was just "going through a little phase, being the cutest bass player in indie rock, and knowing it"—opened the door for her own adventures.

Melissa did play a special role in the band: besides being the band's unofficial photographer, she served as Courtney's editor, given her ability to nix lyrics. She was also the one most likely to be criticized in print by Courtney, who often compared Melissa to her predecessor, Kristen Pfaff, who'd died the year before of a heroin overdose. As Courtney kept pointing out to the press, Melissa wasn't as good as Kristen, but she was learning.

When the bus pulled over for a pit stop along the way to the gorge, the entourage got out and a crowd quickly gathered—but they pushed the band aside and few paid attention to Courtney. Instead, they mobbed cute little Drew. Courtney was pissed.

Her mood didn't improve when she stepped off the bus at the concert grounds, cranky, and having a difficult time walking as her tranquilizers kicked in. The rest of the band headed backstage, knowing full well they were many hours late for the sound check that had been scheduled for that afternoon. Courtney went off to take a nap. When she finally showed up—helped along by two handlers—for the rehearsal the day before the first show, she cursed out the band, slurred her words incoherently, and was so messed up that she fell—an incident captured by the rock magazine *Rolling Stone.*

From the beginning, the tour managers and promoters seemed to be eyeing her every move warily, like nervous baby-sitters. There were rumors of an incident in the catering tent after Courtney supposedly slapped Frances for grabbing a cookie after being told not to. Indeed, Courtney had shown herself to be such a monster, so it was said, that she was almost immediately banned from the other bands' dressing rooms.

Lollapalooza was going to be a drag, all right. Thank God she'd brought her laptop and could tell the real story online. But that first evening, before she'd had a chance to crawl into "the void"—her term for the Internet—Courtney headed backstage to watch the final show of the lineup: Sonic Youth. As she stood in the wings smoking and munching corn chips and candy, she zeroed on a disturbing sight: Kathleen Hanna, the singer for the grrrl band Bikini Kill—the enemy! Or at least a leading name on Courtney's ongoing list of hated ones, most of them female.

Kathleen lived in Olympia, Washington, the college town that was headquarters of the riot grrrl movement, a quasi-political movement whose proponents put their opinions about sexism and the double standard to music. It was a scene that Courtney had come to loathe. She often trashed the riot grrrls in interviews and in songs.

And as much as she hated Olympia, she despised Kathleen more. A friend of Kurt when he lived in the town, Kathleen had actually given him the title of his first major hit when she wrote some graffiti on a wall in his house: "Kurt smells like Teen Spirit"—although back then Kurt didn't know she was referring to a deodorant for teenagers.

Kathleen's band, Bikini Kill, included Tobi Vail, an ex-girlfriend of Kurt's, who'd given him the heave-ho when he became a rock star; like many in the riot grrrl scene she considered him a corporate sellout when he made it big. Bikini Kill recorded on Kill Rock Stars, a small independent label headed by Slim Moon, himself the object of the occasional Courtney tirade. And if it that wasn't enough reason to commence World War III, the label also put out Mary Lou Lord, another woman who'd dated Kurt, and another of Courtney's hate objects. And during the uproar onstage at Lollapalooza, Kathleen had reportedly grabbed a mike and intoned "Hole is a *band*"—underscoring the fact that the group wasn't just Courtney. This was something that Courtney herself had said—but she didn't need Kathleen to point it out, thank you very much.

Earlier that day, when Courtney had seen the Bikini Kill singer hanging out with Sonic Youth, she'd hissed "Oh, so is Kathleen joining your band?"

Now just the sight of Kathleen Hanna, the symbol of so many things Courtney did not love, was enough to make her blood shoot up the temperature charts. Courtney glared for a second and then reportedly flicked a cigarette at Kathleen and followed it with her fist, throwing a classic sucker punch, not giving her victim a chance to dodge the blow. For a moment the people backstage thought Courtney and Kathleen were hugging amid the shower of chips and candy fluttering overhead.

But then Courtney ran off and hid behind her body-guard, later mustering her dignity and calling for Drew, who took her arm and escorted her away. Then, en route, when a bystander returned the bag of chips that Courtney had dropped in mid-battle, she thanked him, then pelted Kathleen with it. "Here, go feed the homeless!" she screamed before disappearing to the cottage that served as Hole's dressing room.

A roadie explained to bystanders, perhaps jokingly, that Courtney had propositioned Kathleen, who had declined her offer, telling Courtney she didn't like silicone.

The ordeal quickly went out on the Internet, courtesy of Sonic Youth's Thurston Moore, who described the mood of the entire Lollapalooza entourage as "bummed." In his report, Thurston didn't even refer to Courtney by name, instead calling her the "Hole singer" and writing that "Kathleen had decided that if the Hole singer attacked Kathleen, then Kathleen should respond by verbally challenging the offender to debate any and all feminist issues at a university of her choice. The Hole singer's retort was supposedly 'Debate? You can't even read!'" His version of the event was followed by Courtney's pithy online explanation, in which she did not deny the clocking charge. "I do believe," she wrote in her post, which was quickly blasted to modems worldwide, "eventually my fist . . . met [Kathleen's] Rathead, and it was orgasmic."

At the next show, Sugar Ray Love seemed unrepentant. In Vancouver, British Columbia, where her bandaged hand prevented her from playing guitar, Courtney explained to the crowd, "I punched some bitch in the mouth, and her teeth got in the way." Endorsing the Canadian beer company that was paying Hole $400,000 to perform at one heavily hyped gig in the Arctic Circle in September, she added, "Fuckin' Molson's, man . . . I douche with it, I wash my face with it, I smash chicks in the head with it."

So very Courtney.

And it was Courtney-like, too, that despite the rumors and the bets that she'd be off Lollapalooza in days, she lasted the whole tour. It was controversial Irish singer Sinéad O'Connor who walked, leaving the Lollapalooza promoters to learn she'd quit the tour when they read about in *USA Today*. The official word was that Sinéad's pregnancy and the sun weren't mixing, but rumor had it, of course, that Courtney and Sinéad had fought. The reality, according to Sonic Youth's Thurston Moore, who blabbed about Courtney over the Internet through the whole tour, was that the two females singers had bonded.

Courtney and Sinéad did have a lot in common. They were both iconoclasts who could induce chills in an audience, Sinéad with her strange, soulful spirituality and Courtney with her anger-choked songs and occasional charisma. One night, while Courtney cried at her table in the catering tent, Sinéad massaged her head, no doubt because of the headache caused by the Kathleen Hanna incident.

Hotheaded, quick-punching Courtney was in trouble: Kathleen had officially charged her with assault; she was also sending out letters saying Courtney was nuts and had to be stopped. These tactics aroused Courtney's fear that Frances would again be taken away. She pleaded with Sonic Youth to reason with Kathleen and later sent her brother to their dressing room with flowers, again asking them to talk to Kathleen and tell her to drop the charges. They declined and instead offered Bikini Kill the opening spot on their upcoming tour.

After the impromptu massage session, Sinéad and Courtney held an all-night talkathon on the bus while watching movies. Courtney later admitted that they hit a few raw spots, though she didn't give details, except to say Sinead convinced her to return to therapy. The next morning Sinéad left, barefoot and pregnant.

During the next three weeks Courtney tossed mike stands into the crowd; dodged flying chairs; faked orgasms; incited more audience members to strip; tossed condoms at her bass player, noting that she herself did not use them, since no one would sleep with her; flashed her privates in conservative Cincinnati, but unlike the lead singer from the Jesus Lizard, who did the same, did not get arrested; tossed her guitar at a man who yelled "Who's your next victim?"; and announced to a cocky fan, "You want to put it in me? . . . I am not a woman, I'm a fucking force of nature. Your dick would fly right off."

When Lollapalooza played Pittsburgh, Courtney abruptly walked off the stage in mid-set, again crying. Someone in the crowd had tossed a shotgun shell at her feet. Not exactly roses. Not exactly the sight needed by a person who already believed everybody wanted her dead, but so exactly suited to Courtney's strange dance of a life, where she battled her public image, herself, and the tornadoes she created. When news of the incident hit the airwaves, some accused Courtney of instigating the stunt in a bid for more media attention.

By the time the tour hit New York, she was so heavily sedated that she fell on her way to the stage. She stayed pharmaceutically numbed for most of the remainder of the tour, so dazed and out of it that the bodyguards simply carried her around and makeup women blushed and mascaraed the sleeping star.

At the final concert, at Shoreline Amphitheater outside San Francisco, she went out with a bang *and* a whimper. It was August 18, Frances Bean's birthday, and the child, who had been shuttled away after the Kathleen Hanna affair, rejoined her mother for the last shows. All day backstage a clown followed Frances about, wheeling a wagon overflowing with wrapped presents. At seven-thirty that night, while Frances watched, wearing earphones, Mommy ripped up the stage—although by that time, Courtney's hour at the mike was about the only hour of the day she wasn't leaning on a bodyguard's shoulder. But even though she cried through many of the songs, Courtney, and the rest of the band, cranked. Red-hot, blistering, awesome: all the clichés applied that night.

Courtney was even being kind, going through the list of bands on the tour, one by one, and demanding that the crowd show a little respect by applauding them. She finished her list with a demand to "show some respect for Frances Bean, who is three years old today." The crowd cheered. Backstage, Frances was ecstatic and wide-eyed when the band broke into "Happy Birthday" and Eric wandered offstage to play a guitar solo to the birthday girl, as Courtney commanded the crowd of thousands to sing along.

The sweetness soured minutes later, however, when the set ended. According to accounts from those close up at the show, the trouble started with two young men in the front row who were obviously not Hole fans. They had glared during the show, and refused to clap at the set's end, standing there cross-armed, staring. Courtney screamed at them, "Louder!"

One of them hissed, "You killed Kurt!"

She stepped into the audience and started pounding them.

Courtney was carried off from her last Lollapalooza show, crying.

But that final slam didn't stop her for long. Days later—around the time Thurston Moore was reporting via the Internet that Courtney had pulled a VIP number, banning the other Lollapalooza bands from the parking lot, forcing them to trudge in for the whole tour, Hole flew to England for the annual Reading Festival, a prestigious three-day event. Patty Schemel, apparently sick of the bandleader, ended that show by pushing her drum set over on Courtney. During the Smashing Pumpkins set, Courtney stormed into the photo pit demanding attention, but her former boyfriend, Pumpkins lead singer Billy Corgan, took no notice from the stage.

After a brief stop in L.A., where Courtney met with *Hustler* publisher Larry Flynt to discuss a part in an upcoming movie about his life, she flew to the Arctic Circle for the Molson's gig on Labor Day, where the headliner once again wasn't Hole, but Metallica. But so what? Metallica didn't fly directly to New York City's Radio City Music Hall for a surprise appearance at the MTV Music Video Awards, as Hole did.

The Music Hall was a mob scene, stars and video screens and upscale, well-heeled, tuxedoed kids everywhere. At the ceremony, Michael Jackson lip-synched as he danced, Madonna gave away awards and received her first, and Drew Barrymore wore daisies in her hair as she presented a special honorary award to R.E.M.

The ceremony's host, comedian Dennis Miller— former star of *Saturday Night Live* and his own talk show—introduced Hole as "Miss Congeniality and her band."

Courtney, barefoot and stunning in pearls and a long pink gown that prevented intrusive glances when she adopted the famous foot-on-monitor pose, remained composed despite Miller's jab. "This is for Kurt and Kristen and River and Joe and Rob and today Joni Abbott," she said in her whiskey voice, eyes raised as she ran down the list of the newly dead, a list longer than that of most award winners' thank-you sheets. And then Hole burst into "Violet," the song written for Billy Corgan of Smashing Pumpkins, though its lyrics also applied to Kurt, especially when Courtney bellowed, "Go on, take everything, take everything, I want you to." She looked radiant and simultaneously zombielike as she whisper-sang about a jeweled amethyst sky and offered sex advice to girls everywhere, singing, "When they get what they want, they never want it again."

Even though her singing was occasionally off, even though she let her guitar hang around her neck while her arms fluttered above her head like wings, it was the most compelling show of the night, and Courtney was the undisputed winner of the Rock Goddess Award. Madonna, after all, didn't perform—onstage, at any rate.

But Courtney was also the undisputed winner of the Backstage Bitch award a few minutes later. She was livid after the show, pacing the halls, carrying Frances, chain-smoking, apparently playing the "Miss Congeniality and her band" introduction over and over in her head. Screw Dennis Miller, what did he have against her? And to think she used to have a crush on him! When a photographer snapped a shot of her, Courtney demanded that she be kicked out, despite the fact that the photographer was authorized to be backstage.

"She was a raving lunatic," one backstage attendee told the *New York Post,* "hurling obscenities, holding the baby in one arm, and throwing everything in sight with the other."

But Courtney cooled down soon enough—for the video camera, at least. MTV newscaster Kurt Loder was supposed to interview her, but he was running late, something Courtney was often known to do, but wouldn't tolerate in others. She could see the back of his head as he stood nearby, so she pitched her compact, which sailed into the interview he was conducting. And then she headed up the curving stairway to push her way in.

Alas, Kurt Loder was interviewing Madonna, the '80s' bad girl of music.

Alas, Courtney didn't care. "Am I fully interrupting?" she asked, grabbing a microphone and taking a seat. Apologizing to the off-camera MTV newscaster Tabitha Soren for previously calling her "a thin-lipped Republican bitch," and reminding Madonna that her label, Maverick, had once wanted to sign Hole, Courtney just barged on in. But she was amusing in her outrageousness, that included chastising Madonna for not even watching Hole perform. "Don't worry," she sarcastically confided to Madonna, who was eyeing Courtney's fist warily and coming off like a high-society gal compared to Ms. Love, "I've never clocked a soul in my life."

And then, unknown to the viewing masses, since the incident was edited from the show, Courtney fell off her chair and stuck her legs straight up like the Wicked Witch of the West.

CHAPTER 2

The Trippy Beginning
(1964–1981)

THE BEACH BOYS' "I GET AROUND" BLARED FROM AM radios nationwide, Neil Simon's *Barefoot in the Park* was a smash hit on Broadway, and Banquet pot pies were all the rage that summer of 1964—a few months before the word "hippie" was coined, and a few weeks after Richard Alpert and Timothy Leary published the recipe for LSD.

On July 9, 1964, the day the Republican convention convened in San Francisco at the Saint Francis Hotel, Courtney Michelle Harrison took her first breath at Saint Francis Memorial Hospital. As usual, Courtney turned up smack-dab in the heart of a happening scene, though for once she hadn't shoved her way in.

The country, which had been hopelessly Donna Reedish for the previous two decades, was in an uproar: the hope epitomized by JFK had been shattered by his assassination the year before, and the nation stood divided by race, party, sex, and age. San Francisco's Haight District, a haven for musicians, rebels, radicals, and spiritual seekers, was a major node in the political rallying spirit that came to be known as the Free Speech movement, though it later embraced free drugs and free love. And it was there, in March of 1963, that Courtney's mother attended a party for jazz trumpeter Dizzy Gillespie and met the loquacious character who would become Courtney's father.

The pairing was odd, to say the least. Linda Risi was a lovely, lithe, tight-lipped nineteen-year-old debutante, the daughter of an optician, and the heiress to a substantial fortune, who had rebelled from her well-to-do upbringing for soul-searching in San Francisco. Hank Harrison, who looked like a cross between the Addams Family's Gomez and Sonny Bono, was an enthusiastic college student and rock scribe whose garrulousness could wear listeners down in ten minutes flat. For three weeks or so, Hank had managed the Warlocks, a band that lasted for three decades—after he left them as manager and they changed their name to the Grateful Dead. Undaunted, he found a new niche in the emerging sociopolitical scene: he started a government-funded hot line to talk people down from bad LSD trips, and he wrote his first book, *The Drug Crisis Handbook.*

The minute Hank's eyes landed on Linda, he wanted to breed. Between her beauty and his brains, he "knew the child would be genetically perfect."

Linda and Hank were married in Reno a few months after their first date. Their union was the result not of insta-love but of insta-conception: Linda was pregnant.

According to Hank Harrison, Linda, who was raised Catholic, refused to use birth control. Courtney has said, from the stage, that the only reason she wasn't aborted was that Linda thought she might be Bob Dylan's baby.

In any case, Linda was twenty when she had Courtney, her first child, and Courtney was informally adopted into the Grateful Dead clan, with the band's Phil Lesh sometimes babysitting her.

Courtney grew up in a San Francisco house bought for the new family by Linda's wealthy parents. The people who passed through their home were emerging pop icons, symbols of the new generation. The Dead could be seen on TV and in newspaper and magazine pictures;

their music could be heard on college radio stations and at concerts that packed the Haight's streets. And sometimes they were on the news—for getting busted.

One of Courtney's earliest impressions was the realization that some people had star quality; they were special. Her father also recognized this quality. The time he spent with the band in San Francisco was apparently some of the most memorable years of his life. Calling himself "the Jane Goodall of rock and roll," he chronicled the era and the band in a self-published three-volume series—*The Dead: A Social History of the Haight-Ashbury Experience,* a mishmash of journal entries, interviews with characters in the Haight scene, recollections of concerts, and assorted essays. According to Hank, the book sold 400,000 copies.

Courtney wasn't too young to sense that some people were perceived as godlike; she was an extremely bright toddler whose first words, according to her father, were "Please get me a bottle." The picture he painted was of a young genius who could spell at age two, could read backwards and upside down, and had a photographic memory. "She was a dream child," Hank said. Linda agreed, stating in a rare interview for *Vanity Fair* that Courtney was "an absolutely, unimaginably calm and happy baby. She hardly cried."

But something happened to change all that before Courtney turned three. Her parents' marriage ripped apart. Hank hooked up with a woman who, like him, followed the Grateful Dead on tour. And according to him, Linda became intimate with their garbage man, Frank Rodriguez, whom she later married. According to Courtney, however, that trauma was only partly to blame for her unhappy childhood. She claims that as a toddler, she was dosed.

In testimony given in San Francisco Superior Court, Hank was alleged to have given the toddler LSD, a hallucinogen that caused childish dream images of monsters and fairies to be projected out of the brain and onto the wall.

"He was alleged . . . to have given me acid and gone around boasting about it, like [I was] some biological experiment," she told the *San Francisco Chronicle.* As Hank knew well, from talking people down from bad trips in the mid-1960s, the acid of that era could fry the brains of adults and freak them out for months.

Hank, however, has always emphatically denied that allegation—and even claims to have taken a polygraph test to prove his honesty. The LSD incident, according to him, was a fabrication, just one of many by Linda to deny him custody, to deny him access to the trust fund established by Linda's father for Courtney, and to turn Courtney against him. The reality? He said one time Courtney took too many vitamins and became hyper. This caused Linda to believe he had given Courtney drugs.

Courtney also told people it wasn't actually Hank who gave her the hallucinogen; it was a hippie girl in a commune where her father dropped her off to be baby-sat while he attended a Dead concert.

In any case, Courtney was not around her biological father for long. Linda left town with her toddler and her new husband, hoping to start a new life in a different state. The family moved to the liberal college town of Eugene, Oregon, following a movement of freethinkers led by the novelist and LSD guru Ken Kesey and other spiritual seekers who had headed to that northwestern state to buy up the cheap land and start communes. Linda herself became a leader to many of the young women in that scene who were fired up about women's rights and who attended the University of Oregon. Hank was court-ordered not to see Courtney until she was an adult, after Linda filed a complaint that he had threatened to abduct Courtney and take her to another country.

Courtney, believed to have been drugged, started therapy at age two. "She was in so much pain," her mother, now known as Linda Carroll, told *Vanity Fair*'s Kevin Sessums. "And that manifested itself ever since she was a little girl, in ways in which I had no clue how to deal with."

Linda was gutsy and defiant in thought and action. And in an era when psychiatrists were widely mistrusted, she took Courtney to counselor after counselor after counselor, exposing the child to every trend, from transactional analysis to transcendental meditation for tots.

Counselors had a difficult time diagnosing and helping the amazingly bright but frighteningly angry child. Courtney was believed to be drug-damaged, and Freud hadn't dealt with that problem. At one point, Courtney now says, she was so disturbed that she simply stopped talking and was diagnosed as autistic. The treatment Courtney received was so frustrating, and the progress so unremarkable that Linda began studying therapy and ultimately became a counselor.

Linda and Frank Rodriguez had two daughters before their divorce a few years later. In the midst of Linda's own emotional turmoil, and raising two other children, she had Courtney to deal with. The child often awoke screaming from nightmares. She had crying fits and tantrums, and she hated school. She bossed other kids around, often not bonding with them; the people in her crayon drawings looked like murder victims. She didn't respond well to authority. And she was very upset by the lifestyle her mother was dragging her through, with its constant moves and exposure to new people. Again, according to Courtney, it wasn't just that her clothes stank so bad for lack of washing that the other children nicknamed her "Pee Girl." What also bothered Courtney was that the spotlight was being yanked away from her.

There are certain children who, in an ideal world, would be given a stage for their birthday, along with a microphone and a video camera; large-screen TVs would display their likeness at the dinner table, on the playground, and on the bedroom wall when they went to bed and woke up. Courtney was one of these need-a-stage kids. She wanted to be the center of attention at all times. But that just wasn't possible, given the way she grew up. In the late sixties and early seventies the lifestyle around Eugene, Oregon, was heavy on granola and Birkenstocks; Linda, who'd once managed a Birkenstock store, made a shrewd investment in a dairy company, Nancy's Yogurt, which became a major supplier in the Northwest.

There was plenty of money, but Linda was no longer interested in capitalism and the nuclear family. Along with dozens of other hippies, she lived in communes, teepees, mansions, and farmhouses—but Courtney was not always comfortable with her mother's free-falling alternative lifestyle.

A poem by Fritz Perls, founder of the Gestalt Approach, which Linda practiced with a fervor, was the credo of the day: "You do your thing, I'll do mine." Stephen Stills advised "Love the One You're With." This was the era when the nuclear family untied its knot and frayed, as young dreamers seeking a better way moved into coed houses with friends—a scandalous concept just a few years before—and into communes, where composting was as routine as home-baked bread.

In short, Courtney was a product of a world where the adults were absorbed in the pursuit of getting their heads together. The communal living arrangements, with lots of what Courtney called "wangly-assed hippies" running naked through the house having "encounter sessions" in the dark, may have worked fine for plenty of other children of that era, but growing up in a gender-free household devoid of "canopy bed [and] jewelry box with the ballerina," with constant competition for attention, was frustrating for Courtney.

Linda was doing everything to find herself, ultimately bringing five children into the world by various fathers, marrying four times, and typically requiring that each new husband formally adopt her existing brood. The other children apparently accepted the program, but not

Courtney, who early on learned the power of being a monster.

She and her mother did not get along. Courtney later speculated that she reminded Linda of Hank, the embarrassing marital mistake, whom Courtney resembled right down to his nose. The mother-daughter tension, Courtney believed, stemmed from "a projection that my mother made on me because of the repulsion she felt for my father, for which I don't blame her."

The older she got, the more she hated the life provided by Linda. At one point, Courtney, her mother, and a slew of other people moved into a mansion in Marcola, Oregon, which Linda inherited from her own mother. But despite all the company, Courtney felt increasingly isolated in her own home.

On a therapist's recommendation, Linda enrolled her in Brownies; but Courtney didn't have time to learn to tie the orange tie or memorize the Brownie oath. It was obvious the first day that she didn't quite fit in. When it was time to show the happy-smile drawings the girls were working on at that meeting, Courtney looked down at her war-victim drawing and burst into tears. Her mother hastily escorted her out.

Courtney wanted to take ballet lessons, to surround herself with lace and frills and dolls, but her wishes were unfathomable in that genderless household and were often denied.

Inspired by Tatum O'Neal's Oscar-winning role in *Paper Moon,* Courtney began taking acting lessons. A big production of *Snow White* was coming up, and Courtney was determined to land the leading part in the play. "I studied the part of Snow White forever and had it down," she later told the British press. "And they gave me, without even auditioning me, the part of the Evil Witch. And that's when I was eight."

Linda never did find a way to deal with her tantrum-prone child. The eldest of her five children was too much for her to handle, and always a question mark in any new relationship that Linda embarked upon.

After Linda met a busboy named David Menely on a rafting excursion, she had an idea for a new lifestyle adventure—sheepherding! Courtney balked at the thought. Courtney later told *Spin* magazine that Linda left her in Eugene with her therapist while the rest of the family packed up and moved, not just to another Oregon commune, not just to the other side of the country, but to the other side of the world: a sheep farm in New Zealand. Might as well have been Saturn. The message was pretty clear: you're entirely dispensable; leave us alone; you're a nightmare.

Courtney seconded their assessment by underlining the point in the emotional equivalent of screaming red lipstick. Within a few weeks she exhausted the therapist and his child and was so utterly uncontrollable that she was shipped off to New Zealand.

According to Hank, she ran away several times—starting with the flight on the way over, when the youngster bolted during a stopover en route. Once in New Zealand, she was sent to live with another friend of the family. Happily, Courtney liked this woman and went on her best behavior. Unhappily, the woman ultimately didn't want the responsibility, and besides, even on her best behavior, Courtney was very demanding.

She was shipped off to boarding school Down Under, but was soon expelled. The mother superior said Courtney was a horrible student who ran around without shirt or shoes, obviously mistaking the strict religious school for a hippie commune. Courtney was then sent to a liberal "free school" in London. A couple of years later, though, Linda returned to Oregon and brought Courtney back with her. But Courtney, then around ten, was sent to live with one of Linda's ex-boyfriends in Portland, while Linda settled in Eugene.

While her siblings lived with their mother and Linda's husband du jour, Courtney was shuttled between foster homes. She complained to Oregon Child Services that she just wanted a home, but whenever she returned to her mother's house, her presence was disruptive. (She later admitted to a reporter, "I smoked rock with my brother . . . when I was eleven.") And so she'd get booted out again.

Nobody wanted Courtney. Nobody could cope with her. She challenged authority, she fought, she cried, she lied, she was a drama queen and a manipulator. She didn't heed household rules. She could be violent.

And then she got worse.

One day it happened: there was a surge of hormones, and she plumped out, broke out, until her entire body, not just her nose, seemed strangely misshapen. The beautiful child had been transformed into something that fell short of the very, very pretty girl she most wanted to be. Courtney by age twelve was the least likely candidate for the Miss World title. The loser years had begun.

"There is no power like ugly, ugly, ugly," Courtney would scream from her first album, *Pretty on the Inside,* fifteen years later, referring to her sudden transformation from lovely cygnet to ugly duck.

Courtney was already angry. The fall from physical grace only ticked her off all the more. It was bad enough feeling unloved and being unwanted. Now she'd lost the power that came with being pretty. It was utterly depressing. This in turn made her even madder. And then it made her bad.

In the mid-seventies, after coming upon "Queens of Noise," an album by the bad-girl band, the Runaways, and whose members included Joan Jett and Lita Ford, Courtney latched on to them as her new role models.

These teenagers out of L.A., whose big hit was "Cherry Bomb," were literally marketed as juvenile delinquents. "They looked like the foxy stoner chicks at my school," Courtney told *Option* magazine, "But they were way cooler and badder . . . That's when I became fascinated with becoming a JD."

And, living up to the name of her favorite band, the twelve-year-old started running away often. She also made the decision to learn to steal and to get arrested. "I thought that crime was the coolest subculture going," she said.

For social life, she turned into a mall rat and a café fixture. In Portland, the main hang was the Galleria, a small three-floor downtown shopping center of jeans stores, jewelry shops, and cafés. Gangs of kids hung out there—from suburbanites to hoodlums and the Mohawked ones—drinking coffee and smoking cigarettes at Café Ritz or La Patisserie. On occasion, Courtney got beaten up, but she learned the fine art of shoplifting. She snagged a lipstick here and some mascara there, but the Kiss T-shirt she stole from Woolworth's was a turning point in her sticky-fingered career. When the store summoned her mother, Linda called the cops.

Courtney was put on probation, which she soon violated by running away from home, a regular routine for her. When she came home, she was turned in and sent to a reform school in Salem, an institution that housed eleven- to eighteen-year-olds who were considered a threat to society.

Salem, Oregon, the state capital, is home to numerous bureaucratic buildings, official-looking, beige, and bland, broken up by residential streets. For Oregon, the town is remarkably flat until one heads toward its outskirts. There, a hilly area is dominated by Fairview Hospital for the physically challenged and by the Hillcrest Youth Correctional Facility. From the road below, Hillcrest is invisible, hidden behind a grove of Douglas fir trees. Fields spread out below it, with geese and deer running through a scene so pastoral it might be a resort. To the right, a semicircle of two-story red brick buildings form what looks like a typical college campus, with a well-manicured lawn, shrubs, and, off in the distance, a swimming pool.

Courtney arrived at this lovely scene in a police car, in handcuffs, her ankles shackled. The sheriff firmly grabbed her arm as she took tiny steps toward the brick administration building, where flower boxes hung from the windows, her chains rattling with every small step and her thoughts, no doubt, foul. She was escorted inside, led to a stairway, pushed down, and forced to kneel on a step, as if praying to the gods of the justice system. Behind her, out of sight, she could hear the sheriff checking her in at the desk. Minutes later, handcuffs and shackles removed, she was led in silence through a tunnel of hissing pipes, her hands out in front of her, stopping at every corner in the underground network. She emerged at the medical office, where she was given a cavity search.

This was worse than being ditched when her family left her and moved to New Zealand. In this place she even had to wear a uniform.

But some part of her no doubt got a thrill from the experience. She was her mother's worst nightmare, a constant source not only of guilt but of embarrassment as well. Linda, after all, was a counselor. And her firstborn child wasn't a very convincing advertisement for her therapy.

Reform school was not where Courtney belonged; this was not part of the plan for greatness that she had already begun constructing in her head. But Courtney quickly ascended in the school's pecking order and garnered a reputation for being tough, foul-mouthed, and likely to attempt escape, offenses likely to land a student in the "Quiet Room," where the walls were padded and every move was monitored by a video camera. She was the sort who didn't care if the lights went out early because she didn't make her bed properly, failed to tidy her room, or refused to be quiet in the tunnel, where the youth walked with their hands out in front of them, stopping at every corner, and where the water pipes were padded so they couldn't be used as weapons.

Her several months' stay at Hillcrest wasn't her last stretch in the reform school system. For the next few years she had a revolving account. She was a chronic challenge whose problems were considered so severe that she was sent to live in schools alongside teenage killers and other menaces to society.

Two important things happened during that time: she reconnected with a man who'd been missing from her life for the past decade—her father, Hank Harrison, who was still living in San Francisco; and she found a new reason for living called New Wave.

Courtney had been in Hillcrest for several months when Hank Harrison got word via one of her stepfathers that she was in trouble and was asking to see Hank. He showed up at the institution, and was immediately informed that Courtney didn't belong there.

After several years of not seeing him, her first words to her biological father were "Why did you abandon me?"

Hank told her he'd been shut out, that he'd tried unsuccessfully to reconnect with her.

"Why didn't you try harder?" she asked.

Hank checked her out of Hillcrest and took her to live with him in California. That arrangement didn't last long—"We didn't get along," he said—but they continued corresponding.

When she turned up at reform school again not long afterward, she wrote Hank letters noting that "life has passed us both by. . . . I'm liable to rot in this hole, but life goes on."

He told her of his plans to go to Ireland to write more volumes of his book and to study the Holy Grail and ancient Irish stones. He invited her to live with him in Dublin once he got there.

The idea appealed to Courtney, particularly after she became immersed in the latest outpouring of music from the United Kingdom. A college intern at one of the other reform schools she lived at, this one in Eugene, had recently visited England. The intern told her to check out the emerging music scene there, and he gave her a handful of tapes—the Clash, the Sex Pistols, and the Pretenders among them. And suddenly Courtney knew what she wanted to do: she would be a rock star. Or at least hang out with some of them.

During her incarceration she dreamed, in the same way the typical suburban teenager gazes at posters or pores over magazine pictures, fantasizing and listening to songs over and over, wishing she knew the singers personally. Courtney concocted scenarios in her head, while she bided her time in reform schools, where her posters and pictures were confined to a small bulletin board, where a messy room meant lights out early, and where bars on the windows blocked her view.

When she was released after several months at the Eugene institution, Courtney headed back to the Galleria to tell others about her dreams of greatness and how she was going to be a jet-setter. Most of them laughed at her: Sure, Courtney, you're gonna go meet the Clash. Let us know how it turns out.

The powerlessness she felt while institutionalized just increased her desire for autonomy. And a young kid seeking money and escape can find independence quite easily—in the sex industry.

One would never guess it at first glance: Portland, the friendly little town with hills carpeted in velvety green forests, a town so wholesome that it seemed to be caught in a different era, like a place invented by Hallmark. But there was another, darker side to the city—and Courtney was soon sucked into it.

The dark side of Portland was as hidden as the shanghai tunnels that wove underneath it, linking some of its buildings to the waterfront. Opium was once smuggled through those dank corridors, and drugged or drunken men were dragged out onto outgoing ships in the late nineteenth and early twentieth century. It's rather revealing of the Portland mind-set that the shanghai tunnels are rarely mentioned in history books.

Although the tunnels were now bricked up, though opium had fallen into disuse and men were no longer shanghaied, Portland was still a center of illegal activities. In the late twentieth century, it was believed to be a hotbed of child pornography, and it was home to an abundance of teenage hustlers and street kids whose nightly activities included being bought by wealthy businessmen. Though there were frequent crackdowns on prostitution, the sex businesses thrived. So many strip clubs dotted the city—more per capita than in any other city in the United States—that the dancers themselves dubbed Portland "Pornland."

With its open-minded ways and live-and-let-live attitude, Portland attracted visionaries and community activists; but it was also a magnet for the shady and weird—from murderous cults to Rajneeshes. Gangs overtook the city, but the residents denied their presence, despite a handful of drive-by shootings; the emerging neo-Nazis in the downtown scene were also ignored—until an Ethiopian man was killed by a young Nazi-aligned skinhead. One of the city's leading social workers was alleged to be misusing his post, offering to help young boys out if they agreed to sex with him. When a weekly newspaper reported the incident, the town's response was outrage—directed at the paper, where the phone rang with bomb threats, and bulletproof windows were quickly installed.

Starting in the late seventies, on the outskirts of downtown, a few blocks from the murky Willamette River, was a parking lot known as "camp." This pickup site for young boys and a hangout for runaways and junkies was the inspiration for *My Own Private Idaho,* Gus Van Sant's movie about the darker side of street life.

It was at this so-called camp, when Courtney was fourteen, that an underworld sort approached her with an opportunity to see Japan. This time she didn't have to worry about anything as mundane as sheepherding in New Zealand. She said she was flown to Japan to be a dancer—as in *erotic* dancer.

The overseas scene was said to be a sleazy world where once they had their performers, club owners' previous promises were null and void, and dancers were forced to do whatever the organizers wished.

Whatever happened in Japan, it came down with a crash; Courtney was deported six months later after a major bust. She came back bragging about a scene that included live sex acts on stage, and telling friends she'd been part of the white slave trade.

Once back in Portland, she bounced around more foster homes, continuing to run away. She frequently confronted Oregon Child Services about their inability to place her. A social worker report written in 1980 states that Courtney "continued her former pattern of challenging adult authority, [and] running away to avoid problems. . . . [She] repeatedly asks for authorities to find her a 'home.' It is apparent that Courtney has been in search of the family life she has been deprived of for so many years."

Shortly after her return from Japan, she got into trouble again. She later told *Spin* she'd been called as a witness to a statewide sex scandal, though none were reported at the time. It's more likely that Courtney returned to the stages of Portland's strip clubs. At some strip joints that didn't serve alcohol, and thus escaped the surveillance of the strict Liquor Licensing Board, the young girls danced entirely naked and pranced through the audience. At the end of 1979, the same time that a children's sexual abuse hot line was installed through the city, three such clubs—all owned by the same two men—were shut down in a sting operation.

Courtney may have been among the dancers rounded up that night. Whatever happened, she was brought back to the attention of the courts. But that unfortunate incident ultimately led to her independence. When a new social worker took Courtney's case and learned that she was an heiress, she requested that Courtney, then sixteen, be granted legal and financial emancipation from her mother.

In 1981, with income of about $800 a month from a trust fund set up by her maternal grandfather, Courtney moved into the first of many coed houses with struggling artists and rock performers. She promptly developed a crush on the lead singer of a group called Napalm Beach.

From her earliest days, the objects of her affection have almost always been the breed that sings.

Hank Harrison, who had essentially been awakened from the dead, made up for the years he and Courtney had lost. He made good on his offer to put her up in Ireland, and several people who knew Courtney at the time say that she showed up with a thousand hits of very strong LSD.

Courtney soon appeared at Hank's doorstep in Dublin, with plans of attending Trinity College.

Oh, joyous reunion! For about ten minutes. Father and daughter didn't hit it off; they both agree on that. Hank claims she was with him for months, but Courtney says she only lasted days. "He beat me so badly I called the cops," she told the *San Francisco Chronicle*. Hank said she spent much of her time in Dublin "hooking on the street."

She blasted out of his life soon enough—the very night she caught a show of a New Wave band, the Teardrop Explodes. Courtney was so taken with their performance that, after introducing herself to the band members, specifically the leader, Julian Cope, she followed them back to their hometown. The girl always had a great nose, and once again it led her to one hot little scene: Liverpool.

If one ever wanted to step into an E-Z Meeting Opportunity, Liverpool was it. The industrial town best known as the birthplace of the Beatles was then experiencing another musical renaissance. And like the Beatles, the new bands coming out of the British scene—Elvis Costello, Echo and the Bunnymen, and the Teardrop Explodes—played music that was melodic, romantic, and catchy enough to get them noticed in the United States as well.

Courtney brazenly blasted into their world, pushing her way into conversations at cafés and pubs, crashing parties, and inviting herself to shows.

And it was in England, Courtney claims, that she stepped out of the onstage pretense of seduction and into the reality of the bed. "I lost my virginity in a council house in Liverpool, listening to 'Isolation' by Joy Division, to a guy called Michael Mooney, who hung out with Teardrop Explodes," she later told the British music paper *Melody Maker*. "After we'd done it I went across the road for cigarettes and I had all this blood and fluids running down my legs. Luuuuurg, real graphic." The man to whom she claims she lost her virginity denied the deed to *Melody Maker*.

For a few months, Liverpool, with its many musicians, was a riot. Julian Cope, of the Teardrop Explodes, supposedly even wrote a song for her called "When I Dream." But as is often the case with Courtney, the situation darkened soon enough. Before long, people were getting annoyed with her constant scenes and loud confrontations; one musician reportedly punched her out. In both looks and personality, she resembled Nancy Spungen, the American groupie who hooked up with Sid Vicious of the Sex Pistols.

Courtney returned to Oregon, bringing back several tales, which may or may not have been true. She said that one of her objects of affection, Echo and the Bunnymen's lead singer, Ian McCulloch, rebuffed her advances and that she snagged his stage jackets in retaliation. More frightening was the story she told about Julian Cope, a self-admitted acidhead: Courtney said she gave him some of her extra-strength LSD, manufactured in the 1960s, when mad chemists brewed up mind-frying dosages. She told her friends that Julian took a little too much of the hallucinogen and had to leave Liverpool and move to a goat farm. That might explain an advertisement Cope took out in magazines over a decade later, when Courtney first coupled with Kurt Cobain. "Free us, (the rock'n'roll fans)," Julian implored in full-page ads that appeared in British music magazines, "from Nancy Spungen fixated heroin a-holes who cling to our greatest rock groups and suck out their brains."

By the time 17-year-old Courtney left Liverpool, she was notorious in the New Wave music scene.

CHAPTER 3

Small Town Girl Makes Loud
(1982–1983)

PORTLAND INTERNATIONAL AIRPORT DIDN'T SEEM TERRIBLY international when Courtney Menely, then using the surname of one of her stepfathers, blew back into town from England, having mentally reviewed her exploits and sexual scores during the entire trip. Now a bona fide New Waver, with a British accent and a fondness for tea, she couldn't wait to hit the cafés to brag. She'd cut a few more notches on her belt, and they were pretty big name notches. She had proved that she could weasel into any scene, even if she had no connections within it.

At 17, she was a New Wave Pamela Des Barre, the infamous groupie whose backstage exploits were captured in the book *I'm with the Band.* Twelve years later, Pamela would write about Courtney for *Interview* magazine, likening her to Janis Joplin, Jimi Hendrix, Jim Morrison, Iggy Pop, and Lou Reed "because she shouts her mind."

Courtney's exploits abroad had confirmed what the mouthy hell-raiser already knew, and what she'd already proved to friends, family, and legal authorities many times: that she was unstoppable. The Unsinkable Courtney. With her new artillery of star-quality names that she had personally partied with, she machine-gunned her way into the swelling Portland music scene—at the time richer, more diverse, and far more festive than Seattle's would ever be.

Portland, Oregon, as Kurt Cobain later said in *Monk* magazine, was the birthplace of grunge. But Portland never got much attention, perhaps because out-of-towners couldn't find it on a map, believing it was a suburb of Seattle, which is actually four hours north in an altogether different state.

There was ready evidence of her potential, her unyielding desire for power and personal freedom, when Courtney returned to Portland in 1982. And this time around, she established herself as a force to contend with, making it clear that she wouldn't be confined to the treadmill of life. It was there and then that hundreds of stories about her—of rip-offs, break-ins, and fires—first snaked through the gossip lines. And it was there and then that she decided to form her own band, announcing bossily that she'd someday be a sex symbol and a rock star, an idea that sent howls through the town.

Over a decade later, when Courtney told *Spin* magazine, "Years ago in a certain town, my reputation had gotten so bad that every time I went to a party, I was expected to burn the place down and knock out every window," she was referring to Portland. And when she returned from the UK and hit the downtown music scene, even those who hadn't heard of her now noticed the obnoxious noisemaker and got out of her way.

Courtney's mouth was her most powerful weapon, as unceasing in its noise as a power tool on a summer day; like a chain saw, it ripped through anything in its way, including the doors of bars that were locked to the underage. In any conversation, no matter with whom, no matter the hour, she could spin a verbal cyclone in tones sultry or shrill, a dizzying whirlwind of ideas, gossip, and confessions punctuated by the names of musicians, authors, and heady books.

The infamous mouth flapped through the day and the night, wrapped around receivers in hours-long telethons to the far corners of the world, in conversations with producers, psychics, singers, at any hour Courtney saw fit. One minute her voice whispered or confessed, the next it hissed and issued death threats or passionate declarations of love; *anything* was possible, and it was always startling what flew out of this yammering mouth.

But Courtney was more than a mouth; her eyes also demanded attention—those piercing eyes that sized people up in an instant, that gushed tears on command, that blazed a scorching brand on those who wronged her. For many years they were the only beautiful feature of the frumpy dynamo that was Courtney, and she knew how to work them for maximum effect.

Her nose, until resculpted, was a blight on her already coarse-featured face, a pointy, twisted nose that appeared to have been broken or bludgeoned, but that could always sniff out a trend faster than the hottest reporter. It could also track down a love object like a bloodhound.

Her legs, originally the pale, flabby, overweight sort, were hidden under old-lady dresses back then. They were long, though, allowing her to tower over others with the confident superiority that came simply from being tall.

Then there were the hands and the thick, coarse fingers, better suited to a steelworker than to a wanna-be tiara-wearing star. Long before they picked up a guitar, those rough hands had learned how to seduce and caress, and how to pummel anyone who got in the way.

Her hands, like her feet, seemed to have been inherited from her father, along with her nose. All Courtney had inherited from her reserved mother, it seemed, was an ability to ignore societal norms—and the trust fund that she quickly ripped through every month.

Courtney Love's features, seen in their original state, offer a clue into the mind-set of the teenager who stepped back into Portland, Oregon, where her tales of firsthand experience with the international music scene helped her to quickly land a job at an all-ages club.

She was not the classic American beauty, this tall, dumpling-bodied yapper, who even then, before it was fashionable, liked to dress in ripped vintage clothes. But Courtney was smart, and she had perfected the compensatory skills required by less-than-pretty girls to get along in the world. Because if you're less than lovely, if you're only "pretty on the inside," there are but two choices: sit back and take whatever comes along, or aim high and devise a bag of attention-getting tricks. Courtney opted for the latter, becoming a self-educated expert on sex, seduction, manipulation, and outlandishness. Before she was a star, even before she had show biz looks and before she took the surname Love, there was simply no ignoring Courtney.

In Portland she quickly became one of the most remarkable characters around; in itself, that was amazing, since the city was chockablock with the colorful sorts so often portrayed in movies and books. While Seattle was a gleaming city of lakes and bays and glassy high-rises built up along the Puget Sound, Portland stood at the confluence of two rivers, the Willamette and the Columbia, one murky and the other radioactive. And it wasn't a sprawling metropolis like Seattle, but a compact hamlet of Victorian houses stacked upon hills cloaked in the morning fog, a pedestrian community where the sidewalks were clogged with café tables, and where a trip to the mailbox involved running into ten first-name acquaintances, eight of whom would bum a smoke.

Whether triggered by boredom or mildew of the mind, creativity seemed to be oozing up from the wet ground of Portland in the early eighties. The city of eccentrics, where the artists and halfway-house residents tended to be crammed into the quadrant known as "Northwest," was creatively charged. Low rents and the lack of a sales tax helped to make Portland a magnet for artists; it was brimming with writers, actors, painters, singers, dancers, and poets as well as plenty of scenesters who threw late night parties, which all the penniless creative types crashed.

But the most prestigious of all the arts was music. It seemed as if half the town was in a band. The guy at the grocery store, the guy at the espresso machine, and the guy who worked by day as a mechanic were all by night cranking away on the stage of Luis' La Bamba, the Long Goodbye, the Earth, or any of dozens of other clubs that popped up every few months and soon disappeared. And unlike bands in many major cities, these groups were writing their own music. While they shied away from performing Top 40 covers at dance clubs in Portland, even the hipster audiences often danced—most unlike Seattle. Ignored by local radio and major record labels, the bands often recorded their own music and released tapes or pressed their own singles.

Like the rest of the nation, Portland had few girl bands, save for the Neo Boys, a female punk band who preferred to play in art galleries, all-ages clubs, and penitentiaries rather than bars. Courtney quickly attempted to befriend them.

In fact, before long, she knew all the bands, and vice versa. Greg Sage, a tall, alienlike albino recluse, headed the Wipers, whose song "Over the Edge" Hole would later record as a cover, first on a single for a small Portland label and later on a Hole EP, released in 1995.

There was Billy Rancher, the recent winner of a David Bowie look-alike contest; based on the contest alone, he started a group called Billy Rancher and the Unreal Gods, whose music was luring major label scouts to town. Billy's little brother, Lenny, had a band called the Pipsqueaks, talented drunks who were likely to continue playing music even after they'd fallen on the floor. There were punk bands like Napalm Beach, Poison Idea, the Obituaries, Final Warning, and Sado-Nation, and there were searing rock bands such as the hot three-piece group, the Confidentials. There were instrumental pseudo-surf bands like Pell Mell. But of all the hot bands in town, and there were many, Courtney's favorite was Theatre of Sheep, whose ethereal dream-rock sounds were landing them covers on the local weekly just weeks after they were formed.

The lead singer was Rozz Rezabek-Wright, whom Courtney called Rezabek. Tall, pale, thin, and punklike, Rozz looked like a cartoonish baby bird mixed with a red-haired British rock star. It was the latter quality that Courtney saw when Theatre of Sheep played the Metropolis.

Portland's music wasn't the domain only of the twenty-one-and-over crowd. All-ages clubs had sprung up, the leading hang being the beat-up Metropolis, located on a transient-ridden strip of Burnside, the city's main drag. Known as the Met, it was heavy on the black-and-red decor, and divided into two parts. One side of the club was the booth-lined "all-ages" section, where the kids danced on an elevated runway while looking into a mirror. One wall away, the over-twenty-one crowd sat at the bar, gazing through the glass side of the two-way mirror at the dancing kids.

The Metropolis was managed by a young visionary named Dean Mathiesen, who would become one of Courtney's longest-lasting friends. Short, sharp, sparrowlike, and gay, Dean was the Andy Warhol of Portland, who always had a coterie of young boys trailing him. The impossible-to-ignore scenester, who could swipe anyone down with a wisecrack or a glare, had a nose for the hip and an ability to make a dive seem like a palace. Dean saw the potential in Courtney, the yappity name-dropper, when she touched down. He hired her as the club's DJ.

Not long into her stint, the dive packed out when a new band, Theatre of Sheep, took to the corner platform of the miniature stage, followed by a flock of teenage girls. The five-piece band looked good, sounded good, and was sometimes described as swanky, in part because of their keyboardist, who looked as if she had stepped out of the flapper era, right down to her long string of pearls.

But most eyes stayed glued upon the lead singer—handsome Rozz, who was as mutable as the synthoglamrock music the band played; he was reminiscent of David Bowie, the New York Dolls, and Boy George. Though straight, he crossed gender lines enough to give the boys fantasy fodder.

Rozz was a ham, the sort who seemed to have spotlights following him long after they were turned off. He reeked of that showbiz quality that groupies can sniff out from many rows back, many years before talent scouts. So dreamy was the set that, from that point on, Rozz would cause a mob scene of kids just by walking down the street.

His potential didn't go unnoticed by Courtney, who'd watched it from the DJ stand at the front, cross-armed and smoking. After the gig, she pushed her way across the room and into his life. "Who do you think you are?" Courtney demanded in her recently acquired English accent, which hadn't worn off. "David Bowie? With your mock rock star poses? You'll never make it wearing those atrocious green checkered pants!"

"And who do you think you are with that fake British accent?" he asked.

She threw her drink at him. He spit on her. She slapped him. Someone dragged her away.

He was scared. She was in love.

He was twenty-two. She was almost eighteen.

"You don't decide you want Courtney," he later admitted. "She decides she wants you."

Rozz says he received a letter two days later, requesting a secret midnight meeting on the fire escape of a downtown café, Metro on Broadway. The note was unsigned. Inside was a rose. And a small packet of blue-and-red pills.

When he showed up, there was Courtney, the loon

with the fake British accent. He considered running away, but something about her compelled him to stay— a feeling of danger, a feeling of traversing the edge. In seduction mode, and a black dress, Courtney looked rather alluring. And she'd done her research well. She already understood that drugs and drunkenness were her friends, that with their help and with the conscious mind numbed, she could get what she wanted. She could lower defenses and seep into a love object's life.

The capsules were an effective means to Rozz's heart. He loved pills—barbiturates and tranquilizers especially, the sort that made his muscles relax and made him laugh a lot; he'd developed a taste for them when he was fifteen, after a beam fell on his back and a doctor prescribed extra-strength painkillers.

The pills she'd enclosed in the letter, the ones they went to her apartment to take, were Tuinals—a pharmaceutical that was half Seconal (a barbiturate) and half truth serum. The effect was to induce a relaxed delirium, where the body was out to lunch but the mind was still half-functioning. Thanks to the truth serum—and yes, there is such a thing—the mouth could utter only truth, which may have been the attraction for Courtney, who many people viewed as a chronic teller of tall tales— though many of her tall tales were true.

The bedroom in the Northwest house that she led him to was a wreck. Clothes, papers, magazines, records, books, and tapes were strewn everywhere. Somewhere beneath the mess was a mattress.

She lit candles and burned incense, which swirled through the room, competing with her trademark scent, Oscar de la Renta, which she'd sprayed on a bit too heavily. They played a scratchy Billy Holiday record. They drank tea and orange brandy. She brought out pictures, told him about all the bands she'd befriended abroad, and how her dad had once been a manager for the Grateful Dead. They talked through the night, about music, love, and about the celebrity Rozz would some-day be. Courtney could see it; she knew how famous he could be—if he changed his wardrobe and got rid of his modellike female keyboardist, whom men often fell for.

Courtney gave Rozz the stage jackets she'd supposedly swiped from Echo and the Bunnymen's lead singer Ian McCulloch, and suggested that perhaps Rozz should let her play in the band—as the new keyboardist.

He was amazed by her command of the language, her brilliance, her stories. She was amazed that in Portland she'd found exactly what she sought: a rising star. He just didn't know how to market himself, she informed him; he needed her to give him pointers and to draw up a rise-to-fame plan. Her determination and business savvy, even as a teenager, were remarkable.

Rozz left and stumbled home. But he didn't escape her for long. Shortly thereafter, they met up at his place, where he showed her his library—a collection of thirty-seven books. All of them *Valley of the Dolls,* the Jacqueline Susann novel about three pill-popping beauties who called their encapsulized happiness "dolls." That book was his bible, and he read it aloud to Courtney while they settled back, high on downs. The novel soon became her bible as well. She identified so strongly with one of the characters, a pudgy wannabe actress named Neely O'Hara (played by Patty Duke in the movie), that she began referring to herself as Nee, a name she would sign on the many love letters she sent to Rozz, sometimes daily, over the next several years. Neely, believed to be modeled after Judy Garland, befriended powerful people in order to promote her career, tossed out husbands when they ceased to aid her, and gobbled pills as a survival technique, occasionally overdosing on them.

The third time Rozz and Courtney went out—to a movie, where they shared a bottle of smuggled-in champagne—Courtney proposed; she also volunteered to support his musical cause with her trust fund. There was at least one major problem with that arrangement. It was not just that her frequent requests for advances from the fund were often denied, or that the trust fund kid was chronically "borrowing" to come up with cash. The real snag was that Rozz was already engaged.

His fiancée, Marion (not her real name), was the perfect suburban rich-kid brat: fine-featured, well-heeled, pretty, the product of a stable family, with parents who were still together. She was everything Courtney wasn't, everything emblematic of her mother, whom Courtney described to Rozz as "a majestic-titted blond debutante without a drop of poetry in her soul." It became Courtney's true purpose in life to shove Marion out of the way. "She's a good visual prop," Courtney told Rozz, "but you don't have to marry her."

Courtney's first step was to announce all over town, in the clubs and through the cafés, that she was going out with Rozz. That was a bit of a stretch, since their relationship was platonic; Rozz was unwilling to succumb to her advances despite his relaxed state. But once the rumors hit the street, the self-appointed advisers flocked to his side—friend and fan, male and female alike, all saying the same thing. "How could you?" he heard over and over. "What do you see in Courtney? She's such a bitch. She's not even pretty!"

But there was something about that big doughy sack of intensity. Something more than her assurances that someday she would achieve greatness and to her claims of being an heiress despite her frequent lack of funds. No one could ignore Courtney, but not that many could then see what Rozz saw: the braininess, the style, the humor, the ambition, the charisma, the way she could charge a room. Nobody else saw what he called her "biblical eyes." Few others regarded her intensity as intoxicating; many found it merely frightening. Most people only saw the fat chick with the funny nose, the one who wouldn't shut up, the one whose name was often connected with theft, lies, and fires. Despite their intense beginning, the continuing warnings that she was nothing but trouble ate away at his image of her. Rozz shoved Courtney away, nipping their budding relationship, and spending more time with his fiancée. One night while Marion helped him staple up posters for an upcoming show, they ran into Courtney right on Northwest Twenty-third, a main pathway of the pedestrian community.

At the sight of her competition, Courtney became enraged. "Guess you must not know how to treat your man!" Courtney screamed at Marion. "Guess that's why he's been hanging out with me."

Marion ran after Courtney with the staple gun, and Courtney darted between cars, Marion in hot pursuit, while Rozz admonished her to go away and leave them alone. Finally she split, shouting all the way. Rozz claimed Marion then began trying to shoot staples into her own head, a preview of things to come.

Courtney was more forward after that, simply dropping by Rozz's place with pills, wanting to analyze *Valley of the Dolls,* reading his short stories, wanting to hear his tales about the music scene in San Francisco, where he'd lived a few years before while playing in a punk band called Negative Trend. Sometimes he sent her away. And sometimes he didn't. The secretive nature of their rendezvous only added to her allure.

Besides, it was increasingly obvious: Courtney Menely was unlike anyone else. Though at eighteen, she was four years younger than he was, she was smarter, funnier, more driven, more dangerous, and more cunning than most of the people Rozz knew in bars. He had plenty of fans, but Courtney made him feel like a star, continually etching the possibility of international fame in his head. Even though their relationship wasn't sexual, sometimes they'd stay in her bed for days, just writing through the night or singing songs from the *Valley of the Dolls* movie. That was always the way to her heart, no matter her mood: sing to her, like a mother to a child.

Courtney could create an atmosphere of jet-setting debauchery, the twentieth-century equivalent of an ancient Roman feast, this one serving tea, brandy, and blues. They lay around saying lines out of their own personal romance novel. "Who has the prettiest eyes?"

he'd murmur, referring to hers. "The ocean," she'd reply. Whenever Rozz awoke from a short nap, he found the bed littered with books and notebooks filled with scrawled lyrics and ideas for movies, and Courtney would be working the phone, calling bands and producers in England or Asia. She could simply wear a guy down and induce creative mania: she never shut up and she never got boring, even after seventy-two hours of straight talking.

And when she wasn't with Rozz, she wrote him long love letters, always signed Nee. "You may be blessed with charm," she wrote in one, "but I'm blessed with the emotions of a four-year-old." She begged him to write one to her. Finally, simply to stop her whining, he did, asking in the letter, "When you get what you want, will you ever want it again?"

Fifteen years later the answer showed up in Hole's hit song, "Violet": "When I get what I want, I never want it again."

One love letter from fickle Rozz didn't exactly constitute a commitment, however. With her eyes, her coaxing, her proposals, and her pills she still couldn't persuade him to sleep with her, or to dump Marion. But Courtney was getting to him, putting his whole value system up for debate. She was pulling him in, as she spun a narcotic web and a silken dream. He was growing more and more fond of her and of the decadent days they spent together. "I hate men," Courtney would tell him, "but that's okay. I don't think of you as a man." Sometimes they'd talk for five hours straight entirely in rhyme.

Rozz even found himself affecting her fake British accent, asking from the bed, "Oh, Courtney, love, might I have a spot more tea?" Bingo! She soon announced her new name: Courtney Love.

But when he saw her on the street, in cafés, or at clubs, Rozz ignored her, the girl with the funny face, who dressed in a dumpy style that might have been called Early Old Bag Lady. It was much simpler to pretend he didn't know her than to catch more flak about hanging with Courtney. His friends thought she was nothing but trouble. His band called her the Black Tornado.

Courtney had other friends, fortunately. Dean Mathiesen for one, and a theater group called the Bad Actors, which had just started up. Snotty, bratty, funny, and dramatic, the mouthy bunch was aptly named. They put on productions of darkly amusing performance-art pieces, which they wrote themselves and which were filled, as one might expect, with very bad acting. Courtney was queen around Dean and the gay boys, able to match their stinging wit and sarcasm, able to upstage their dramas.

She could also outdo their most intense crushes. She was obsessed, asking everyone, everywhere, if they'd seen Rozz. On nights when she wasn't working and wasn't able to secure a bedside appointment with Rozz, she often stood around outside a new club, Satyricon, a dark cave of a space with black lights and graffiti-covered walls splashed with neon murals, where Napalm Beach and the Wipers often played. She was too young to get inside the first year it was open, so she waited on the sidewalk smoking cigarettes until the sweaty masses flooded out during breaks.

It was there one night that she was kidnapped. At least that was the story. A group of neo-Nazi skinhead girls, sick of Courtney's chronic mouthiness, grabbed her one night and drove for six hours up to Bellingham, Washington, near the Canadian border, where they dumped her out on the highway—naked.

She was livid, and humiliated. And while she apparently never avenged herself against those girls, her absorbed anger from then on was a barrier projecting a warning: "Do not fuck with me!"

The story, when it was flapped through the town, was just another rumor about the hellion—and one of the few where Courtney was the victim. By then there was already a volume of Love stories. Courtney could make subculture headline news any time she walked out the door. Her living arrangements were a continuing source of gossip. She'd move, owing several months' rent and sky-high phone bills. People had to be careful with their clothes, drugs, and boyfriends when Courtney appeared; around her, they had a tendency to vanish.

She was rapidly making enemies, but even some of *them* liked her. One Portlander despised her so much that he later confessed (on the Internet) that he had set fire to a house she lived in—as if Courtney wasn't capable of doing that herself—but even he admitted that when she was in a good mood, nobody was more fun than Courtney. It was just that she had a mean side as well, and no one knew when her mood would darken. One minute she'd be cracking up the crowd she'd invited to her place, and the next she'd be insulting them and hissing at them to leave.

To make sure that musicians noticed her at their shows, she would grab at them, yell at them, and make a huge scene whenever she spotted them; she was rumored to blow anyone who was even vaguely connected to a band, just for a chance to talk to the singer.

But of all the handsome musicians in town, Rozz was really the only one she deeply desired. For seven months, their friendship had been on again, off again, and though they'd spent many nights together, she still hadn't had sex with him. Her trump card had yet to be played.

Finally, the opportunity arrived. She received a major installment from her trust fund, and she used it to woo her beloved. Courtney showed up at a Theatre of Sheep show with an offer that Rozz could not refuse: champagne, more pills—and tickets to San Francisco. The idea of slipping off with this wildly determined girl who wreaked havoc wherever she went, who knocked over tables as she crawled around on all fours looking for spilled pills, appealed to his love of danger and of the clandestine. They flew to California that night, before he could change his mind, and before he had a chance to recall his engagement to Marion. They holed up for two days in a four-star hotel, singing in bed, writing, laughing, popping pills. And this time, after months of her cajoling, they finally consummated their relationship.

Rozz, however, felt guilty for betraying his fiancée. He refused to look at Courtney's face, and he made her write poetry during the act. Not exactly romantic, but nevertheless a victorious moment. She was getting in, blurring the line, throwing his upcoming marriage into serious question. She was wild in bed, where her hands were instruments of seduction. And the pills made it all seem like a subconscious dream. Even though he refused to look at her, they both knew after that first night that Courtney had him. "The War of the Roses," as she called their relationship, had begun. He agreed to continue the sex and to have a bona fide affair—but on one condition: it had to be kept secret. In public he would still pretend he didn't know her. She agreed.

The next night, back in Portland, Theatre of Sheep played Starry Night, an old church that had been converted to a balconied all-ages club. The place was packed, the videotape was rolling. And in the middle of the show Rozz looked up to see a fury in white literally splitting the crowd. It was Courtney. In a wedding dress, a visual reminder of her determination to marry him. She shoved fans out of the way, as she stormed up to the stage. Once there she glared up at him and tossed onto the stage a bottle of peach brandy and an empty Tuinal bottle—left over from their hotel party in San Francisco the day before. So much for discretion.

Marion, who was present as well, freaked. Courtney was back in the picture. The fiancée went on a self-annihilation binge and turned anorexic. She called Rozz, threatening suicide again and again. Courtney, not to be outdone, began threatening suicide as well. Rozz himself was becoming an emotional wreck—his life divided by two demanding females, one beckoning him to a traditional way of life, the other luring him toward the dangerous unknown.

All three of them were getting frighteningly skinny, Courtney gobbling speed to shed weight, Marion losing more to stay in the lead, Rozz becoming emaciated out of sheer anxiety and dread of another late night suicide threat. Courtney suggested Rozz market himself as a diet plan. He'd spend a few days with Marion, then a few with Courtney, then slink back to Marion again. The status of their engagement was questionable.

On one occasion, when Courtney was with Rozz at his apartment, Marion stopped by unexpectedly. Courtney scrambled under the bed, where she was forced to hunker down for hours, listening to the fiancée whine about her, saying she knew Rozz was still seeing Courtney, because the apartment reeked of her perfume.

Wining, dining, and drugging Rozz with pills procured from her psychiatrist, Courtney was eating away at her trust fund; but then again, Rozz was an investment. She was charting his course.

Rozz wasn't ready for a commitment, but hanging with Courtney was intriguing and addictive, something he'd never experienced before, especially as they sought out stranger and stranger places for their secret meetings. One night, as they sat drinking champagne in a boxcar parked on the railroad tracks, she passionately proposed once again. Suddenly they were startled by the emergence of a wino rolling out from his under a cardboard shelter. "Oh, go ahead," he drunkenly growled. "Marry her!"

Another night they were the eavesdroppers: as they lay in bed, dazed again by Tuinals, Marion called and left a long-winded message on his answering machine accusing him of being with Courtney, who was in fact at his side. She and Rozz laughed away as Marion droned on about Rozz hanging out with a pushy groupie, asking what could he see in her. "And she's not even pretty," Marion lamented before hanging up. Courtney used that line as the title of her fanzine: *And She's Not Even Pretty* eventually became the official Hole newsletter.

Courtney was so obsessed with Rozz and his band and a few dozen other groups that he finally suggested she start up her own. Courtney bought a Casio keyboard, and soon the word was out: Courtney was bragging that she was going to form a girl group and be a rock star. Laughter echoed through the bars.

Girl bands were a rarity at that time, the early eighties, and not only on the local scene. Chrissie Hynde, Patti Smith, Joan Jett, Nina Hagen, Lene Lovich, Pat Benatar, Suzi Quatro, Toni Basil, Kim Wilde—the names of female rockers couldn't fill a page, even if you included relatively obscure but noteworthy artists like screamer Lydia Lunch. Even though more girl bands and bands led by females had emerged since the late seventies— Siouxsie and the Banshees, Blondie, Heart, Bow Wow Wow, Romeo Void, X-Ray Spex, the Go-Gos, the Delta Five, the Raincoats, the Motels, the Bangles, the Au Pairs, and the Slits among them—the idea of Courtney as entertainer was pushing it: she had shown little more than a penchant for ticking people off.

She ignored the snickers, called up the town's wildest women, and asked them to join her new band. Every single one of them turned her down.

So much for that.

And so much for her affair with Rozz, which seemed permanently triangulated. Courtney could not get and keep the lead; then again, neither could Marion.

It was time to try a new tack. With her next trust fund installment, she traveled alone to San Francisco, with one purpose in mind. She was going to relive everything Rozz had done when he lived there, back when he was in a rowdy punk band called Negative Trend, whose claim to fame was opening for the Sex Pistols at the infamous Winterland show on the night the Sex Pistols broke up.

Rozz would live to regret having told her about his past. Because Courtney turned information into a weapon.

CHAPTER 4

San Francisco, Here She Comes
(1983–February 1995)

THEY WERE STILL THERE. THE PUNKS ROZZ TOLD HER ABOUT. Still hanging at the Tool and Die, a sleazy firetrap with beat-up greasy sofas in an upstairs room that had once been the employees' lounge of a tool-and-die shop. In the basement was a tiny band room and a speakeasy where Courtney could drink and where some of America's most underground bands partied. Members from Black Flag and the Dead Kennedys hung out there, and rising punk groups like Jodie Foster's Army played there while skaters rode up and over ramps brought in for special events.

The illegal bar was a perfect reflection of the street. Its grit, its kinks, and its twisted humor were all there, along with ground-level habitués, including runaways, rejects, and addicts, bonded together in the dank subterranean hole.

The postcard charm of San Francisco—the city of bay-windowed Victorian houses, trolleys, and Rice-a-Roni—faded in this world of black leather, army jackets, Mohawks, and tattoos, where the mood was way more big city, way more hardcore, than Portland. In Portland, cocaine was still the champagne of drugs, too expensive for most, and heroin was still hidden, used mostly by musicians who'd started in the sixties and hadn't yet quit.

But in the Tool and Die and the world that oozed out from it, heroin was everyday news, as common as herpes, often regarded as a punk battle scar.

Courtney knew Rozz's stories well, and she knew what to expect. When he had stumbled in from a small Oregon town a few years before, his initiation was swift. One night at a party he waited impatiently at the locked bathroom door. After half an hour, with no response from its occupant, he had kicked it down. Inside, a young man was slumped on the floor, dead from an overdose, the needle still sticking out of his arm. The response to his death was as harsh as the sight itself. "Hey," said the dead man's friend, pulling the needle from the corpse's arm, and tapping it. "Still a hit left."

In 1983, when Courtney first moved to San Francisco, the scene wasn't much different from the one Rozz had left a few years before. Almost everything about it, from the drugs to the living conditions, was a parent's worst nightmare. Bloody needles littered the hallways of battered apartments, where Mohawked musicians shared scuzzy bathrooms with video artists who made snuff films of kidnap victims being slowly tortured. Theft, guns, violence, and death hovered over the scene, sometimes much closer than a thin wall away. And that was if you were among the lucky ones to land an apartment. Faced with the highest rents in the country, San Francisco's musicians often just climbed into abandoned buildings and turned them into squats.

The most famous squat was the so-called Vats, a defunct beer distillery with tubes that tenants crawled through to reach the tanks, which were partitioned into informal apartments. Residents of the Vats typically left someone to guard possessions and space, until a "secretary of the squat" was installed in front, to bar access by the uncool. A few years before, Rozz had spent time there. Courtney made a point of hanging out there as well, as though checking off items on the to-do list in her Fodor's Punk Guide.

She headed to the clubs seeking out every band that Rozz had ever been in or been near, tracking down every person whose name he had mentioned in their late night rambles and stuporous talks. And she slept with most of them. Or so she told Rozz.

For money, she turned to dancing again. The $800 or so she got from the trust fund each month was not really enough. Had she been able to budget or save, it might have been plenty, but she was busy buying presents for potential boyfriends and occasionally renting houses for groups of her friends; she also had psychiatrist's bills, prescriptions to fill, and champagne tastes. To be a trust fund kid, but have it doled out in small parcels, was frustrating; by the end of the month, she'd be borrowing money, which she often didn't pay back.

Though she was from a wealthy family, she couldn't play by the rules, and she couldn't get along well enough with her mother, the conduit of heiress status, to tap into large chunks. Her fund allowance was just enough to make it a financial tease, a carrot that she dangled in front of people to impress them and that was dangled in front of her.

She intended to be rich someday. She lay on her bed writing list after list, figuring out how to be famous, how to be a millionaire. Courtney had dreams, and she shared them with everyone, boasting that she would someday be well known and that she'd marry somebody famous and live a really grand life.

In the meantime, she turned to the legal sex industries.

Dancing, whether topless or nude, was an entirely acceptable form of employment in downtown artistic circles all along the West Coast. After all, erotic dancing and stripping gave young women the best wages they could garner: $60 to $200 a night was the typical take-home pay in Portland; in big cities she could get $300 or more for prancing around in various states of undress and having men tuck bills into her g-string. In some markets, such as Hawaii, Alaska, and Asia, dancers could make $1,000 a night.

And besides, dancing offered Courtney something she'd been searching for since she was a child: a stage. Sure, it wasn't Broadway, it wasn't the Coliseum, and it wasn't the stage of the Tool and Die or Portland's coolest club, Luis' La Bamba. But in that slimy world of stripping and strutting, Courtney found the only stages that would then take her. And erotic dancing brought with it guaranteed attention.

So what if she spent her afternoons gyrating in smoky bars for old codgers, drooling geezers, and smarmy businessmen in leisure suits with popping eyes and hands in their pockets? Blinded by the lights that she imagined were eyes, shedding fantasy costumes to Fleetwood Mac, she could pretend she was somewhere else, dancing for someone else; she could practice for a time when the fans would number in the thousands, not dozens, when the seats were filled with cute guys, not leering frat boys and bored retirees, and when the audience had come to watch her perform in bands or in movies, not just strip.

In San Francisco, however, the competition was greater, the market was bigger, the sleaze factor higher. It was easier to get a gig in a peep show doing provocative things with a soda bottle behind a glass partition than it was to land a job as a plain stripper. So, along with gigs as a dancer at the Lusty Lady, she began doing peeps. One night a few guys from Portland who happened to be in town looked Courtney up and found her working with a bottle behind glass. The story goes that they started rapping on the glass, jeering her and her great gig, and she fled in tears.

While Courtney was in San Francisco, she earned a few more badges in underground living. She had more sexual conquests, some of which were humiliating. It wasn't always glamorous being a groupie in an increasingly S&M scene where people were into bondage, domination, and an occasional "golden shower"—the nickname for an act in which one party is peed on. And, as one might expect in that highly sexual crowd where condoms were then considered a joke, the scene was a breeding ground for sexually transmitted diseases, which were running in epidemic proportions.

That experience merely deepened Courtney's knowledge of life, her understanding of how the world worked and how depraved it all was. All the more reason to stay messed up. And along her merry way into the dregs of the subculture, she picked up a new intrigue or two. She tried methamphetamines, the speediest of the uppers, which were known to cause extreme violence and insanity with prolonged use. And she embraced heroin. In San Francisco she learned how to score dope in quantities then called "spoons," which were sometimes sold in balloons or wrapped up in paper, and which sold for about $60 a gram.

Courtney delved into the world of potent opiates, with its many rituals, which varied from the East Coast to the West. Along the Atlantic seaboard, heroin often came in powder form conducive to sniffing. On the West Coast, it was typically sold in a black tarlike form. That made it easy to smoke; but it packed more of a wallop when it was injected.

She was taught the mystical and celebratory rites surrounding heroin use; she learned how to wrap a tie or belt around her arm and "tie off," then tap her veins until one popped out; how to cook down the balls of black tar or powder in a spoon, melting it with a little water over a candle; how to soak up the liquid in a section of cigarette filter and pull the liquefied opiate up in the needle; how to stick the needle in her vein, first drawing a little blood into the syringe to ensure it had hit a blood vessel; and how to slam it. It was a brutal way to get high, but one that came with the honor of being hardcore. Proof positive that life sucked.

Even though Courtney was really more of a pill freak, prone to go to a doctor and complain of sleeplessness to score a prescription, or to bum pills from whoever recently had surgery, she now had learned how to fake being a junkie. And even though her musical tastes ran more toward New Wave and folk, she could now pretend to be punk.

Some of the "true" members of the punk underworld, the ones who lived on food stamps and drug deals or maybe a low-paying job at a bookstore, doubted her authenticity; not only did she care too much about her perfume, she could actually afford to buy it.

The only problem with San Francisco, and her immersion in Rozz's history, was that Rozz was still in Portland, so she returned there after a few months. It had been very enlightening, that jaunt through Rozz's past, which she now dangled in front of him, updating him on his former bandmates, all of whom she claimed to have had sexual dalliances with.

When she arrived back in the Northwest, she had new artillery with which to win friends and influence people. She had found power in a little ball of black tar. She was one of the endarkened few, and now when she went downtown, she could mingle with the new influx of junkies who seemed to ride in on the punk scene like a virus from the California coast.

Not that the whole drug scene was sordid; much of it was creatively rich. Punk, with its anticorporate sentiment, spawned amazing do-it-yourself art—from handmade books of paintings and poems, to photocopied fanzines containing interviews with bands and streetcorner characters. From this world emerged the crude tunes of bands that may have not have graduated from the garage but had the determination to save the money necessary to put out their own record. The scene produced the precursors of grunge—and the self-sufficiency that went hand in hand with small independent labels, which eventually captured the sounds of these bands and distributed the music across the globe.

At around the same time Courtney returned to Portland, Bruce Pavitt, a transplantee to Seattle, was sending out a fanzine called *Subterranean Pop*. Initially, in 1981, the cover boasted artwork by cartoonist Lynda Barry, and the inside contained record reviews. Subsequent issues included tapes that Bruce had made of unknown bands from the Northwest and the Midwest—anywhere that wasn't L.A. or New York. He boasted that someday he'd help make Seattle the music capital of the world. Everyone laughed.

The creativity and low-tech, do-it-yourself attitude spawned a whole movement of notable artistic accomplishments. But the "life sucks" sentiment that punk symbolized created a social climate that often made heroin use not just acceptable but admirable, a symbol of underground legitimacy.

The drug itself was not the sort that triggered violence à la drive-by shootings. Instead, it induced a feeling of spiritual euphoria; its users were blissed out while on it, not even minding the nausea and itchiness that was typically part of the effect. The vileness of the drug was what people would do to get it and how, once on it, the other aspects of life lost all meaning.

By late 1983 heroin was more obviously infiltrating the Portland scene, exposing the dark side of the city that was always there, just veiled. Syringes could be found on the floors of sleazy bars, in fine restaurants, and in alleyways behind a strip where teenagers cruised. A handful of artists, certain bands, and their followers made up a group of the new users; the social scene, which had once been affable and trusting, quickly changed. Hosts of late night parties now hid their jewelry and other valuables, knowing that junkies would steal them without a second thought.

And Courtney was part of the cabal. Some said she was an influential member who glamorized the use of heroin to others. It was hard to be really punk if you weren't shooting up or smoking heroin, or at least being tolerant of its use. Besides, needles were disgusting and alarming, two qualities that were esteemed in that scene.

When she barged into the hard-core scene in Portland,

Courtney became known as a betty—a groupie who was easy to bed in exchange for a backstage pass or some dope. The social scene that she became immersed in was neither wholesome nor feminist; she was roughed up physically and emotionally, put down and used by various musicians.

It was a degrading and dangerous life, and the fact that she delved as deep into it as she did reflected her low self-esteem. It spoke of the same insecurity that drove her to bring drugs of some sort into most every romantic scene she entered. Back then, Courtney felt big and fat, and every time she looked in the mirror she saw her father's nose.

When she wasn't hanging with junkies, she turned back to Rozz. He was the fantasy man who offered escape from the sleaze of the heroin scene through the promise of fame. He could be a huge star, she knew it. But he didn't exactly treat her like a prince, especially when he returned to his real world, and his fiancée.

But Courtney and Rozz's moments together were intoxicating for both of them. When they dreamed, they dreamed big, and it wasn't hard to imagine that Rozz's band was going somewhere. Theatre of Sheep was growing hotter by the gig. They'd recently won a battle of the bands against Billy Rancher and the Unreal Gods, and the groupies swarmed around him in the cafés, roving bands of teenage girls and gay boys who seemed to live only for Rozz. He even started a fashion trend by tying a shoelace around his head.

He was so charismatic, and she was so dangerous, the personification of temptation, the wrong choice, the road that should not be taken. But Courtney was daring and funny, and brilliant. Rozz loved to lie around drinking tea while Courtney painted their future. The houses they'd have. The stages he'd play on. The roles she'd land in movies.

When she was around him, Courtney put away the heroin and brought out the pills. Together they enjoyed their dolls. Pills, pills, the beautiful world of pills that could shut out reality as effectively as heroin but a lot less brutally.

Together she and Rozz could soften the harshness of the world, they could write poetry, and they could sing and escape everything that was real, including his fiancée. Despite occasional efforts to kick Courtney out of his life, or at least his heart, Rozz was falling for her. She was blending with the drug itself, inducing the same subconscious blur. He began writing songs about her, with titles like "Courting Disaster" and "Angel Face from Outer Space." He also began to refer to Courtney as "my cure for happiness." Nevertheless, he was intrigued by her persona and the creative mania that being around her produced.

But even as she wove her way back into his life, Courtney could never push Marion completely out of the picture. And Marion was becoming more extreme; her relationship with Rozz was as rocky as her encounters with Courtney were dramatic. One night she broke into Rozz's apartment, convinced he was there with Courtney. When the apartment manager got wind of Marion's break-in, Rozz was kicked out.

He'd barely finished unpacking at the new pad, when Courtney this time broke in. She smashed his artwork, ripped his clothes, stole his books, and she admitted doing it. "But why, Courtney?" he asked.

"Anything *she* can do," Courtney explained, *"I* can do better."

Days later she was back with more pills. He told her to leave, incredulous that she would return after the break-in. "Oh, God," she said, "are you still mad about that?"

She did slip back into his life, though. And the triangle raged on, with continuing threats of suicide from both girls. Courtney at one point was whisked away to the hospital, where she nearly died from too many Tuinals; the ambulance bill was forwarded to her trust fund trustees. According to written statements, the trust fund administrators were concerned about her continuing requests for advances and by her use of the money. She would have bought Rozz a house if she'd had access to the funds. That was her latest strategy to get, and keep, his slippery heart: buy the boy a home, preferably in the Northwest part of Portland, where they could practice twenty-four hours a day, where the band would hang out, and Marion would be barred. A house for Rozz was the obvious solution to her quandary, and Courtney set about to make it manifest. And if that meant going overseas again, she'd do it.

It wasn't long before someone offered her an opportunity to make at least $30,000 by dancing for a few months—in Taiwan. A few months of sacrifice, and violà! Rozz would be hers. And with the new house and more practice, the band would get famous, and she could replace the swanky keyboardist and share in their wealth.

Taiwan was dangerous. There were stories of dancers being stranded over there and turned into indentured servants after their passports were taken away. But for Courtney it was worth the gamble. Besides, she didn't have to worry about Rozz's relationship with Marion while she was gone—because Marion was being shipped overseas as well. Her parents, who attributed her anxious state to her relationship with Rozz, sent her to study in Germany for the summer.

As for Courtney, she could earn substantially more money in Asia than in the United States. There was only one problem: dancers in Taiwan were sometimes expected to do more than dance.

Courtney arrived in Taipei in the early summer of 1984, just in time for Ghost Month, when the Taiwanese believed that spirits trapped in hell were released to come out and party. The streets were filled with parades and chanting ceremonies; Pagodalike temples, permeated with incense smoke, were piled with sacrifices of food; haunting operas were performed in the parks; and paper lanterns shaped like small houses were set afloat in the harbor.

The city was exotic, and she described her life there in long, soul-baring letters to Rozz that arrived daily during her three months abroad. Those letters were filled with moving descriptions of walking past funeral pyres where the masses chanted and burned money—sights that seemed all the more moving when she took them in after chewing bits of opium. She bought pills, speed, downs, and assorted odd drugs from old hunched-over pharmacists and sent them to Rozz in small boxes.

When she turned twenty in Taipei, Courtney wrote lamenting that she was now almost middle-aged. It was hard work, she told him, and she was so depressed. "Now I just play a game with myself—'Let's stay sane one more day.'" In another letter, she wrote, "I borrowed Scarlett O'Hara's soul, and put it in a fat woman's body and added poetry." Courtney had a lot of drive, but she hadn't done anything important yet. She had never played on a stage that wasn't selling sex. "I stole for you," she wrote, "I lied for you, I prostituted myself for you. I hope you appreciated it."

And with every letter she penned, Rozz was more enchanted by her poetic persona, which translated so well in print.

But as visually inebriating as Taiwan was, as magical and engaging as its rituals were, it was not the money-making paradise that she'd hoped for. When Courtney returned to the States several months later, in 1984, she had a small bundle of cash—emphasis on "small". A thousand dollars wasn't nearly enough for a down payment on a house, but it was enough for a good night on the town.

She and Rozz checked into the Heathman, a four-star hotel in downtown Portland for a weekend of reacquaintance. They promptly had a fight.

Rozz liked her better in her letters. In person, Courtney was just too much—too demanding, too manipulative, too intense—and she was always making a scene.

So he abruptly left the hotel—and she chased him through the lobby and along the main downtown drag, her bathrobe flapping open all the way.

Rozz was obviously slipping from her hold. But at least she had succeeded in wrenching him away from Marion. He'd had enough of both of his lovers, whose absence he'd relished. He started adding twists of his own to their mind-trips, little things like asking a female friend of his to wear his sweater out to the clubs, simply to drive Courtney nuts. His "lucky sweater" was a ripped and hole-filled navy-blue number, but Courtney had always loved it. When she saw Rozz's friend in it, she flipped—and began calling the girl continually in the middle of the night, demanding that she return the sweater to her, even though it belonged to Rozz.

And as for Marion, one night shortly after her return from Germany, she smashed a beer bottle over a policeman's head and was shipped off for a brief stay at a psychiatric hospital. The next night, Courtney broke into Rozz's apartment again. Coming home from a show, and seeing the ruckus-in-progress from the street, Rozz called the police from a pay phone. They told him not to enter, so he watched the spectacle from outside, standing open-mouthed as Courtney ran through the apartment, shredding clothes, and smashing everything in her way. Then she picked up a bamboo rod and, one by one, knocked out the many windows in his second-floor apartment.

Before the police arrived, Rozz sent a roadie in to intervene. At the sight of him, Courtney jumped out the window. The roadie caught her by one foot, and Rozz looked up to see Courtney swinging back and forth over the sidewalk by her ankle. When the police finally arrived, she was sitting on the stairs, wearing his robe, crying.

The incident marked the breaking point for Rozz. He called his band and announced he was moving to San Francisco. Courtney, who was at least half of the reason for his speedy departure, wanted to follow, but he told her he needed a break. Marion tossed back the engagement ring, which Rozz gave to a waitress at a café as a tip, while waiting for the Greyhound for hippies—the Green Tortoise bus—out of town.

Theatre of Sheep broke up. Shortly thereafter the Confidentials faded out. Greg Sage, leader of Portland's premier punk band, the Wipers, moved to New York, then went to the Southwest and became a recluse. Billy Rancher and the Unreal Gods were the only band of the bunch to land a major label deal—with Arista Records. The record was almost ready to go when Billy died of lymphoma, a fast-acting cancer, and the project was shelved. About the only band that remained from the scene was Napalm Beach, who went on to rage for another decade without much major label attention.

Out of the entire Portland music world of the early 1980's, Courtney—who had been merely a groupie— was the only one who eventually emerged as a star.

With Rozz out of the picture, Courtney made new friends, among them a petite doll-faced blonde by the name of Kat Bjelland. Initially, Kathy—her name in high school—was a brunette, a straight-A sort from a small town in Oregon. But she changed her name, fell in with the downtown music crowd, bleached her hair, and, like Courtney, looked to dancing for money. They both had dreams of being famous. And they both were competitive: Kat envied Courtney's intoxicating presence and adventurous spirit, while Courtney envied diminutive Kat and her little-girl looks, which were a boy magnet. They were instant enemy-friends who supported each other in between put-downs.

And they both shared a love of vintage clothes. Antique garb wasn't hard to find in Portland; back then, those who liked old stuff didn't have to toss out much money to buy it. Portland was a Dumpster-dive kind of town, a place where every weekend the porches and garages were filled with old clothes and junk. Goodwill was the hip place to shop: you could rifle through bins of stuff from the recently deceased and buy piles of it for fifty cents a pound.

Those bins spawned many an odd fashion: dust coats and old-lady dresses, frocks and frills. Girlie girl, the look forbidden in the genderless household that Courtney grew up in, soon became her fashion statement. But the baby-doll origins of the "Kinderwhore" look, with its many bows and frills, was locally credited to the artist Ava Lake—although Kat and Courtney would later fight about which of them started it.

Courtney and Kat had more in common than their taste in clothes and drugs and their desire for fame and cute boys. They both suffered from missing-mother syndrome. Kat's mother had taken off when she was five, and Courtney never could connect to hers. Both girls looked to role models in pop culture, devouring books like *Edie,* the biography of model Edie Sedgewick, an Andy Warhol starlet, whose life was ravaged by drugs. Kat and Courtney were also fascinated with Nico, the Velvet Underground singer who suffered a similar lifestyle and drug-overdose death, and they loved the poetry of Sylvia Plath, who killed herself by sticking her head in a gas-filled oven. And of course there was the continuing fascination with *Valley of the Dolls* and its fictional celebrities powered by pills.

The available role models were hardly saints, although at least one had adopted the nickname of the Virgin Mary. Around then, Madonna, the first really really bad girl of music, who would parade around in pointy bras and call men her "boy toys," was starting to make her name known in the world.

Not that Courtney needed to take lessons from Madonna in being outrageous and shocking. She could easily devise her own ways to tweak people's brains. And she loosed that ability on Rozz. Even though he was out of town, he wasn't out of her mental picture. In mid-February, several months after he'd moved south, the phone rang in his San Francisco apartment, with a very special Valentine's greeting from Portland: On the line were Courtney and Marion—together at last! Courtney, he was told, had shot Marion up with heroin and was in the midst of seducing her. They were doing very wild things to each other, and they told him all about it, every last detail, as they moaned into the phone.

Rozz referred to that call as the Valentine's Day Massacre. Courtney had once again proved herself queen of the head trip. And before long she showed up at his door.

CHAPTER 5

California Dreaming
(1985–1988)

STUPID OLD PORTLAND. BORING, BORING, JUST INCREDIBLY boring. Same people every night, everybody on a first-name basis, knowing everyone else's secrets, like a small family. The so-called city felt like a village, where the population of available men seemed to number eight—make that seven with Rozz gone.

Kat Bjelland felt the same way. It was time for some big-city action. Seattle was a mere four hours away, but it didn't have that much of a scene then. So when Courtney got a bundle from her trust fund—theoretically for college tuition—she headed with Kat to San Francisco, leaving many stories and diaries in assorted houses she'd lived in.

They moved to the outskirts of the Haight District, seven blocks from Rozz. Marion moved down a few weeks later, renting an apartment five blocks from her former fiancé.

Sometimes Courtney would stop by Rozz's apartment for tea and end up staying for three days—days filled, as usual, with writing and pills. At other times, though, Rozz wouldn't even let her in, and before long her crush faded, at least slightly. After all, there were rising rock stars to meet, and Rozz's was no longer on the ascent.

There was a problem, though: whenever the two girls from Portland encountered new social life opportunities, guys typically chose petite Kat over big-boned, big-mouthed Courtney. "Kat was far better with the men," Courtney later said. "They'd all fall in love with her, and she would break their hearts. She was like a sex symbol who always hung out with the coolest musicians, and I was fat and zitty and hanging out with the roadies. That power was something I wanted."

Kat and Courtney took jobs as hat-check girls at a music spot called Club Nine, where the owner berated them routinely, calling them ugly sluts. There were, however, perks to the job, like meeting musicians and watching the bands rehearse. One night the absurdity of the situation struck Courtney: it was ridiculous that she was only the coat-check girl, when she wanted to be one of the performers on that stage. "Why was I not allowed to play guitar?" she later recalled wondering. "I just made myself think, 'I will not covet what boys have. I'll just create it myself.'"

Courtney and Kat began more seriously dreaming about having a band, instead of just chasing after musicians.

Jennifer Finch, a young musician from Los Angeles, with whom Courtney had become pen pals via a classified ad in a music paper, came up to visit her. Jennifer was disheartened because she been nixed by an L.A. band called the Pandoras, who'd said she wasn't pretty enough.

One night, the three girls headed out to hear an all-girl band called Frightwig. The men in the audience were heckling the performers for their less than glamorous looks. But Courtney, Kat, and Jennifer were inspired: if this band could pull it off, they could too.

Thus was born Courtney's first band, Sugar Baby Doll, the raw beginning of three of the hottest girl bands of the 1990s: L7, Babes in Toyland, and Hole.

Courtney, Jennifer, and Kat sat around the San Francisco apartment, jamming and creating pretty acoustic songs. One of their first was called "The Quiet Room," named for the padded cell at Hillcrest, where Courtney had spent time in solitary confinement. That song later showed up on a Babes in Toyland CD. Another, called "Best Sunday Dress," would end up in Hole's repertoire.

Courtney, who then couldn't play any instrument very well, was the lead singer. Kat played guitar, and Jennifer played bass; there was no drummer. During the first show, stage-shy Jennifer was a mess: she vomited twice before their appearance, cried onstage, and played with her back turned to the audience. But a few weeks later Courtney used some of her trust fund money to buy them time to record demo tapes in a studio.

Nevertheless, the group broke up after three gigs. It was amazing that they lasted that long, since they were always fighting. Courtney wanted to play melodic music in the New Wave genre; Kat and Jennifer leaned toward punk. And one night at a practice session, Kat kicked Courtney out, and the band broke up before they'd even attracted a following.

As pitiful as their beginning was, they were actually triggering a revolution: all three would go on to change the role of women in rock, starting a girl rocker movement that Sonic Youth labeled "fox-core." Jennifer would go on to play with hard-hitting L7, who in 1993 would be pictured on the cover of *Spin*. Kat would later start up Babes in Toyland, one of the first female groups to inspire a hardcover book. And long after Kat and Jennifer became working musicians, Courtney would finally form her own band, Hole.

Not knowing that fame and notoriety lay ahead, Courtney grew depressed when her first band fell apart weeks after it was formed. Some friend Kat was, booting her out of a band she'd cofounded.

Then again, Courtney herself was always testing the limits of friendship. One night she slept with the boyfriend of one of her closest pals in San Francisco. The karma payback was instant: the next morning while she was taking a shower, suddenly there were firemen pulling her out of the house. The bathroom wasn't filled with just steam, it was choked with smoke: her place was on fire. It burned almost entirely to the ground, torching all her notebooks filled with lyrics. And there were many more fires to come.

With no band and nowhere to live, Kat called her father, who drove down and moved her back to Oregon. Jennifer went back to L.A., leaving a note that said, "I love you, I love Kat, but I love the [Red Hot] Chili Peppers more. I'm going home."

With nowhere else to turn, Courtney again tracked down her own father, who by now was back in San Francisco. Their relationship was still turbulent. She accused him of going through her things and stealing from her; he accused her of stealing from him, and he was mortified that she was using heroin. She didn't stay long. She took another job as a dancer, and moved to a corner room in the Europa Hotel in a sleazy section of the Haight.

She went through an Iggy Pop phase, and sliced her skin with a razor blade as part of her erotic dancing act. Cutting provided a sexual high: the pain, the drama, the thrill of the forbidden. She liked to slice herself up whenever she was working through an emotional trauma.

There was plenty of blood in her life back then. She continued to court the junkie crowd, some of whom she'd known in Portland. She was funny and daring, and she would stop at nothing to prove how hard-core she was, but many of them were put off by her brash personality, her compulsive name-dropping, and her bragging—about her trips abroad, about her brushes with the underground celebrities, about her sexual conquests, about how she'd hung around with bands such as the Slits, an all-woman British group that Courtney admired, later giving her band, Hole, the American equivalent of their name. Most people thought of her as a rich kid, an heiress who danced at strip joints such as the Lusty Lady just to give herself subculture credibility.

"It's Courtney at the door—don't answer" was the frequent response at one of her favored junkie households, where she was regarded as a faux user who shot up simply to gain access to the scene.

Some people liked her, though. As always, while many found Courtney intolerable, a few were genuinely taken by her intelligence, wit, and charm. Roddy Bottum, for instance, a musician in a new band called Faith No More. Recognizing her star quality and seeing that she possessed both charisma and talent, he actually got her a gig as the singer for the group. A local fanzine reviewed Faith No More's first show with Courtney. The writer said the group was unremarkable, except for the lead singer, who was definitely going somewhere. Nevertheless, the rest of the band was unimpressed, and she was such a pain to deal with that she was quickly ousted.

She danced some more, got into heroin again. "It was such a druggy summer," she later recalled. Occasionally she'd look up Rozz. Sometimes she'd take him out with her stripper friends, or they'd go to see a fortune-teller. On one occasion the reader told Rozz his aura was gold and he would always be rich in friendships. Courtney's stripper friend, the reader said, would always be lonely. But for Courtney, the reader predicted a lot of turmoil and a tumultuous life, adding, however, that Courtney would eventually triumph.

On other occasions Courtney barged back into Rozz's life with more serious matters to attend to. She would show up unannounced at his apartment, sit at a small table near a lace-curtained window, and turn his apartment into her rehab center, junk-sick as she kicked her heroin habit, shivering, throwing up, sweating, and swearing she'd never do dope again. He'd nurse her back to health with tea and cold towels, and a few days later she'd flit off, sticking him with a five hundred dollar phone bill.

Courtney was floundering—until, in Los Angeles, her friend and former bandmate Jennifer Finch launched a new part-time career playing small parts as a punk in TV shows. So Courtney followed Jennifer down to the land of palm trees and glitz, where she got a gig stripping at seedy clubs near the airport during the daytime, when they let the less attractive girls dance. She took the name Crystal, bought some white pumps, and was back in the money.

One of the places where she frequently danced was Jumbo's Clown Room, a dimly lit, sleazy joint in a mini-mall, sandwiched between a video store and a Thai restaurant. Across the street was a twenty-four-hour pie shop, where Courtney often dined after work. A few blocks away from Hollywood Boulevard, the club was tiny, boasting little more than a bar, a half dozen tables, and several stage-side stools. Off in one corner were a couple of video games and a Fritos dispenser, but the main attraction, of course, was the twenty dancers trotting around from 2:00 P.M. to 2:00 A.M., sliding up and down a gold pole onstage amid potted plants. Though the crowd was made up mostly of blue-collar workers, along with a college student and a rock star or two—Guns n' Roses were said to be occasional customers—at least it wasn't a peep show or a full-strip joint. The dancers at Jumbo's bared their breasts, but they kept their bikinis on. And like a theater revue, all the dancers returned to the stage at the end of the night and bade the customers an onstage adieu.

Dancing was just a temporary thing, of course. Just like Neely, Courtney was going to be an actress, or so she boasted to everyone she met. Many doubted it—but she showed them. Her will, her timing, and her connections paid off.

Life took quite the upward turn. Jennifer helped line her up an agent, who happened to be representing Uma Thurman as well, and soon Courtney landed a bit role on *Quincy,* playing a punk rocker at a nightclub in scenes with star Jack Klugman. Not exactly something that would rate her a gold-filled footprint in the sidewalk outside of Mann's Chinese Theater, but it was a beginning.

And while hanging around the TV circle, she met with the director Alex Cox. After the surprise success of his cult classic *Repo Man,* Alex wanted to turn his camera to the tragic, debauched tale of Sid Vicious and Nancy Spungen.

Sid, who (sort of) played bass in the notorious British punk band the Sex Pistols, hooked up with an American groupie by the name of Nancy Spungen, with whom he often did heroin. The duo became infamous for getting so dangerously wasted that when they set fire to their room in New York's Chelsea Hotel, they just stayed in it, too messed up to move. Sid is believed to have ultimately killed Nancy with a knife; shortly thereafter Sid died of a heroin overdose.

When Courtney found out about Alex's upcoming project, she had a new reason for living. She was meant to act in that movie, she believed. Her childhood—being the tyrant whom the family feared—mirrored much of Nancy Spungen's. Courtney had lived in England, hanging around musicians; she had a feel for the music scene. She'd even stayed at the Chelsea Hotel, where she had once used heroin in the same room, number 101, where Sid and Nancy had lived, and where Nancy died.

The part of Nancy was written for her; that was obvious—to everyone except the director. Alex Cox did take her pleas seriously. He liked her, and when he said the most subversive thing he could do would be to loose her upon the world, she knew she'd be cast in the movie. But he cast another, then-unknown actress—Chloe Webb—as Nancy.

Courtney was furious. And depressed. Once again everything was turning to dust. And once again she had to fall back on dancing for money. As hard as she tried to get out of the sex industry, it often presented itself as her only alternative when her attempts to become a star again crumbled. This time she packed up her dancing gear and headed for Guam, another spot where the bucks could be plentiful, although the island could be dangerous and dancers were often put up in tin shacks.

But Alex Cox tracked her down overseas and wrote her a letter saying that he and the producers loved her and had written a part for her in *Sid and Nancy*. The role was small, just a few mumbled and screamed lines, including one in the opening when she yelled *"Nooooo!"* But hey, it was her first big—well, bigger—break. Gary Oldman, who played Sid, was way more her type than the middle-aged Jack Klugman.

Courtney quit the dancing gig in Guam and flew back to Portland that fall of 1985, with a week to kill before being flown to New York for the filming. While in Portland, she crashed at the so-called Bad Actors House, an old Victorian in café-cluttered Northwest, where Dean Mathiesen, the former manager from Metropolis, lived along with half a dozen other smart-ass artists and creative types. She hadn't been in the house more than a few days when her habit of lighting candles and dozing off almost killed her. In the middle of the night, the house went up in flames.

Among the ashes were the melted-down remains of a movie production company that wanna-be filmmaker-musician Michael Hornburg had just bought, with plans of launching a movie career. (A decade later he wrote *Bongwater,* a novel that, despite its unmoving story line, made entertainment news and was even being optioned for the movie—because of a foul-mouthed, drug-popping character named Courtney, who burned down a house. The book's publicist would make much ado of the fact that Hornburg had once gone out with Courtney Love and had known her in the biblical sense.)

After only a few days in Portland, Courtney was again infamous, leaving ashes in her trail, but so what? She boarded a plane and flew to New York to start her new life as a star. Most people didn't even really believe she'd landed a part in a film; they regarded her claim as just another of Courtney's big lies.

The movie cast moved into the Chelsea, the century-old Manhattan hotel on West Twenty-third Street that had once housed Dylan Thomas, Arthur Miller, and Thomas Wolfe. In more recent years, it had served as a temporary home to many a musician, including Bob Dylan, who wrote a song about one of its rooms, not to mention Sid and Nancy. The principal actors moved into the suite next to Nancy's death site, and the rest shacked up in several other rooms down the hall. Even the desk clerk was cast as an extra in the film, which would occupy the Chelsea for two months.

Even though she had only a minor role, Courtney felt like a star and was on her best behavior toward almost everyone, including the hotel staff. A decade later they would recall her as extremely sweet, though they didn't realize she was Courtney Love from Hole.

This was yet another time when her dreams and reality merged. She was reliving modern mythology, walking down the same yellow halls tiled in black and white that some of the leading creators of the past decades had padded down. Even though it didn't take long to memorize her lines (including "She was *really* nice, she *was*," and a less comprehensible garble about scoring heroin), she pored over the script, taking it upon herself to help rewrite it, penning notes in the margins: "They'd never say this."

The making of the movie was the high point of her life thus far. She was part of one of the most popular cult films of the 1980s; she got along with the crew, and she actually made good wages doing exactly what she wanted to do. She was even given a job with the production team so that she could earn more money. "I got loaded," she later said. "I got like $185 cash per diem, plus $365 scale, plus twenty percent on top of that. . . . Plus they [kept] me around for extra weeks just 'cause they liked me. So it was really cool, and I made a lot of money."

Two months later it was all over, and she began city-hopping up and down the West Coast from Portland to Los Angeles. She returned to San Francisco for a time and talked Kat into coming back down as well. Her former flame, Rozz, had moved back to Portland but had kept his San Francisco apartment; Courtney moved in for a while, convincing the building manager that she was Rozz's fiancée. She also went to Rozz's psychiatrist, paying $200 an hour. At Rozz's next visit, the psychiatrist mentioned a fascinating young woman who claimed to be Rozz's fiancée and talked of nothing but him. Of course it was Courtney. Rozz was ultimately notified that she was "subletting" his apartment, and he okayed the arrangement. Courtney decorated the place with lace, knickknacks, miniature tea sets, baby rattles, and old vases that she filled with violets. She dug through stacks of Rozz's notebooks, his journals, and the piles of love letters from his former fans—grading them all, and writing comments in his diaries. She was terribly upset, however, when she came across the love letters *she* had written to Rozz; many of them were unopened.

She also went through another flurry of drugs and did more dancing and plenty of bragging about her part in *Sid and Nancy,* which was then being edited for a fall 1986 release.

During the premiere at the New York Film Festival in Lincoln Center, Courtney sat on the stage next to Gary Oldman and Chloe Webb, drunk with her first real taste of celebrity. Being part of the movie paid off in many ways. She made her film debut, and she used a portion of the money from *Sid and Nancy* to get a nose job, which she modeled for her friends back in Oregon.

When *Sid and Nancy* opened, people in Portland were stunned. The braggardly nightmare whom most had shrugged off as a liar was staring back at them from the big screen. Maybe she hadn't been such a pipe dreamer after all. Like Courtney, though, they were surprised that she hadn't landed the part of the in-your-face Nancy.

Back in San Francisco, however, Courtney fell into a rut. Between the drugs, the go-nowhere situation with Rozz, who flitted back to San Francisco intermittently, and the stagnant feeling creeping into the San Francisco scene, she and Kat decided to look for a new home. They headed to Minneapolis in late 1986. Kat's father had moved to that part of the country, and they also wanted to search down the Replacements, one of their favorite bands from Portland days. Out of the subzero temperature, the brutal winters, the mosquito-filled summer, and the isolation, a music scene was pushing through like a crocus in the tundra, right there in the middle of the country—Minnesota. Bands like Soul Asylum, the Replacements, and Hüsker Dü were taking over the stages, and the music industry's eyes had been watching the city's scene since the emergence of the Artist Then Known as Prince.

For Courtney there was new music to check out, and there were new boys to date. "It was so exciting, it was winter, it was like going to Japan, it was grain belt beer, the CC Club, and all the guys were cute," Courtney later recalled. "Oh, God, every guy was cute."

Within a few hours, Kat was snagging the attention of the city's eligible bachelors and Courtney was scouting out possible candidates to play in a new band. Her eyes fell upon Lori Barbero, a charismatic waitress at a rock club. They decided immediately that she was the city's most popular girl. Kat and Courtney talked her into joining up, and together they formed a band. Courtney wanted to call the new group Swamp Pussy, but she was overruled, and they decided instead upon Babes in Toyland.

Around then Courtney got a call from Alex Cox. He wanted her to act in another film—*Straight to Hell.* When she left for a month, the band found a replacement.

Oh, well, screw music. Courtney had her acting career to consider. This part, which she said Alex had written specifically for her, was much bigger than her role in *Sid and Nancy.* The film—"about sexual tension," as Alex described it—concerned a town occupied by 750 men and five women, including Velma, the part Courtney was to play. She described her character as "a white trash pregnant bitch, some weird hillbilly from an incestuous background who's fascinated with charms and magic. She's into tackiness."

She flew to Europe, where the movie crew set up in Spain's Sierra Nevada mountain region. She worked alongside Joe Strummer of the British punk band the Clash. The Pogues and Elvis Costello also had parts. According to Brad Morrell, author of an unauthorized British book called *Nirvana and the Sound of Seattle,* Courtney told the press on the set that she was sleeping with almost everybody: "the director, the director of photography, the assistant director . . ." but she later retracted that claim. "During that time I did not sleep with anybody. I was fat, and when you're fat like that you can't call the shots. It's not you with the power." Power or no, she was sticking with her original sex-laden story, listing her many sexual exploits when she showed up in Los Angeles shortly thereafter where she crashed with friends from Portland.

When she blew into Portland several months later, her ego had swollen considerably, and she started to mythologize herself even before the movie came out. At parties she often bragged so much and acted so snotty that no one would or could talk to her. She headed to New York, anticipating the release of *Straight to Hell,* which she believed could catapult her to stardom. A write-up about her in the February 1987 issue of *Interview* magazine preceded the movie, and made Courtney Love look entirely glamorous.

Jaws dropped. She wasn't kidding after all. Courtney Love was going to be a star. Almost everybody was sure of it, especially Courtney.

Well . . . at least until the movie came out.

"Pan-o-rama" was putting it mildly. Leonard Maltin called the movie "self-indulgent." Though it featured such big names as Dennis Hopper, Elvis Costello, Grace Jones, Jim Jarmusch, and the Pogues, Maltin said, "It has the insistent air of a hip in-joke, except that it isn't funny. In fact it's awful." The movie was such a bomb that Courtney later made friends promise not to see it.

Hoping for something bigger, better, and more successful, she remained in New York, where Dean Mathiesen and some of the other Bad Actors had taken up residence. Never landing an apartment of her own, she stayed with friends for weeks at a time, at one point living in a closet; she hung out at East Village bars such as the Pyramid Club, getting drunk and often doing ecstasy, the euphoria-inducing designer drug that had just come into vogue in the underground. With the Bad Actors, she did performance art at tiny clubs such as ABC No Rio, a ratty East Village dive where the bathroom was doorless, boasting only a curtain. The group was known for absurd pieces involving the worship of a plastic doll called Mrs. Wong, which Dean "channeled." They also smeared a naked woman with mashed pumpkin gunk; and occasionally they put on more disturbing performances, such as throwing lit matches on a person lying on the floor until someone in the audience objected.

Meanwhile, between telling anyone who would listen her dreams—becoming a Hollywood movie star with a mansion that boasted a pool in back, and having Belinda Carlisle of the Go-Gos as her best friend—Courtney tried out for roles in plays and continued to network with theater and movie types. Despite her chronic shortage of funds, she was determined to avoid the sex industry. After befriending a group of avant-garde artists, she was hired as a receptionist at the Bond Street Galleries in the East Village, "so that I didn't have to go down to Forty-second and do a peep."

She had a few callbacks for plays and movies, including *Last Exit to Brooklyn,* about the gritty scene in that New York borough, but nothing materialized. Nothing much was panning out, and Courtney was becoming pathetic. *Straight to Hell* was appropriately named. Her acting career went spiraling downward, right along with the film.

That was a brutally cold winter, and she had little

money and only one pair of shoes—with holes in them. "I was famous in that real minor way when you're first famous," she said. "I felt like I couldn't strip. I didn't know what to do. I had no agent. And I was getting too fat, my weight problem was crazy, you know. I had no money, yet every day I'd eat like this big cheese Danish and go to these Polish delis, and I would eat and eat and eat. I mean I was 170 pounds."

It apparently wasn't a look that Dennis Miller liked. Miller, a regular on NBC's *Saturday Night Live,* was one of Courtney's few non-singing crushes. A friend at *SNL* would sometimes sneak her backstage, where she would sit in the greenroom, just hoping to hang out with the comedian who "anchored" the comedy show's news segment, during which he continually cracked up at his own jokes. She had taken up chanting, the simple Buddhist formula for success that involves repeating the words *nam-myo-ho-renge-kyo,* but it apparently had no effect on the comedian. In fact it didn't seem to improve her life much in general.

Courtney was already an emotional mess, and then she became a physical mess as well. She found out she was pregnant as a result of a fling in Minneapolis, and she learned that she had hepatitis B and something called microplasma—all from the same guy. In fact, he'd also given hepatitis to two other of her friends. That time in New York, she said, "was a miserable, miserable three months." She called her mother, but Linda refused to help her out, or so Courtney said. So she pinned the pregnancy on someone who wasn't the father, and he tossed her some cash.

Courtney returned to Minneapolis, terminated the pregnancy, moved in with a friend, and freaked out. Her problems weren't aided by the fact that the guy who made her pregnant was living downstairs with another girl. "They would take acid and do heroin and fuck," she said. "So one morning I got up early . . . and I started screaming, 'Fry, fucking fry, fucking fry, fucking—' I screamed it for like twenty minutes." Someone told her to quit her banshee cries, and she thought, "Hey, you know, I'm into this."

She was kicked out of the crash pad. Then she was taken back into Kat's band—and kicked out of it again.

But Courtney had some new ideas up her sleeve. She made friends with Bob Dylan's son, Jesse, whose father and uncle owned the Orpheum, and she devised a new plan for making money and becoming successful: putting together rock shows. Courtney had a gift for it, she had to admit. Within a few days of working the phone she organized an Orpheum show with the Butthole Surfers and a slew of other bands. She persuaded two local radio stations to get involved, and she borrowed thousands of dollars. Then she immediately started planning a trip to India with the beaucoup bucks she would undoubtedly make.

But once again things didn't exactly turn out as planned. The show was a financial fiasco. Not only did she not make money, Courtney ended up owing various parties $20,000, and she was unable to pay the bands. People were furious with her, and she was essentially run out of town—"I had no friends," she later recalled. Taking along a drummer who was smitten with her, she ran back to Los Angeles and sank into depression.

It was a real drag of a time—1988 was the low point of her entire twenty-four years. Her trust fund permanently dried up. She'd blown through all of her movie money. Every band she touched either broke up or booted her out. Her film career had vanished, and her roster of friends was thinning. She wasn't on good terms with either of her parents. Glory and fame were not materializing; every time she got up to bat, she fell on her butt. She needed money, and the drummer boyfriend wouldn't even look for a job, even after she informed him he'd have to sell his stereo or she'd sign up with an escort service. Instead, she made a call to a strip club— this one in Alaska—falling back on the skill she could get the most money for. The club agreed to fly her up to dance. So she dumped the drummer, packed up her stripper costumes again, and headed in the winter to the land where days were mostly dark but where the owners of the club had offered her room and board.

It was common for West Coast dancers to head north, where the money was better and the clubs were packed with younger men employed in canneries or on fishing trolleys who, by demographics alone, were female-deprived. The conditions, however, were often disheartening: accommodations were often stark dormitory rooms with little heat, and some of the other dancers in Alaska were hard-core, willing to turn tricks to support their drug habits. The only real plus, beside the higher pay, was that there were few places to spend the money. The drawbacks were substantial; besides the isolation and the low-grade housing, Alaska was dangerous—particularly at that time. One resident was a baker by day and a killer by night: he dismembered dozens of women in Anchorage, often targeting erotic dancers and prostitutes as his victims.

There in Alaska, in the winter's darkness and solitude, while gazing at the aurora borealis every night, Courtney had an epiphany. This wasn't going to happen again. Like Scarlett O'Hara declaring "With God as my witness, I'll never go hungry again," Courtney all but raised her fist at the heavens and decided that, damn it, she was going to *be* a star, not just a stripper in Alaska gazing at them.

At that point her ambition kicked back in, and Courtney got motivated. She made some decisions, scrawling her goals in notebooks that served as journals. At the top of the list: lose weight. She peeled off forty pounds while peeling off her clothes. And she decided that once and for all she was going to have a band. There'd been too many near misses on the rock 'n' roll stage.

"The clock [was] ticking and I was just like, Jesus Christ, I've got to kick some ass, you know, and I don't want to be twenty-five and not have a band," she later said of that time. "I'd been trying to have a band since I was sixteen, and I still wasn't successful. . . . I'd been kicked out of Sugar Baby Doll, the most retarded band in history, I'd been kicked out of the hardcore band in San Francisco, I'd been kicked out of Jennifer's band, I'd been kicked out of a million and one bands."

After a few sun-deprived months, she left Alaska and traveled down to Vancouver, British Columbia, via bus and ferry, since she'd suddenly developed a phobia about flying. Vancouver was a stripper's paradise, however, and most of her competitors had silicone breasts, so she could only find work as a "Sunday girl," when the busty dancers were off-duty. Despite her flat chest, though, she won wet T-shirt contests, because she added seductive dancing to her strutting. But that got old quickly, and after a few weeks Courtney bussed down to Seattle. She hopped off the bus, walked around the city, and immediately got chilly vibes. Besides, she realized it wasn't much bigger than Portland.

"I walked two blocks away and went to get a room," she later said. "And in those two blocks I figured out it would take four months before everyone in [Seattle would] hate my guts and want to kill me." She ran back to the station and hopped back on the bus, turned on the tears, and convinced the driver with her sobs that she'd been given the wrong ticket and was supposed to go to Portland all along.

So Courtney was back in the sleepy hollow again. Well, at least it was familiar. She had some friends left, so she could regroup and figure out what to do next. She briefly took a job at the Blue Gallery, a new club, where she became known as one of the town's grumpiest bartenders.

Courtney began hanging out at places like Satyricon, where punk music blared most of the week, but open mikes and plays sometimes took over the stage as well. One of the organizers of the loud, drunken poetry scene, which was raucous long before the advent of the "poetry slam," was an old Santa-like lawyer by the name of Don

Chambers. He'd always liked Courtney and thought her poetry showed promise. When he became bedridden from diabetes, Courtney was one of several poets who cooked for him and cleaned his house—though she had never been well known for her domestic abilities.

Subsequent organizers in the poetry scene didn't share Don Chambers's fondness for the wild poet, though. One night at Satyricon she hassled Doug Spangle, the new poetry organizer. Courtney wanted a spot directly after a certain woman poet whom she greatly admired. The organizer had her scheduled for a later spot, and she bugged him every three minutes or so until he finally gave in to her wishes.

Once onstage, Courtney straddled a chair; the organizer made a point of concentrating on the sound board and ignoring her poetry—until someone pulled on his arm and screamed, "She's jacking off! She's masturbating onstage!" The organizer didn't even have the nerve to push her offstage. But luckily, by the time he became aware of her antics, her performance was over.

Shortly thereafter Courtney moved to a town near Corvallis, Oregon, where she shacked up with the owner of a record store. There were plenty of benefits to the arrangement: he supported her and brought home free records and tapes, many of which she sent off to Jennifer in L.A. and to Kat, who was still in Minnesota; and with all the free time being a kept woman provided, Courtney finally learned to play the guitar.

It was always fun to get a medical exam, too, since her mother was then well known in the area as a therapist. "I liked to go to the doctor and go, like, 'Well, I've been a junkie and a stripper and my mother is a respected member of the community,'" Courtney later told a reporter. "I thought it was really fun to terrify her." But even between the trips to the doctor, the records, and learning guitar, she lasted only a few months in the small Oregon burg.

Courtney was bored. She still hadn't done anything to further her pursuit of stardom. So she packed up and took a train to Los Angeles, stealing the $180 train fare from the man who'd been so generous to her for months.

In L.A. she demanded that Jennifer help her out, recalling all the times she had used her trust fund money to help Jennifer. "I just got my shit together, I just made Jennifer loan me money, like 'You'd better just fucking loan me money now!' so I could get an apartment."

Jennifer caved in. Courtney again took a job at Jumbo's Clown Room, where she could make a few hundred a night working in the "blue-collar titty bar." She went on government aid, but could still afford perfume—at the time, Fracas. "I always felt like half a person when I was poor and would run out of perfume," she later said in an interview for *Mademoiselle*. "I'd find a way to get some even when I was on food stamps."

She hung out with glam-rockers, with whom she ingratiated herself by buying dinners, scoring drugs, or harassing people for them. She became infamous in the porn and music crowds for being obnoxious, especially to live with.

Despite the constant excitement of the big city—where she typically traveled around by bus, since she didn't drive—she was always breezing back up north, often bragging about how someday she was going to have a hot band.

There was a new wave of girl bands on the rise. And Courtney was determined to ride it.

CHAPTER 6

A New Boy to Conquer
(1989—1991)

DURING ALL THE YEARS WHEN COURTNEY HAD FELT ALONE
and deserted by her family, hating almost everyone, and
plotting to get revenge by becoming a star, there was
someone else who shared the same sentiment. He knew
all about feeling worthless and neglected. He knew the
lure of the stage, how stepping upon it could temporarily
negate the deep wells of self-loathing. While Courtney
was dancing up and down the West Coast, he had been
sleeping under bridges in the logging town of Aberdeen,
Washington, or in the music section of the locked-up
library. While she was getting beaten up emotionally,
being told she wasn't pretty or desirable enough, he was
getting beaten up by the locals in Aberdeen, who thought
he was effeminate and weird.

He was a slight man, beautiful, with deep blue eyes
that were as dazzling as Courtney's. His name was Kurt
Cobain.

A spark passed between them the moment they met;
the sky should have opened and issued a loud warning.
Because what was to transpire would turn Courtney's
black comedy into a melodramatic tragedy, and Kurt's
search for an escape from pain would become a night-

mare that he ultimately believed could be stopped only with a bullet.

It was just a typical night at Satyricon, which by then pretty much held a monopoly on underground music in Portland. It hadn't altered its black-lit cave feel much in the years it had been open, except to add new murals and another layer of posters to the walls. Nirvana—now known by the latest in a series of band names that included Throat Oyster, Pen Cap Chew and Ted Ed Fred—had driven down from the college town of Olympia, Washington, where they then lived, to open up for the Dharma Bums, a local band that boasted some of the town's cutest boys.

Courtney didn't think Nirvana's music was that hot, but the lead singer was a different story. He was quite handsome. And he seemed to be drawn to her as well.

Her reputation had preceded her, and when someone told Kurt that the girl sitting in the booth was Courtney the wild dancer-scenester-starter-of-fires, Kurt swaggered up to her table, sat down across from the Nancy Spungen look-alike, poured himself a beer from the pitcher, and glared at her. She mirrored the punk greeting, glaring back. Before long, he was giving her stickers of a logo he'd designed for his band, bearing a picture of Chim Chim, his beloved toy version of the monkey from the cartoon *Speed Racer*. They wrestled a bit, and then she got up and left.

At the time of this first meeting, in 1989, Nirvana had just released *Bleach,* a promising album that featured screaming punk, scrappy rock, and John Lennon–style ballads. Hole was just a name bouncing around in Courtney's head. By the time Kurt and Courtney next saw each other, much would have changed.

That was a good year for Courtney, even though being in her mid-twenties made her feel middle-aged, bringing the fear that she'd die an unknown. But at twenty-five, she had at least set the framework: she'd traveled the world several times, danced in numerous clubs, lived with a few guys, bedded many more, and hung out with the famous and the up-and-comers. She also was showing the fruits of having been a human sponge for a decade. From Echo and the Bunnymen's lead singer Ian McCulloch, from whom she admitted snatching rockstar poses, to Rozz, she'd been studying the people whose lives she paraded through, gleaning insight into power moves and personalities. She borrowed jokes, she borrowed styles, she borrowed clothes, and she borrowed boyfriends. Courtney was a flashy compilation piece, the walking best of Portland, Liverpool, Minneapolis, San Francisco, L.A., and New York, all mixed up with a little of Edie, Blanche DuBois, Lydia Lunch, and the O'Haras—both Scarlett and Neely. She was an attention-getting production all right, for Courtney always did have a taste for the outrageous, and an ability to pull her personality parts together with a bright, funny charm that could darken in a second.

Her persona hadn't been enough to get the sort of attention she wanted—yet. But that year she pulled it together, stopped making a creative mess of her life, and started really creating—her music, and her new life. She prioritized her dreams, once again made lists, and decided what she really wanted: a hot band and a rock-star husband. And she diligently and daily chanted the Buddhist prayer for success—*nam-myo-ho-renge-kyo*—in finding such a band and such a man.

For money, Courtney was still dancing at clubs around the L.A. airport, often working the day shift at the Star Strip or the Seventh Veil, but she was also making an effort to start a band. That year she married a musician—James Moreland, the cross-dressing lead singer of the Leaving Trains. Some people in that scene believed the marriage was a career move on her part. James was widely respected in the Los Angeles punk community, whereas Courtney was shrugged off as a punk poseur. And some of her friends thought she showed more affection toward other men in her life such as Roddy Bottum, whose band Faith No More was by then in demand.

After just a few months she and Moreland were divorced. Their relationship, barely a blip on the social barometer, had not been terribly helpful in helping out her career, so she took an even more extreme step. Courtney placed a classified ad in several rock papers: "I want to start a band. My influences are Big Black, Sonic Youth and Fleetwood Mac."

Eric Erlandson, a twenty-seven-year-old accounting clerk at a major label, replied. Before he met Courtney, as he later told the press, he'd never "done anything bad."

"She called me back about two weeks later," Eric later the *L.A. Times,* "and talked my ear off until three in the morning." When they met, he was wary but intrigued. "I met her and thought, This is not going to work," he told *Option.* "She didn't know how to play, and she had a really crazy lifestyle. I didn't think she would get her shit together."

But once again Courtney surprised all the Doubting Thomases by lining up a neighbor who played bass and then borrowing a drummer for their practices. After running through quite a few players, the band ultimately settled down to work with bassist Jill Emery and drummer Carolyn Rue. After three months of practice—and a brief fling between Courtney and Eric—Hole made their debut at Raji's in Hollywood, having persuaded L7 to let the fledgling band open their show. Not many took immediate notice of Hole, but Courtney would soon bully her way into the spotlight, pulling the rest of the band with her.

She called a man by the name of Long Gone John, who'd started up a small L.A. label called Sympathy for the Record Industry. Courtney's approach was direct. "Are you gonna be the cool label or what?" she asked, not waiting for a reply. "Because if you are, you have to put out Hole's record."

John had never heard of her or the band, but her brash hustling maneuver intrigued him enough to make him check them out—and he liked what he heard. Though many people tried to talk him out of getting involved with Courtney, John adored her and thought she was quite glamorous, even then. He gave Hole $500 to record their first single—"Retard Girl" and "Phone Bill Song"—at Rudy's Rising Star Studio. It was released in March 1990, and it sold well enough that John offered to put out their first album. But he hadn't jumped soon enough. Caroline Records had already signed up the act.

By then Courtney had roped in management in much the same assault-and-conquer way. Peter Davis, a manager from Creature Booking in Minneapolis, had flown to Los Angeles to hear Jennifer Finch's band, L7; he was considering signing up the new all-girl rock group. When Peter was pointed out, Courtney was immediately in his face, demanding that he check out Hole, too. And when he saw their show at a tiny club called the Gaslight, he was impressed enough to begin managing Hole as well as L7. Before long Hole had a national tour, playing small clubs across the United States and meeting other bands that recorded on small labels, such as Smashing Pumpkins. Courtney was quite taken by their lead singer Billy Corgan, with whom she developed a passionate friendship.

Hole played at Courtney's old haunts in Portland, including Satyricon. But this time when she walked back into Portland's punk club, she wasn't a whirling dervish hissing accusations and causing a scene. She was quite civil, very polite, extremely nervous, and almost humble. "Well," she said to the club owner as she surveyed the room, "is anybody going to show?" They did. It wasn't exactly a sellout. But the general buzz around Portland was that, surprisingly enough, Courtney and her band weren't half bad.

Meanwhile, the very face of music was changing radically, gearing up for a movement that would revamp the whole record industry. More and more, the hottest bands—at least from the underground aficionados' point of view—weren't to be found on the large labels. They were being signed to the tiny independent, or indie, labels that were springing up all over, though many were in Chicago and along the West Coast. One of the leaders was Seattle's Sub Pop; owned by Bruce Pavitt and Jonathan Poneman, who pushed their own "singles club" (a mail-order club for 7-inch records), the label sold records of little-known bands with music that was raw, vibrant, and sometimes recorded on colored vinyl, often with artwork drawn by the band.

An underground aesthetic had developed. People who were truly into the avant-garde music scene were often listening to records, not CDs; the most interesting music was heard less often on commercial stations than on college radio. And labels in the Northwest were leading the way in this alternative movement.

In addition to Seattle, another Washington city—Olympia—became a major hotspot for indie record labels and new bands.

Olympia, Washington, didn't appear a likely spot for a revolution. The state capital was a laid-back town where the social life revolved around two bars, a couple café's, the local theater, and the Evergreen College auditorium. It was a place where doors were left unlocked and where the three taxi drivers couldn't stay busy even on a rainy Saturday night. Lacking even that most basic of institutions—a Dunkin' Donuts—the residents baked a lot of pies for fun.

But boredom-induced inspiration, a new uprising of feminism, and at least a modicum of talent transformed Olympia into a significant node in the Northwest music scene. It started in the late 1980s, when a few upstarts such as Calvin Johnson formed small record companies capturing on vinyl songs that were usually performed at parties.

The town's young women were writing their own fanzines as well as forming bands, holding conventions, and rallying around political and feminist causes. Before long, the loose-knit movement had a name—riot grrrl—and a motto "revolution grrrl style now." It was an informal network made up mostly of females—many from Olympia and Washington, D.C.—who strove for creative expression and retaliated against society's programming by taking many of its insult words, such as "slut" and "whore," and scrawling them in lipstick across their stomachs and arms.

Any attention given the riot grrrl movement by the press, except for the small fanzine corps, was generally greeted with resentment and quips of "We are not just a media item." When reporters came to review their shows, musicians escaped out back doors.

Despite the annoying, "cooler-than-thou" attitude and the cliquish feeling, it was a fertile scene, out of which came a new breed of girl musician. Subculture bands and small labels, many of them headquartered along the West coast, were kicking up something new, something exciting, something that the major labels dismissed, initially, as unimportant. But those in the social scenes knew better.

And out of this rich, subcultural environment came two bands that would change the face of music in the late twentieth century: Nirvana and Hole.

The next time Courtney saw Kurt Cobain, Hole was touring around small clubs, and Courtney had become an underground legend, as much for her impulsive business maneuvers as for her screaming on stage. Never mind all the years she'd fought with Kat, wanting to play pretty songs; now Courtney sang-yelled her melodies. She was the soul of the street child, singing songs about prostitution and abortion. Hole's music lashed out; it was the attack of a woman for whom PMS was a permanent personality trait.

In March, shortly after Courtney stormed into Jonathan Poneman's house demanding that he sign Hole to his label's roster, Sub Pop released a seven-inch record, a 45, of the grating Hole songs "Dicknail" and "Burnblack." Around the same time, the group recorded an entire album of semimelodic screaming—*Pretty on the Inside.* Produced by Sonic Youth's Kim Gordon and Gumball's Don Fleming, the album earned instant subculture credibility. To give the songs a raw edge, Courtney guzzled whiskey before taking to the mike.

By 1991, when Kurt and Courtney next hung out together, she was up and coming on the alternative scene, and he was about to turn alternative into mainstream: Nirvana had just signed with a major label—DGC, a division of Geffen Records.

Nirvana had a knack for dramatic timing. On their first tour to Europe, they were heading to Germany just as the iron curtain opened, and they got caught in the westward traffic jam where, at Checkpoint Charlie, the guard now handed out champagne and baskets of fruit. Nirvana had emerged in the Northwest just as independent labels were becoming established. Pure punk was fading, as was the interest in just being screamed at from the stage, but few were ready for pure pop cooing. Nirvana bridged the gap.

And in 1991 the band saved Sub Pop, the Seattle indie label that thought it could, but was at that time proving otherwise. Despite underground popularity and a stable of bands that included Nirvana, Mudhoney, Screaming Trees, Soundgarden, and the Fastbacks, the label was overextended and needed money fast.

Little did they know that a frantic late night phone call from a drunk bass player would ultimately deliver it.

One night at the Comet, an endearingly scuzzy tavern on Seattle's Capitol Hill, where many a musician drank at long, carved-up wooden tables, Nirvana's bassist, Krist Novoselic, freaked out. Not knowing that DGC would approach Nirvana within weeks, he decided that their contract with Sub Pop didn't offer enough security. After a few pitchers of beer, he called Bruce Pavitt from the phone at the end of the bar and requested a late night meeting to hammer out a multi-record deal.

By the end of the night, Krist and Kurt had walked away with a deal for three albums on Sub Pop. A few weeks later that contract didn't look as if it would amount to much. Sub Pop seemed destined to fold, so co-owners Bruce Pavitt and Jonathan Poneman hit the town desperately seeking investment capital. At the twelfth hour, a miracle occurred: David Geffen's new label, DGC, signed Nirvana, which meant that Sub Pop got a chunk of the deal. The underground empire was saved.

According to *Come as You Are,* the semiauthorized Nirvana biography by Michael Azerrad, the ensuing events went something like this: bassist Krist Novoselic and his wife, Shelli, drove a van to L.A.; Kurt and Nirvana's new drummer, Dave Grohl, followed in a Datsun that broke down an hour outside of Olympia, and they pulled off the side of the road and pelted the car with rocks. Kurt and Dave finally made it to L.A., and the band set up in the Oakwood Apartments to start recording "Nevermind."

By pure happenstance, Courtney Love lived only one block away.

Kurt didn't exactly show up at Courtney's door with flowers, though. In the beginning, at least to his friends, Kurt referred to her disparagingly as "that junkie from L.A." From the beginning, drugs were a part of the picture. "We bonded over pharmaceuticals," Courtney told Nirvana biographer Michael Azerrad. "I had Vicodin extra-strength, which was pills, and he had Hycomine cough syrup. I said, 'You're a pussy, you shouldn't drink that syrup because it's bad for your stomach.'"

Since the mid-eighties, Kurt had been plagued by horrible stomach pain that would sometimes prevent him from walking three blocks without resting, and that could reduce him to a heaping ball of agony writhing on the floor.

To Courtney, the entry of Kurt into her life must have initially seemed like a repeat of Rozz; as much as Kurt desired her pills, he didn't want to sleep with her. "I couldn't decide if I wanted to consummate our relationship," Kurt told Azerrad. "She seemed like poison." But he was attracted nonetheless, in a roundabout, head-trippy way.

"It was really up and down," Courtney later recalled of their budding relationship. "He didn't really give me any incentive to sort of think he liked me. And yet he would, like, call me at six in the fucking morning and be drunk and say like, 'You're really cool, you know,' then hang up." And he kept calling in the middle of the night, she said, asking to come over and do drugs. On one occasion, when she demanded a real date, Kurt told her to call him the next night. Then he took his phone off the hook for the week. Though his message seemed clear, it deterred her only briefly.

Courtney had already made a point of befriending Nirvana's handsome drummer, Dave Grohl, a former beau of her old friend Jennifer Finch. Being pals with Dave was an easy way to keep tabs on Kurt. Courtney and Dave soon became fast phone friends, talking for hours; she was in high charm mode, and in typical Courtney form, her conversation never slowed, never got boring, and was peppered with music industry gossip. She mentioned to him that she had a big crush on Kurt; Dave confided that, despite his seeming ambivalence, Kurt had a crush on her.

Through Dave, she passed a present on to Kurt: seashells, pinecones, a set of tiny teacups, a miniature doll, all wrapped up in a Valentine box. The gift would later inspire a Nirvana song.

It's not unreasonable to conjecture that there might have been another miniature substance included in that box. After all, by then Courtney did have an M.O. for entangling men in her life, and that M.O. was already working on Kurt. Given the lyrics of "Heart Shaped Box"—"I was drawn into your magnet tar pit trap"—there is cause to wonder if Courtney, whose first letter to Rozz reportedly contained pills, didn't toss in a bit of black tar heroin, or at least a few of her favorite "dolls."

Although the contents of the heart-shaped box are a

matter for speculation, one thing is certain: in response to Courtney's gift, Kurt didn't so much as call.

That May, at a Butthole Surfers and L7 concert in Los Angeles, Courtney was actually allowed to go backstage despite the fact that she'd turned the Butthole Surfers show in Minneapolis into a debacle. At the show that night, according to Everett True, a reporter for the popular British music paper *Melody Maker,* Courtney was "off her head . . . forcing whisky down my throat and rampaging wild." Everett, who was reviewing the show, ended up interviewing Courtney as well for the music paper. He later claimed she had a breakdown the next day as a direct result of his probing questions.

Maybe. But to others it seemed that Everett was the one having a nervous breakdown, he was so enchanted by the singer. Midway through the interview, Courtney even called her manager to brag that Everett was madly in love with her. But that night she had another man on her mind—Kurt—and he was there.

When she approached him, her greeting came in the form of a flying fist: she immediately punched Kurt in the stomach, fully aware that he suffered from chronic stomach pain. He punched her right back—"a mating ritual for dysfunctional people," she later called it. The "short-lived and stupid" affair Courtney had with Kurt that spring had left her with what she called a "semi-broken heart." And although they hung out together that night, the encounter didn't cement their relationship.

Courtney had other love interests in mind—among them Billy Corgan, the head of Chicago-based Smashing Pumpkins. Billy had more than a few similarities with Kurt. Born three weeks after the Nirvana singer in March 1967, Billy was also a spiritual, poetic Pisces whose parents had divorced early in his childhood. He too was bounced around to assorted relatives. And, like Kurt, he felt like an outsider and was a depressed, drug-prone but extremely compelling and talented musician, who back then recorded on small independent labels like Sub Pop.

In 1989, when Billy formed Smashing Pumpkins, a lyric-driven rock band whose fluid music was dreamy and sensual, there was talk that this band was going to be big. In 1990, when the band signed with the mid-level label Caroline Records—larger than an independent label like Sub Pop, but not a really big major label like DGC—he developed another similarity with Kurt: Billy was extremely taken with the up-and-coming whirlwind of energy known as Courtney Love.

The two, it was said among reporters, had met at a drug dealer's house. It was obvious from the start that both Courtney and Billy, who then looked almost her-maphroditic with his long, dark brown tendrils, had visions of becoming internationally known. Both were obsessed with the poetry that formed the shell of their music, and they wrote songs together as they lay around in bed; Billy would later credit Courtney with having a profound effect on his work.

Though Billy had a girlfriend of seven years, his relationship with her was rocky by the end of 1990. Courtney, legendary in her lovemaking abilities, raved about Billy's prowess.

Billy had another similarity with Kurt in 1991: Smashing Pumpkins' first semi-major label recording, *Gish* was produced by the talented Butch Vig, who would also soon produce Nirvana's *Nevermind* and would go on to play in one of MTV's most popular bands, Garbage.

The year 1991 was an incredible one for music. It was obvious midway through it that something was about to break. And Courtney, of course, was right there in the center of it.

The alternative music scene was about to be knocked loose from its underground pinnings, and many of its major players, including those with major roles in Courtney's life, were in Europe that summer. The British, particularly, seemed to have a much keener sense of what was hot than the Americans did at that point.

That summer Nirvana toured abroad as the middle act

for Sonic Youth. Kat's band, Babes in Toyland, was in England as was Mudhoney, another Seattle band that was expected to become hugely popular. Courtney flew to Europe, tagging along for a while with "Billy Pumpkin," as she called her lover, and later touring with her own band, which was opening for Mudhoney.

It was amazing. All these people who were Courtney's friends and acquaintances, all these young alternative bands—whose music the bigwigs had deemed too fringe for the masses—were selling out shows, rating the highest critical praise, and rising almost to star status right before her eyes. For that matter, so was Hole.

The new music reached critical mass that summer, and cameras caught many behind-the-scenes moments for the documentary *1991: The Year Punk Broke.*

There was already a buzz about Nirvana, whose record, due for release in September 1991, had been previewed many times within the music industry. Those pioneers of the alternative sound, Sonic Youth—which included *Pretty on the Inside's* coproducer Kim Gordon, were growing in influence as well. And Smashing Pumpkins, having released *Gish,* was hot. Babes in Toyland was noteworthy; like Nirvana and Sonic Youth, Kat's band was playing the three-day Reading Festival in England. Hole was about to do its first English tour, and there was lots of talk about Mudhoney.

The first rave review that summer came out about Courtney and Hole—in a British paper. *Melody Maker* writer Everett True, whose words are respected in the industry, had done more than gush. He may have been hot for Courtney, but he was a professional who wouldn't have stuck his neck out simply for his heart; he was equally blown away by her band.

Everett started a media blitz with a full-page feature on Hole, half of which was a picture of Courtney. He gave a thumbnail sketch of her past, writing "she was a self-confessed 'Teenage Whore,' a slut who would sleep with anyone going." And without even knowing that

Courtney had briefly played with them, the writer compared Hole to Kat's group, noting "Think of a harsher, far darker Babes in Toyland and you'd almost be there."

But the clincher was the last line of the piece: "Hole is the only band in the world right now, and they're going to be so fucking huge, six months from now you're going to wonder how you survived without them."

Not a bad way to launch Hole's European tour. Especially since the flattering photo of Courtney appeared on page eight of the well-read paper, eighteen pages ahead of a much smaller photo of Kat, which appeared in the calendar section and merely mentioned that Babes in Toyland was touring.

The tour was romantically charged as well. Although Courtney was ostensibly Billy Corgan's paramour at the time, she had her eyes focused on Kurt. Billy was loath to commit to her; he'd recently gotten back together with his former girlfriend in Chicago. And some speculated that Kurt was still hung up on an old grrrlfriend, Tobi Vail, who played with Bikini Kill in Olympia and had broken up with him prior to the tour.

Acting the part of wanton woman at her most obnoxious, Courtney tried to carve her way into Kurt's romantic picture. Though he consistently rebuffed her advances, he could hardly overlook such a pest, and he must have been somewhat flattered at how taken she was with him.

At the Reading Festival, Courtney hung out with Kat Bjelland and Sonic Youth's Kim Gordon, slamming whiskey in a trailer. When the documentary camera for *The Year Punk Broke* swung by, Courtney peered into the lens and announced, "Kurt Cobain makes my heart stop. But he's a shit."

That quality in a man had never stopped her before, though, and it wouldn't this time, either.

Billy Corgan didn't seem to much care initially that Courtney, his occasional lover for the past year, was so taken with Kurt. Billy wasn't terribly worried in the beginning about Nirvana's upcoming album, but in a couple months it would eat at him horribly. And in interviews for years to come he would compare his band to Nirvana, and even to the much less well known Mudhoney.

Mark Arm, lead singer of Mudhoney, looked rather like Kurt—except for his big nose—and that summer Courtney considered going for him instead. "I was so in love with that guy," she later told *Interview* magazine. "In fact, it was sort of a contest there for a while between Kurt and Mark over who was going to be the love of my life."

One night, when Mudhoney played England, Mark body-surfed atop the crowd and back onto the stage.

Courtney was inspired. The next night in London she stood on the edge of the stage wide-eyed, hesitating only briefly before taking the plunge into the audience—and being tossed about by the crowd, groped, and attacked. She was livid by the time she was shoved back toward the stage—almost naked. Rabid with anger, fear, and humiliation Courtney smashed her only guitar. "I probably did about $5,000 worth of damage that night," she recalled. She felt as if she'd been raped by the crowd, and she stood onstage screaming at them, unleashing a storm of insults that she had, up until that point, reserved for authority figures.

The British press, agog and amazed, had found its new rock goddess. There was a flurry of adoration in European papers.

But if Courtney's ego was swelling there for a second, Kurt quickly put her back in her place. That encounter started out sweetly enough. One night when all the bands were hanging out in a hotel room, Mark threw a bottle of oil at Courtney, soaking her head. She ran out of the room, sobbing, later explaining that she'd always been put down in school and that the incident triggered the memories. When he saw her later, Kurt murmured that he would never put her down.

That same night a group of musicians, including members of Nirvana, Babes in Toyland, and Hole, went out in London. One of the best things that had happened so far was that when Courtney had introduced Kat—always her competitor—to Kurt, Kat hadn't seemed at all interested in him, and vice versa. But that night, while sitting around a pub, Kurt turned to Lori Barbero, the drummer for the Babes, the band from which Courtney had been booted, and asked, "Hey, you want your band to open up for me sometime?"

Courtney slugged him.

When he asked the reason for the hard-packed wallop, she said, "It's just like you just asked my best friend for a date right in front of me."

Taunting her further, Kurt informed her that he was going to be a big star and planned on buying a big house and lots of antiques for his future wife, whoever she might be. And then he promptly left with two British girls while Courtney yelled, "I hope you get laid!"

In two months, when Nirvana played L.A. and Nirvana mania was just getting under way, Babes in Toyland did not open for them. Hole did. And by then Kurt and Courtney were almost an item.

The revolution shifted into full force that September.

Back in the States, Courtney's career was on the runway starting to take off. In mid-September, Caroline Records released *Pretty on the Inside,* Hole's tribute to the fine art of screaming and hissing, à la the punks, whose style the band was rather late in adopting. The lyrics were radical, dealing with topics from teenage prostitutes to abortion, and every song gave voice to a rage last seen only in Lydia Lunch.

"That record was me posing in a lot of ways," she later told *Spin.* "It was the truth, but it was also me catching up with all my hip peers who'd gone indie on me and who made fun of me for liking R.E.M."

Courtney's breathy vocals, while sometimes off-key, were power-packed; her lyrics—"Slut-kiss girl, won't you promise her smack, is she pretty on the inside, is she pretty from the back"—showed the cynicism that was already well developed. But though it gave a hint at Hole's potential, the music wasn't entirely easy on the ears. Even "Clouds," the Joni Mitchell song Courtney had been forced to sing while traveling with her family, sounded discordant. "It was a major dis at my Mom," she later admitted to *Rolling Stone.*

That album, and Hole, were often well reviewed by critics. *Spin* called it "a lovely noise" and, in a profile of the band, said that "it shouldn't be long before everyone jumps on the Hole bandwagon."

But by and large, Hole wasn't widely known by the American public and its clubgoers. Many of the people who did check out the band in small clubs were there mostly because they'd heard of the wild woman whose antics had given her a reputation in music circles around the world.

Shortly thereafter, Kurt had an international reputation as well, but for different reasons: his music, which was so moving that it quickly drew comparisons with John Lennon's.

A week after Hole's album came out, Nirvana's *Nevermind* was released, with a modest 50,000 copies. Before long, it was selling 50,000 copies a day. And for this album the press was out-and-out raving, as were the fans, who adopted its melodic hits as their anthems.

Some of *Nevermind* was loud rock and roll interwoven with the alienation and sarcasm that are evident in "Smells like Teen Spirit": "I feel stupid and contagious. Here we are now. Entertain us." Others were acoustic ballads such as "Polly," a tragic song about rape. And others were just catchy, such as "Lithium": "I'm so happy 'cause today I found my friends. They're in my head." Kurt Cobain, most of his life a social misfit, was suddenly enveloped with love from masses of fans of all types and several generations.

One night Courtney was sitting in a bar with Kat when *Nevermind* came on. "So we sat there and we drank and drank and drank," Courtney later told a reporter, "and got really mad. Because we realized no girl could have done that. I [wanted] to write a really good record and I [hadn't] done it yet."

Billy Corgan felt competitive about Nirvana's new record, too. "We put out *Gish,*" he later told *Rolling Stone*. "It was a huge success. We were on tour, selling out everywhere. . . . Suddenly . . . boom, Nirvana. We went from being seen as future stars almost to has-beens, people saying, 'Well, if you were so good this would have happened to you.' . . . After Nirvana, we were considered a riding-the-coattails band."

Despite her mild resentment, though, Courtney—like much of the rest of the world—simply adored Nirvana's record. She played it constantly—on the road, on her way to be interviewed for magazines, at parties. And she gushed to everyone about her huge love not only for Nirvana's music but also for Kurt.

Nirvana's unforeseen popularity was inspiring as well—a kick in the pants to the woman who wanted to be a rock star. If he could do it, so could she.

Courtney decided she had no time for mediocrity and dilly-dallying; she finally had a band that was holding up and not kicking her out. She wanted attention and she wanted it pronto. She let it be known that if Hole wasn't booked on the next summer's Lollapalooza tour, the band's managers were going to be merely stepping-stones in her career. Hup, two—get with the program. Hole was going to be hot, she assured them all.

Hole left on its second national tour, pushing *Pretty on the Inside* and, later in the fall of 1991, flew back to Europe, where, thanks to the British press, there was a fervor for Courtney Love and her band. Hole was snatching more and more ink, and Courtney—if she wasn't too drunk from the whiskey she chugged before each show—kicked up a storm onstage—when she felt like it. She had a tendency to bail in times of emotional turmoil—of which, even back then, there were plenty.

Once, when the band was scheduled to play on the West Coast, she simply took off to Chicago, and back into the arms of Billy Corgan. A few days later the tour resumed, but in October she bailed again—back to Chicago. But this time she ended up in the arms of Kurt Cobain. They were soon the hot new grunge item.

Before things could really progress, however, there was at least one obstacle to push out of the way: Mary Lou Lord, who'd turned up in Kurt's life when Nirvana toured the East Coast that September.

Small, soft-spoken, and shy, Mary Lou was pretty much Courtney's opposite. The dichotomy was obvious in their musical styles as well. Whereas *Pretty on the Inside* was filled with Courtney's irate screaming, Mary Lou's acoustic music, then unrecorded, was folksy and sweet. Whereas Courtney sought fame and big stages, Mary Lou was best known for playing covers on her guitar in the Boston subway.

One night in September, Mary Lou went down to the Rat, the legendary club that was appropriately named, being located in a rodent-infested block of Boston. On stage were the Melvins, an underground rock band that once had a roadie named Kurt Cobain, and who were still one of his favorite groups. Mary Lou recognized the trio known as Nirvana, whose album *Nevermind* was days away from hitting the record stores. The doorman was denying the band free entry to their friends' show, until she walked over and suggested that they be let in.

Minutes later Kurt thanked the blond urchin for her help and asked what bands she liked. She ran down a list of favorites that mirrored his own.

The next day Mary Lou took Kurt with her when she went down to play in the subway. Being from a subwayless part of the world, he found the subterranean venue charming; the upcoming rock god loved playing the role of a street musician. A few days later, when Nirvana played New York, he asked Mary Lou to join him in Manhattan. Even though his stomach was acting up again, he was ecstatic about the release of *Nevermind*. He was awestruck that week when "Smells Like Teen Spirit" was played for the first time on MTV. At that time he didn't seem to be using heroin, and he certainly wasn't known as a junkie.

Before long, all that would change.

After hanging out for several days in New York, Kurt invited Mary Lou to join Nirvana for the upcoming Midwest dates on the tour. She traveled with the band to Columbus, Cleveland, and Detroit, falling more deeply in love with Kurt every day, and the feeling appeared to be mutual. Kurt wanted Mary Lou to continue on with Nirvana to Chicago, but out of fear of losing her record-store job, she left him and returned to Boston.

Twelve hours later, in Chicago, Courtney stormed back into his life—with a bag of lacy lingerie.

If there was one thing that Courtney really prided herself on—one thing that her musician friends couldn't muster—it was "doing lunch." Though the overpriced-networking-meals concept was entirely anti-punk, Courtney had an agenda, and lunching could help it along. After all, she considered herself Hole's entire public relations department, and she was trying to maneuver the band into a more visible position. One day that fall, after Hole's return from Europe, she dined with a record industry manager, who asked, "What do you want?"

Taking full advantage of the schmooze potential, she replied that she wanted to be flown to Chicago to see Nirvana play. The next day she was at O'Hare International, having ditched her own tour.

But if she was pining to see Kurt again, she took a circuitous route. She first stopped by to see Billy Corgan at his Chicago pad, who threw her out of the apartment. She grabbed up her undies, stomped over to the Nirvana show, and later went to an after-hours party, looking for Kurt.

It was some scene, when Courtney stepped into that party carrying the fantasy wear. When Kurt discovered the treasure chest in a bag, he put on assorted items and pranced about the club. They spent the night together— a sleepless one for Nirvana's drummer Dave Grohl, who

COURTNEY IN HER CHRISTENING DRESS, 1964

Born July 9, 1964, the baby that prompted the marriage between Hank Harrison and Linda Risi was christened Courtney Michelle Harrison.

BABY'S FIRST CHRISTMAS, 1964

"She was such a happy baby," say parents Hank and Linda, shown here with Courtney in the family's San Francisco home.

IN JUVENILE HALL, 1979

Often ignoring her mother's advice ("Don't wear tight sweaters, they make you look cheap"), Courtney had entered her self-proclaimed "loser years."

COURTNEY, AGE 14

At her father's California home during a break from the reform-school track.

ROZZ REZABEK

Portland rock star and Courtney love-object. The man who gave her her new name.

(© Cathy Cheney)

(© David C. Ackerman)

AT THE SATYRICON, 1987

Courtney (second from left) with friends at Portland's premier punk club, Satyricon. Boasting about her bit role in the new film *Sid and Nancy*, she urged the photographer to snap her picture.

THE NEW PARENTS—DECEMBER 4, 1992

Courtney and Kurt Cobain. Having just regained custody of daughter Frances, the couple relax at a Mudhoney concert.

THE OZZIE & HARRIET OF GRUNGE—
SEPTEMBER '93

Arriving at the MTV Video Music Awards in Los Angeles, Kurt and Courtney with Frances in tow.

READY TO ROCK—FEBRUARY '94

Hole—Kristen Pfaff, Eric Erlandson, Courtney Love and Patty Schemel—embark upon a star-crossed publicity blitz for their album, *Live Through This.*

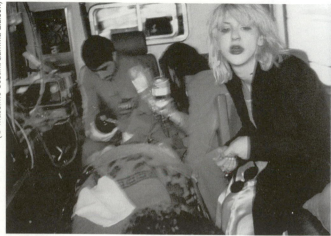

WARNING SIGN—APRIL 3, 1994

As comatose Kurt is rushed to Rome's American Hospital, a distraught Courtney is snapped by a paparazzo. She later assaulted the overzealous photographer.

AT COBAIN VIGIL

Courtney with "enemy-friend" Kat Bjelland, at the candlelight vigil in Seattle where the young widow would give away Kurt memorabilia.

MOTHER AND DAUGHTER—APRIL 9, 1994

Returned to Seattle from L.A. after news of her
husband's suicide, Courtney consoles Frances at their home
on the bank of Lake Washington.

**COURTNEY TWINS—
MARCH 27, 1995**

Courtney and then-best friend, Amanda de Cadenet. The staggering duo were hard to ignore at the Academy Awards.

**GRAVITY-BOUND—
SEPTEMBER 7, 1995**

Apparently exhausted by her extensive summer tour, Courtney hits the ground at the MTV Video Music Awards in New York.

GETTING RIPPED—JUNE '95

Courtney in the mosh pit—the zone of frequent orifice probing—at the WHFS festival in Washington, DC.

was in the next bed. Many moans later, he gave up and split. That was only one of the many times Dave would regret acting as Cupid, delivering the damn heart-shaped box.

Courtney continued calling Kurt while he toured the United States and Europe. She also asked every reporter who interviewed her to tell Kurt that she loved him.

Their fling, however, was not enough to perma-glue the couple together; Kurt continued calling folksinger Mary Lou, saying he was thinking about buying a house in Boston. And he called friends in Olympia saying the same, adding occasionally that he was considering marrying the folksinger.

Some thought that was just his way of trying to get back at Tobi Vail, his old flame from Olympia who played in Bikini Kill. In *Come As You Are,* that relationship is portrayed as ending by Kurt's hand, but that's not the way a lot of people recall it. In the fall of 1991 Kurt was still trying to regain the hand of flinty-hearted Tobi, who had once been proclaimed "the meanest grrrl in the world."

Kurt had asked Tobi's band, Bikini Kill, to open for Nirvana when they returned to Seattle's swanky Paramount in October. In many cities, Nirvana's Halloween gig would have been a homecoming of sorts, where they would have been lauded for their success; after all, the band that had been playing dives for years had graduated to one of the sweetest venues in town. But Nirvana's return to Seattle was met with disdain by the punk purists, who didn't like the idea of Kurt Cobain turning into a rock star.

By the end of October, it was clear that Kurt was becoming just that. *Nevermind* wasn't just another little record selling to the tune of 30,000 or 40,000. It was a total shock: Nirvana's first major-label LP was flying out of stores; it had made $1 million—going gold—within a month of release. It was selling so well that even their record label noticed and started putting major advertising dollars behind it. The company aggressively pushed their new "alternative" product, and suddenly Nirvana opened the doors for a whole new brand of music that was once considered commercially unviable. Its lead singer, however, was now branded as a sellout. Kurt promptly dyed his hair pink.

"The other day," he told a writer for *Sassy,* "I was driving around . . . listening to a college station. . . . And then the DJ came on went on this half-hour rant about how Nirvana is so obviously business-oriented and just because we have colored hair doesn't mean we are alternative. And I felt really terrible. Because there is nothing in the world I like more than pure underground music."

Many of the people Kurt knew from Olympia were disgusted by the rock-star stamp and couldn't believe he'd "stooped so low." The attitude embraced by the underground scene against such commercialization was evident in the very name of one of the town's indie labels—Kill Rock Stars.

Most painful was the shove-off he was given at that Halloween show by Tobi, whose band opened for Nirvana at the Paramount, where suddenly Kurt's good friends had a hard time getting backstage due to increased security. Tobi let him know that she wanted nothing to do with his personal success story.

Kurt wanted to get married, but Tobi was not interested. So he assessed the available grrrls in the potential-wife pool. And his eyes fell upon Courtney, one of the few people who was happy for his success, who thought fame and money was just fine. Kurt's gaze also fell upon Mary Lou Lord, who likewise didn't regard him as corporate scum for becoming so popular.

When Nirvana played England in November, Mary Lou flew over and joined Kurt. Something about him seemed different to her, but he denied anything was up. Nevertheless, he acted chilly and reserved, and Mary Lou stayed for only a few shows before flying home.

The night before she left England, she tuned in to a popular British show, *The Word,* at a friend's flat. The show's host was a sexy blonde by the name of Amanda de Cadenet. And Nirvana was that night's musical guest. Kurt dedicated the band's set to Courtney Love, announcing over the airwaves, "I just want everyone in this room to know that Courtney Love, lead singer for the pop group Hole, is the best fuck in the world."

"Who the hell is Courtney Love?" Amanda de Cadenet wondered from the stage.

"Who the hell is Courtney Love?" Mary Lou Lord wondered from in front of the TV.

"Who the hell is Mary Lou Lord?" screamed Courtney, who was playing Boston. Having just heard someone refer to Mary Lou as Kurt's girlfriend, Courtney unleashed a slew of put-downs from the stage of the singer she had never met.

Upon hearing about Kurt's broadcast announcement, Courtney soon flew to England, and Mary Lou flew back, brokenhearted.

When Courtney showed up next to Kurt's side, she was hell-bent on sealing the deal. As part of the typical one-two love punch, more drugs were added to the seduction formula. Granted, they'd already had plenty of pills to bond over. But now they plunged into Real Drugs. They headed to Amsterdam.

"I was the one who instigated the search for dope in Amsterdam," Kurt told Michael Azerrad. "But I didn't really know how to get [heroin], so Courtney was the one who was able to get it somehow."

The Dutch canal city that suffers from architectural anorexia, being filled with skinny buildings and ridiculously steep, ladderlike stairs, is home to more than the van Gogh museum, coffeehouses where hash can be ordered from a menu, and a legal red-light district. Its leniency toward all vice could as well be seen in its view toward heroin, which was cheap and often ignored, making Amsterdam a haven for junkies.

And when Courtney bought some dope off the street, their junkie bonding started.

* * *

There is a special link among those who use heroin. It's more than the I'll-have-one-if-you-have-one behavior seen in drinking and cigarette smoking.

Heroin is mostly about living a lie—a big fat multi-corded one that's all twisted up in denial: denying that the user is high, denying that using it is a habit, denying that the user is using again. And unless the addict is wealthy, it necessitates denying having conned or stolen—often from friends—to supply their habit.

The fear and hatred of the mind-numbing opiate by non-users merely brings the users even closer together. The junkie community is bonded by the ritual of secret deals and the privileged knowledge of who has a habit, and it even has its own folklore. Among the things heard from regular users: heroin was invented by an analgesic manufacturer a few years before they stumbled upon aspirin; novelist William Burroughs, a well-known hero-in user, is proof that an addict can live to be old; any junkie who overdoses is committing suicide; never do it with alcohol, and never do it alone. And of course, there's a well-known motto among heroin users, and those who know them: "Never trust a junkie."

But what most strongly bonds junkies, particularly couples, is the fact that they can often nearly die and bring each other back to life. The near-death experience could be caused by cotton fever when a strand from a cigarette filter or cotton ball (used in preparing the dose) is accidentally let loose in the blood. Death can result when the dope is tainted, the strength is unusually pure, or the user takes too much. Whatever the cause, when a heroin user passes out or turns blue it's time for his fellow users to jump into action by throwing him in the shower and dousing him with cold water, walking him around, shooting him up with another drug, trying to get him to vomit, or—as a last resort—taking him to the hospital.

It's not uncommon even for an experienced user to overdose, and Kurt did so often enough that some people wondered if his overdoses were suicide attempts.

But each time, Courtney was there to bring him back to this world. She saved his fragile life many times over.

Heroin was Kurt and Courtney's secret. The other members of Nirvana did not acknowledge the couple's plunge into opiates for many months. Initially Kurt and Courtney weren't using every day, but after a few binges, then another and another, they would get sick without it. Heroin, said Kurt, did have its pluses: the best thing about it, claimed Kurt—far more enjoyable than the dreamlike state it produced and the way it numbed emotional pain and vanquished all worries—was that it soothed the pain gnawing at his stomach, which sometimes plagued him so badly he passed out onstage.

Doctors had tested and prodded, sticking tubes down his throat, x-raying him, and prescribing assorted medication, but nothing was effective in treating his stomach problems, which they couldn't even diagnose. It wasn't an ulcer. There was some inflamed tissue, but doctors had no idea what the problem could be.

Whatever. Heroin wiped away the pain, and Courtney was there to soothe him as well. By December, when Nirvana returned to the States, Courtney was his main squeeze.

People were absolutely mystified by Kurt's choice in a girlfriend. Loud, brash Courtney, a bitch on wheels who didn't look like a model back then, seemed to be Kurt's total opposite. She loved attention; he reviled it. She could yak away nonstop for days; he was quiet. She was a compulsive name-dropper; he shied away from the concept that anyone was famous, especially him. "It's like Evian water and battery acid," he admitted to the British press. "It doesn't matter whether she's a male, female, or hermaphrodite, or a donkey. We're compatible." Certainly, in other ways, Courtney was the ideal choice. She was a slob; he was a slob. She didn't cook; he didn't cook, at least not anything more technical than macaroni and cheese. Eating required nothing more substantial than Lucky Charms, pizza, Twinkies,

Nestlé's Strawberry Quik, and cold cuts. Also, Kurt was a feminist; so was Courtney, in her own way. He loved her for her strength, her audacity, her burning ambition, her refusal to be bossed around. She took care of him, and every morning she gave him oral sex. The sex was mind-boggling, for him at least.

In Courtney he found an intellectual equal who could debate him on any topic, question his motives, play architect with his life. She was the only one with whom he could lounge around in bed singing and writing lyrics—and she too would fill notebooks. She knew the pain of abandonment and the reality of raising oneself, the feeling that nobody really cared, and of being given up as a lost cause. She was more powerful than he was, at least in direct confrontation. Even more remarkable, he didn't mind her power. Like heroin, she served as a buffer between him and the outside world.

While other people put him down for his growing rock stardom, Courtney didn't mind it. She liked the music, the money, the fame, the possibilities it brought.

And Courtney was endlessly entertaining. The girl never got boring. She'd be joking one minute, screaming the next, seducing the one after that, and all of that day's mini-dramas were broken up by the phone and assorted deliverymen or psychics dropping by. She was like twenty-four hour cable TV, but with many more channels. When she left their nest, God only knew what would happen. The appearance of Courtney in any situation, from boutique to bar, changed the atmosphere entirely—and never calmed it.

Even more importantly, though, Kurt found in Courtney the mother he'd never really had. His real mother, Wendy O'Connor, had apparently been overwhelmed by her son, who was placed on the prescription drug Ritalin to combat his perceived hyperactivity. The youngster reportedly received beatings, and one year was given a lump of coal for Christmas. After his parents divorced when he was eight, Kurt was tossed around among assorted relatives, including his father, who was upset because Kurt didn't want to play sports. He eventually moved in with a friend's family. Later he lived outdoors or crashed in the library. Sometimes, when he begged, his mother would let him sneak over for lunch.

If his real mother neglected him, Courtney made up for it. She comforted him when he was in pain. She made sure he got the food he wanted when he was on the road; since his stomach acted up worse then, most of his meals were bland affairs such as brown rice and broth. Courtney would scream and yell to make sure everything was to his liking. She doted on him when they were together. And even when they were apart, she would call him during a shopping spree just to see how he was doing. She loved him, she gave him strength, she saved him again and again and again when he overdosed and nearly died. Slovenly though she was, Courtney could create a home, with her candles, incense and lace.

And she was as talented as he was, at least that's what Courtney told the press. Granted, Kurt was a better singer; but she had "a lyric thing" going. She would be more "culturally significant."

Courtney definitely had some reporters agreeing with her. Her musical career, and Hole's popularity, was rising by the end of the year, though certainly not as fast as Nirvana's. But *The New Yorker*'s music critic, Elizabeth Wurtzel, wrote at year's end, *"Pretty on the Inside* is such a cacophony—full of such grating, abrasive, and unpleasant sludges of noise—that very few people are likely to get through it once, let alone give it the repeated listenings it needs for you to discover that it is probably the most compelling album to have been released in 1991."

Pretty on the Inside was rated one of *Melody Maker*'s top twenty albums; the cut "Teenage Whore" was one of Britain's top twenty singles. Hole had a following in France and Germany as well. And Everett True didn't stop raving—even after Courtney slugged him for writing that she was "a self-admitted Teenage Whore." Hole was a force to contend with. The band was going to rage.

On New Year's Eve 1991, Nirvana played San Francisco, and Courtney tagged along with her new love. While there, she stopped in to see Rozz. Unannounced, she buzzed the door to his San Francisco apartment. She knew he still lived there because in the windows were the white lace curtains she'd hung there a decade before. And Rozz was often in San Francisco during the holidays.

He was shocked to see her after several years of keeping track of her mostly through rumor, but in minutes their rapport was the same as it ever was. She was the same old talk-at-the-speed-of-light Courtney, showing him her newest nose job, her boob job, asking if he'd heard her new album, and going on and on about her famous new boyfriend.

That visit was vaguely disturbing, not to mention ironic: the very life she'd fantasized about with Rozz, she was actually living with Kurt. Nirvana was hot, Hole was on the rise, and by then Rozz was a self-proclaimed has-been. Nevertheless, there was still that spark between them: she was still the compelling presence that could light up a room; he was still intriguingly slippery Rozz.

She invited him to come to that night's Nirvana show at the Cow Palace and to hang out with her backstage and meet Kurt.

Rozz declined. He'd had little interest in music since Theatre of Sheep broke up. Besides, it was New Year's Eve. He had other plans.

But she kept begging him, and he finally agreed to join her in Salem, Oregon, where Nirvana would play in a few days. Courtney promised to get him backstage.

When Rozz turned up at the Nirvana show in Salem, he was amazed at the turnout. The place was packed. And when he lined up, and dropped his name at the window, he wasn't on the list. Courtney walked right past him, entirely messed up, and didn't even say hi, she was too busy making out with some girl. Rozz left, disgusted.

A week later, as 1992 kicked off, Kurt and Courtney flew to New York. They would spend the next couple of years and many dollars trying to erase that fateful trip to Manhattan from the public memory. They were on a bender. And unbeknownst to them at the time, Courtney was pregnant.

Nirvana was heading to the MTV studios to play a short three-song set to be taped live by the MTV cameras. Then they were going to be on *Saturday Night Live.* And then they were going to be interviewed for a cover story in *Sassy.*

Nevermind had sold three million copies.

It was as though Courtney had scripted their life— except that Kurt wasn't supposed to have the leading role. This was the legendary rock and roll lifestyle. Money, adoration, and fame. The only thing missing, temporarily, was the drugs. So they reportedly put on disguises and went to the Lower East Side to score.

Christina Kelly, the writer for *Sassy,* was the first to liken the Cobains to Sid Vicious and Nancy Spungen, and the first to ask Kurt his views about kids: he wanted to wait until he had a house and was financially secure. She captured the couple's affection toward each other and Courtney's insecurities. "Sorry about this zit," Courtney had said, pointing to her cheek. Kurt had replied, "Zits are beauty marks." Yes indeed. Courtney had met her prince charming.

It would later be revealed that during their *Saturday Night Live* appearance, Kurt was high on heroin. But his impassioned performance was every bit as legendary as the passionate kiss he gave from the stage—to Nirvana bass player Krist Novoselic. And the short performance he recorded for MTV that week would be played many times a day for the rest of the year.

It was around January that Courtney found out she was pregnant.

That was a problem. Granted, they'd talked about having children together—a year or two down the line. But the timing was frightening. Their heroin binge in

New York had taken place during the earliest weeks of the pregnancy.

Fearing the worst, Kurt suggested an abortion, but Courtney wanted to consult a specialist first. Her physician offered good news: heroin in the early weeks of pregnancy did not cause birth defects. And if the mother's withdrawal wasn't too traumatic, the baby would be fine. The sonogram showed the fetus to be perfectly normal. Because of the kidneylike shape of the sonogram image, they took to calling the fetus "the Bean."

They decided that if "the Bean" was a boy, they would name him Eugene, after the lead singer in one of Kurt's favorite bands, the Vaselines. If it was a girl, they would call her Frances, for Eugene's wife. Both Kurt and Courtney were also fans of Frances Farmer, the Seattle-born actress whose (then-scandalous) pushy anti-Hollywood attitude had landed her in a mental asylum, where she was later lobotomized.

Before she and Kurt got married, Courtney called her ex-husband, James Moreland, whom she'd left in the dust after only a few months of married life. For reasons that mystified him, she asked to legally change the divorce to an annulment. He agreed to it. Courtney also demanded a prenuptial agreement from Kurt—to prevent him from gaining access to her money if they divorced, despite the fact that she had little at the time.

Kurt and Courtney then flew to Waikiki for the wedding. Krist and Shelli had wanted to come, but Courtney didn't care much for Shelli and banned her from the ceremony. With the Novoselics (and Dave Grohl) no-shows in Hawaii, a few roadies stepped in for the nuptials instead.

On February 24, 1992, they were wed on a cliff, with Dylan Carlson, Kurt's friend from Olympia, serving as best man. Though he'd considered wearing a dress, Kurt instead wore pajamas. The bride was clad in an old dress that had once been worn by Frances Farmer. Back at the hotel, they consummated the marriage in the bathroom:

Courtney still wearing the gown, sat on a tube of toothpaste, which shot out all over the dress.

Kurt seemed genuinely happy. Now he would have the family he'd been deprived of for much of his childhood. Courtney was elated. This was her dream come true. She now had everything she'd ever asked fortune-tellers about, everything she'd ever chanted for, prayed for, and written on her many "to do" lists. Money, fame, love, and opportunities galore were all wrapped up in one beautiful commitment.

Now if it just didn't get screwed up.

CHAPTER 7

The Fast Track
(1992)

IT CAME TOO FAST, IT WAS TOO MUCH, AND ONLY A FEW
months after it arrived it ripped him apart. Fame was
entirely overwhelming for Kurt. It changed everything,
mostly in a bad way.

Two years before, he'd been sending handwritten
letters to record companies, begging for recognition,
promising to tour wherever, whenever, wanting only to
have a successful rock band.

But when his wishes came true, success ruined so
much, forging a barrier between Kurt and his friends, his
past, and his future. More and more he sought refuge in
heroin, the greatest numb-er of them all.

By the time he'd been married for a month, Kurt was
an icon. He was featured on the cover of every music
magazine; Nirvana's success even rated writeups in
such mainstream magazines such as *Newsweek* and
Time. They were the forerunner in a new kind of rough-
hewn, brash, but extremely catchy style of music, and
Seattle, home of Nirvana's first indie label, Sub Pop,
was the capital of this new low-tech sound called grunge.
Unintentionally, Kurt and other Seattle bands triggered
a fashion wave of ripped jeans and flannel that was

soon copied by famous high-fashion designers like Perry Ellis.

His success made him feel guilty, though, especially when people called him a sellout. And they were—on the radio, and in the clubs. He started apologizing in interviews for making such a commercial record as *Nevermind,* saying it had all been a joke.

Courtney was also being interviewed for magazines— about her dresses and makeup, her barrettes and perfumes, and about her new husband. Few, however, were asking about her music. She was fast falling into the number two spot as little Mrs. Nirvana. She wasn't pleased at being shoved in the shadow.

Then a new problem quickly boiled to the surface and bubbled over: competition. It was a quality that had soured many of Courtney's previous friendships, including the one with Kat Bjelland. She even felt competitive toward Kurt's ex-girlfriends. Courtney taped lists of household chores, written by one of Kurt's former live-in loves, all over the house, to remind him of how much better he had it with her. She was competitive toward her bandmates, who were routinely expected to toss over their boyfriends for a trial run with Courtney—or so they told their friends. She even competed with *his* bandmates. And now competition was seeping into her marriage.

So what if she was the person closest to him? She still wasn't *him.* It was Kurt's money, not hers. It was his face on the magazine; he was the one the big-name reporters came to interview, even though he frequently allowed her to butt in. She was merely the wifey-poo, and it rankled that she was the second half (emphasis on *second*) in their rock and roll formula. She was the one who wanted to be famous; by then Kurt didn't.

When they'd first become an item, Hole's snarling punk record was selling on a par with Nirvana's first album, *Bleach.* Now Hole was dwarfed by Nirvana's success. So was Kurt. And so was Courtney.

It wasn't that she hadn't been warned, as she pointed out in interviews. "So me and Kurt get married and we're peers—his band was always ahead, but they started before us. Then suddenly his band gets real successful and we're not peers anymore," she told *Melody Maker* early in the marriage. "He's involved in free trade in America, and I'm not making much of a dent."

She *had* been warned, she continued. "Kim Gordon, like every woman I respected, told me this marriage would be a disaster for me. They told me I'm more important than Kurt because I have this lyric thing going and I'm more culturally significant, and they all predicted exactly what was going to happen."

But even if Hole wasn't that well known yet, Courtney was savvy enough to manipulate what she had so far: she used what the press had been saying even before she married Kurt and coupled it with the opportunities afforded her by being Mrs. Cobain. And she created a bidding war.

Hole was making history: the battle for Hole was reportedly the first major label fight in the history of female, or mostly female, bands. Madonna's own label, Maverick Records, was interested in signing the band, but Courtney didn't want Madonna—then the reigning bad girl of music—as a boss. Def American and Arista were both reportedly interested; so was Virgin Records, but she thought Virgin's head man was clueless, and boasted that she'd had to give him a crash course in punk rock. She ultimately went with DGC—Nirvana's label—after reviewing Nirvana's contract and demanding the same terms, and more. In the end, Hole landed a contract reportedly for $1 million that was far, far better than Nirvana's. Of course there were rumors that DGC had signed her simply because of her close connection to Kurt. "All roads lead to Kurt Cobain," she lamented.

Then one day the attention finally switched to her. Somebody wanted to do a profile of Courtney, not her husband, for *Vanity Fair*. Well, it was about time.

Before the interview sessions with reporter Lynn

Hirschberg, who was known for well-crafted fluff pieces, Courtney ran into *Melody Maker*'s Everett True; as always, he fawned over her. She asked him how she should act for the interview, and he told her she should just be herself.

The next time Courtney saw Everett, she said, "You gave me bad advice."

It was a strange, stressful time even before Lynn entered the picture. Courtney was pregnant and demanding, the Nirvana members were fighting about drugs and royalties splits, and Kurt was threatening to break up the band—a move that was drawing new comparisons to John and Yoko.

Though Courtney said she had stopped using heroin when she found out she was pregnant, Kurt continued to shoot up—but he did so in a car or a closet, so as not to tempt his pregnant wife. And he continued to freak out at the repercussions of Nirvana's ever-swelling success, and at the amount of public interest in his dope habit.

Several papers reported that his eyes were "pinned" during interviews: small pupils are one of the telltale signs of heroin use. One magazine just came out and said he'd been "dancing with Mr. Brownstone"—slang for doing dope. He was getting increasingly paranoid, too, and his tendency toward compulsive behavior was increased by the stress; he'd sometimes wander about the house, repeating one phrase or number sequence over and over, trying to let it escape from his head.

When it was reported that a girl had been raped while her attackers sang the Nirvana song "Polly"—the beautiful but disturbing song about rape—he was guilt-ridden. He made sculptures and paintings of headless babies, and he shot more dope.

Lynn Hirschberg walked into a rich story, one that should have been hushed up by management; instead she found fruit for an exposé, which she provided.

Courtney was outspoken, controversial, colorful, audacious, outrageous, and incredibly naive; Lynn Hirschberg couldn't have invented a better character. She was by then visibly pregnant and still smoking, in an era when pregnant women were being kicked out of restaurants for daring to order a drink. Over a series of interviews with the *Vanity Fair* writer—in chichi restaurants, at the Cobains' L.A. residence, and during shopping sprees—when even an earthquake didn't stop Courtney from flipping through the clothes racks—the Hole singer put on an audacious display of drama, candor, and stupidity, once again proving that her strongest asset—her mouth—was also her biggest liability.

Her life, persona, music, reputation, and mouth were unbelievable, and she spilled out her past in long whirlwind stories filled with names and hot gossip and peppered with references to literature and history. Courtney told Lynn about growing up in communes, about the years of dancing, about her views on everything from Shelli Noveselic to men in bikini underwear. She spoke frankly about her pregnancy: "Kurt's the right person to have a baby with. . . . The whole feminine experience of pregnancy and birth—I'm not into it on that level. But it was a bad time to get pregnant, and that appealed to me. Besides, we need new friends."

She let the reporter into their trashed rental house in the Fairfax district of L.A., where dolls lined the mantel and clothes were heaped in the corner. Phone numbers had been written on the walls next to a huge lipsticked apology—"My Best Friend"—which Courtney had scrawled after a fight. It appeared to Lynn Hirschberg that Kurt was high.

When Dave Grohl called Kurt with news that Krist Novoselic was talking of quitting the band, Courtney quipped, "Just call me Yoko Love. . . . They all hate me. Everyone just fucking hates my guts."

Courtney, Lynn reported, admitted to doing heroin with Kurt in January, while she was pregnant, though she later said she did not know she was in the family way at the time.

When Lynn talked to a few of Courtney's friends, ex-friends, and industry insiders, they said that despite Kurt's recent denial of drug use to *Rolling Stone,* the couple had been heavily into drugs. Kurt was still using, and some people believed that Courtney was, too.

When the article came out several months later, the word "heroin" was mentioned six times, twice in quotes from Courtney. It might as well have been mentioned six thousand times.

CHAPTER 8

Damage Control

(August–October 1992)

IT ALL HIT DURING THE SUMMER OF 1992, WEEKS BEFORE
Frances was born. Life was like an automatic weapon,
and every day brought a new wound. The Cobains were
plagued by rumors: Kurt was quitting Nirvana, Kurt was
terminally ill, Kurt was dead, Courtney was a junkie
mother-to-be who was breaking up his band.

The truth was grim enough. When Nirvana returned
home from a European tour that summer, Kurt discovered that all his notebooks and tapes for the upcoming
album had been destroyed; they'd been left in the
bathtub, which apparently served as his "grunge security
box," and they were entirely trashed when the pipes blew
a leak.

The Action Swingers, a Manhattan-based punk band,
released a single called "Courtney Love" with lyrics that
noted her love of material riches. "She wants what
money brings, she got diamond rings." Then Babes in
Toyland released an album with the song "Bruise Violet"
that was said to be a comment about Courtney's deceit-
fulness. The lyrics included the line, "You fucking bitch,
I hope your insides rot. Liar, liar, liar!"

Even "Weird" Al Yankovic joined the slam fest, doing

a parody of the biggest hit from *Nevermind*—"Smells like Teen Spirit." Al's version was called "Smells like Nirvana." But the band at least saw the humor in Al's mockery.

Other events were simply absurd. A London-based band called Killing Joke claimed that part of "Come as You Are" was lifted from a song they'd released in the mid-1980s. They filed a lawsuit alleging plagiarism. A band from the U.K. named Nirvana claimed that the Seattle band had stolen their name and was causing irreparable damage to their career; A California band named Nevermind claimed the same. Both cases were settled out of court with little fuss.

And then the *Vanity Fair* piece blasted in and sent them into shock. There had been pre-quake tremors that hinted at the upcoming disaster. During the first week in August, *Vanity Fair* sent out a press release about its September issue. "Rocker Courtney Love is a charismatic opportunist and proud of it," the release announced. In a later paragraph it voiced concern about her possible drug use during pregnancy.

In the second week of August, the day before the magazine came out, Kurt and Courtney issued a press release of their own, saying the profile of Courtney "contains many inaccuracies and distortions and generally gives a false picture of us both." The couple "unequivocally" denied that Courtney used heroin after she learned she was pregnant. "As was made clear to Ms. Hirschberg . . . [Courtney] and Kurt did experiment with drugs early in their relationship, which they now deeply regret." It added that as soon as she discovered she was pregnant, Courtney "immediately contacted an obstetrician and a doctor specializing in chemical dependency and has been under their care since then and has been assured she can expect a healthy baby."

On August 11, *Vanity Fair* hit the stands, with Geena Davis on the cover and an eight-page feature on Courtney inside titled "Strange Love." Courtney blew up when she read the article. A nightmare had come to 3-D life in her hands. Her most memorable experience of 1992, she later told *Melody Maker,* was "Opening up a magazine that my grandparents read, to find a squirming living nightmare of lies and myths . . . seeing my future flash darkly before me and have all my paranoid fantasies come true." All the things she'd said off the cuff came off sounding calculated. Her jokes fell flat. Things she thought that the writer would censor out, stared back at her in harsh black-and-white.

The article began like any other, with the reporter remarking on Courtney's habitual tardiness, her dramatic entrances and her marriage to Kurt. It made reference to the many bands and musicians who she felt had ripped her off: Faith No More ("The new record is called *Angel Dust*—they stole that from me"), Jennifer Finch, who she claimed had lifted lines from her songs, and especially Kat, who she said had stolen "Dresses. Lyrics. Riffs. Guitars. Shoes."

It was almost amusing, given Courtney's reputation as the high priestess of sticky fingers.

But then the article released a spray of bulletins, proclamations, insinuations, and quotes by unnamed sources—understandable perhaps, since Courtney's anger was so legendary that people often asked not to have their names used even when they praised her. The inside sources quoted in the piece not only feared for the health of the baby; they also worried over the health of the couple, and where they were heading. "She's going to be famous and he already is," one music exec told the reporter, "but unless something happens, they're going to self-destruct. . . . I just don't want to be a part of it."

The story portrayed her as a manipulator. It all but called her a gold digger. And Lynn Hirschberg reported that at least twenty unnamed industry sources were worried about the health of the baby.

Who were those people? Courtney wanted to know. Her paranoia was activated as she ran through the possible unnamed sources. At least she didn't have to guess about Kat Bjelland's involvement. Quite a few of the quotes had Kat's name trailing the quotation marks. "Only about a quarter of what Courtney says is true," she had told Hirschberg. "Courtney's delusional," and "Last night I had a dream that I killed her. I was really happy." And Kat admitted that she too was "worried about her baby."

Well, that left nineteen unnamed concerned parties to be accounted for. How could *Vanity Fair* get away with publishing a story based so largely on unidentified sources? Courtney accused Lynn of being a self-appointed journalist social worker.

But as much as the Cobains wanted to blame their alleged drug use on what they claimed was Lynn's misinterpretation of the facts, the most damning words in the entire article were Courtney's own. "We did a lot of drugs," Courtney was quoted as saying of the trip to New York when Nirvana was to appear on *Saturday Night Live*. "We got pills and then we went down to Alphabet City and Kurt wore a hat, I wore a hat, and we copped some dope. Then we got high and went to *SNL*. After that, I did heroin for a couple of months." Although the Cobains later denied she used heroin while knowing she was pregnant, those printed words would haunt her for years, and they would kick the public outrage machine into action.

But the clincher was the picture taken by photographer Michel Comte. The magazine didn't have to draw in a broom. They didn't need to include instructions "Burn at the stake." They didn't need to paint "Bad Mother" in dripping red paint across the very scary image. It was all implied in one harsh full-page photo.

Courtney, shown pantyless, was eight months pregnant. Her stomach protruded through a gauzy green negligee, her hair hung in Medusa coils, her eyes looked evil and drugged. The fact that the cigarette she was holding was airbrushed out by skittish *Vanity Fair* editor-in-chief Tina Brown only made it more gossip-worthy. Magazines around the globe queued up to buy the other pictures from the shoot—the ones with the mother-to-be's cigarette still intact.

The photographer offered to sell the roll of negatives to the Cobains. For a mere $50,000. Fearful of more adverse press, they took him up on the offer.

The profile was like being busted in front of millions, all stopping to watch the scene. The Cobains considered the article twisted, exaggerated, and contorted to make her look like a money-hungry, drug-shooting, bad-mommy witch. The rest of the world considered it shocking, but a damn good read.

It was tragic, though, and not only in the implications it held about the health of the baby. This was Courtney's first really big national press in the United States, and in her first lengthy feature she'd been strangled by her own umbilical cord, knocked flat by her flapping mouth once again. Her self-destructive streak had won out, at least temporarily.

How could she have been so naive? she later wondered. Why didn't she realize there may have been an ulterior motive when the magazine approached her, cooing about Hole and how hot they were going to be? She suspected that Madonna was behind it; Courtney believed the pop star must have been ticked when Hole didn't sign with her label, Maverick. This seemed obvious to Courtney when the article quoted Madonna flippantly asking "Who is Courtney Love?"

Whatever had prompted the horror, Courtney vowed then and there that nothing like that would ever happen again.

The Cobains began making household help and private contractors sign confidentiality agreements.

The most chilling and ironic part was the ending of the *Vanity Fair* piece: "Things are really good. It's all coming true," Courtney had said to Lynn early that summer. "Although it could fuck up at any time. You never know."

It screwed up big time about the second *Vanity Fair* hit the stands.

The profile of Courtney put her into such a spin that she checked into West Hollywood's Cedars-Sinai Medical Center on August 7, eleven days before Frances was born, fearing she'd do herself in.

Kurt went on a binge, then reluctantly checked into rehab, in a different wing of the hospital. But his determination to quit heroin was not particularly strong; Courtney later said that while he was in the detox unit he had dealers actually shooting heroin into his I.V. bag. One apparently gave him too much; Courtney said the dealer told her that at one point Kurt appeared dead.

Kurt definitely had death on his mind. Apparently fearing the worst, he'd brought a gun to the hospital—though it was quickly removed by Eric Erlandson. Besides, as Courtney later pointed out to the press, if they'd gone through with their suicide pact that day it would have been "sort of rude [when Frances was told], 'Oh, your parents died the day after you were born.'"

Even with the weaponry removed, it was like dropping a kid in a war zone. Kurt was out of it, in the zombieland of nausea, sweating, and skin that felt as if insects were crawling over and simultaneously burrowing under it. Instead of nervous grandparents, reporters for the tabloids paced outside in the waiting room; worse, a mysterious hospital source faxed Courtney's records to the *L.A. Times*. Meanwhile, the *Vanity Fair* article was reportedly making its way through the Los Angeles child services department.

When Courtney went into labor on the morning of August 18, 1992, she shocked the medical staff, or so the legend goes, by standing up and wheeling her I.V. stand with her all the way to Kurt's wing, where she demanded that he join her for the birth of their child. Then, in the delivery room, Kurt passed out as the baby pushed out, while Courtney chanted, "You will only have one head."

Frances Bean weighed in at seven pounds and was

entirely normal—two hands, two feet, one heart, one head, the works—perfect, in fact. Their managers at Gold Mountain quickly announced the baby's normality and healthy status in a press release.

Courtney's relief was short-lived, however. Postpartum depression hit her the moment she returned to her room. She felt entirely alone, once Kurt went back to his wing, and the new mother wasn't exactly surrounded by a coterie of congratulatory friends. Who was she going to ask to be at her bedside—Kat? Rozz? Her mother? Her father? Her relationship with all of them was strained. She felt abandoned.

And then the door swung open and an unsmiling woman, a stranger, stomped to Courtney's bedside, flapped a copy of *Vanity Fair* in her face, and hissed that child services was going to take the baby away.

It was not a happy beginning for the baby they named Frances Bean. And it was about to get worse.

There were a few moments of happiness, however, a few days of pure bliss before the wrecking ball crashed into their cozy world. When they brought the baby home, the couple—suicidal only days before—quickly took to the concept of family. Kurt was crazy about the baby, holding her, feeding her, writing "diet grrrl" on her stomach for one photo session. Even though they had a nanny, a young woman named Jackie, Kurt could often be found late at night, warming up the baby's bottle. He was the one who insisted they spend at least two hours with Frances daily.

And Courtney had never been more pleased. For a short time, she experienced a close brush with happiness and contentment.

But when Frances was five days old, an article appeared in the *L.A. Times*—a result of Courtney's illegally faxed medical records. According to the article, a pregnant woman had checked into the hospital under an assumed name, listing Kurt Cobain as her husband. The article reported that the woman had received "daily doses of . . . methadone, a heroin substitute used to treat narcotics addiction." The piece included a possible explanation for the use of methadone, quoting Dr. David Murphy, medical director of a nearby rehab center, as saying current thought was that an addict should not detox while pregnant: "The standard practice is to continue the use of methadone through the pregnancy and deal with the chemical dependency when the pregnancy is over. And when the baby is born, then the baby is chemically dependent and it will go through methadone detox. Babies go through that well."

David Murphy was not Courtney's doctor, however. He had no idea whether she was on methadone or not. The couple would later assert that the hospital records reflected her drug use in the first month of pregnancy, not in later trimesters.

The public announcement that Courtney's possible drug use may have resulted in a drug-addicted baby didn't help the Cobains' case with Los Angeles child services. And the Cobains were incensed that their confidentiality had been breached and that once again they'd been hurt by the press. They were also not aided by photographs showing up in the press of the new parents looking as if they were on drugs. Perhaps their appearance had more to do with their usual ripped attire, stringy hair, and trademark poor grooming. Maybe they were once again relying on personal style to challenge society's notions about who and what parents should be.

Meanwhile, a new nightmare sprang to life, or so the increasingly wary parents feared, in the form of Victoria Clarke and Britt Collins. The two British women were working on an unauthorized biography about Nirvana for Disney's publishing arm, Hyperion. They apparently had dug up some choice morsels from Courtney's past and had even interviewed *Vanity Fair*'s Lynn Hirschberg, who certainly had unkind words to say about the couple. The Cobains claimed the biographers were even sifting through their trash.

The couple's management, Gold Mountain, quickly notified friends and colleagues, requesting that they not cooperate with the biographers. Meanwhile, MTV continually reported all the news about the first family of grunge. Kurt and Courtney became convinced that one of the newscasters, Tabitha Soren, was out to get them and that when she spoke of them she had daggers in her eyes.

In any case, there was no use in holing up any longer. It was time to get out and fight and to show the world that they were all alive and well.

Six days later, Nirvana flew to England for the 1992 Reading Festival. Kurt mocked rumors that he was on his deathbed by wrapping himself in gauze and having Everett True push him onstage in a wheelchair. He began singing "The Rose," from the movie loosely based on the life of Janis Joplin, and fell on the floor. While some in the crowd panicked, Kurt jumped to his feet, ripped off the bandages, and proceeded to tear up the stage.

Two weeks later he and Courtney attended the MTV Video Music Awards in Los Angeles with the baby in tow, carrying her bottle and looking like the grunge version of Ozzie and Harriet.

But despite the appearance of a happy family, Kurt was irate that night. When handed the award for Best New Artist, he looked into the camera and said, "It's really hard to believe everything you read." The *Vanity Fair* article was only one of the things ticking him off. Courtney and Axl Rose had gotten into a fight backstage, Axl telling Kurt to "shut your bitch up or I'm taking you down to the pavement." More annoying was that MTV had forbidden Kurt to play a new song that he'd written. Courtney would later say it was inspired by music insiders who had leaked information to *Vanity Fair.*

It was a caustic, slow-burning indictment called "Rape Me." "Appreciate your concern. You'll always stink and burn." That was only a snippet of the lyrics born of betrayal. It could also have been a song about Seattle, because a year after *Nevermind* was released, Nirvana mania lived on, and it was common sport in the downtown scene to put down Kurt for being so popular.

Perhaps he didn't feel the resentment so keenly when Nirvana returned to Seattle in September to play at the Coliseum, where Courtney showed off their infant backstage in a smoke-filled room, and where bits of foil littered the floor. It wasn't likely that the partiers backstage were just chewing lots of gum and tossing the wrappers. To some, the litter appeared to be the foil from a cigarette pack that was used to "chase the dragon"—to smoke heroin. While that method isn't as cost-effective as injecting smack into the blood, it does have the advantage of not leaving telltale needle marks on the user's skin.

Then again, maybe Kurt and Courtney weren't using it.

In an *L.A. Times* article that appeared on September 21, Kurt said drugs were "a total waste of time." He maintained that he had developed only "a little habit" for three weeks earlier that year and that since the birth of Frances he was entirely clean. "Holding my baby is the best drug in the world," he told the paper's pop music writer, kindhearted and trustworthy Robert Hilburn, who had proved himself an ally.

Lynn Hirschberg soon after called up Hilburn to inform him that Kurt had not told him the whole story. And the war was officially under way between the couple and the writer, to whom they reportedly made threatening remarks over the phone.

Upon the new family's return to Los Angeles, the fireworks started. The social worker had not been making idle threats. The baby was hardly two months old when they had to hand her over in court, losing custody for several weeks. Kurt was ordered back into rehab for thirty days.

While child services deliberated over the family's fate, Frances was put in the custody of Courtney's half sister, who lived in Oregon. Kurt and Courtney weren't allowed to see their child without supervision. More humiliating, they were required to take drug tests; according to Courtney's father, Hank Harrison, that process was overseen by Courtney's mother. Surprisingly, though, the *Vanity Fair* debacle and the heartache that ensued actually brought Courtney closer to her mother, who Courtney said had never been more supportive.

The Cobains' case was a test balloon in the prevailing winds of society's views. How many hundreds of rock stars before them had done drugs and had kids, without having them taken away? Granted, not that many had been pictured in a major magazine, brazenly admitting to having used drugs, and seeming unrepentant and cavalier in their attitude. Maybe it was just that the Cobains seemed immature and came off like rich, disrespectful teenagers who brazenly challenged the world on everything from music to fashion, or that they chain-smoked, seemed unapologetic about doing drugs, and didn't look clean (in both senses of the word). Whatever the reason, the situation was ironic. As messed up as they were, the fact was that they could afford a nanny who could be more responsible than their own parents had been.

The incident was like a war for the couple. Its everyday reality was horrible. They had gone from the high of success to the low of public humiliation. Life for them was like a roller coaster running off track while rounding a high-speed curve. Lynn Hirschberg became the scapegoat for everything that was wrong in their life. They made angry calls to the magazine, and the writer became a constant target in the Cobains' interviews, even rating a mention in a piece Courtney wrote in *Mademoiselle* about her perfumes. The worst smell in the world, she claimed, was emitted by "evil journalists [who] smell like brand-new couture clothes that are too tight, acrid dishonesty and loneliness."

The trauma bonded the couple like psychic glue, though, and not just when they were in the public eye. Kurt and Courtney's relationship took on a siege mentality, an attitude of "you and me against the monsters"—who included the media, the state, and sometimes even the fans. From that point on, the whole world was divided into friend or foe, and almost everyone fell into the latter category.

Even the other band members were becoming estranged from Kurt. Part of the problem was Kurt's new vision of royalty splits. He wanted 100 percent of the royalties from the lyrics—which, granted, were mostly his creations. And he wanted 75 percent of the music royalties (not including group collaborations), with Krist and Dave left to split the remaining 25 percent (of the music Kurt wrote solely) between them. "I think that's fair," Kurt told *Rolling Stone*. And he also thought it would be fair if the split was made retroactive. The fact that he was suddenly making such seemingly money-hungry requests seemed to be a reflection of Courtney's influence.

During October, when the couple visited their baby at Courtney's sister's house, their mood was glum, and they later confessed to being suicidal. But $240,000 in legal fees later, the baby was back in their custody.

They promptly headed to Seattle, out of the jurisdiction of L.A. child services. In the Pacific Northwest, things tended to be a bit more relaxed.

And with the child back, they had a new project: damage control.

They called Jonathan Poneman of Sub Pop, who got them the cover of the December issue of *Spin*. They called Everett True at *Melody Maker*, who gave them a two-part article that would run at the beginning of 1993. They called Michael Azerrad and suggested he tell their tale in a book.

And then, somewhere amid the flurry of calls to the media, responding to a request for an altogether different article, Courtney called me.

CHAPTER 9

Seattle Revisited
(November 1992)

"I GOT HER! I GOT HER GOOD!" COURTNEY LOVE SAID WITH A proud smirk, swinging open the door to the Cobains' suite at the Four Seasons, downtown Seattle's swankiest hotel, which boasted marble columns and a lavish ballroom-like foyer. I laughed. What a character: she seemed to have tumbled out of a book. Courtney was instantly likable, this knock-'em-sock-'em grunge queen, whose hair was now cocoa brown, with pink plastic barrettes clipped in randomly, and eyes that were dazzling blue and capable of piercing your soul.

When Courtney had called me from L.A., a few days before, and dropping so many names that she had me wishing for a current issue of the Underground Who's Who, her Call-Waiting clicked in.

Victoria Clarke, one half of the British duo writing the unauthorized, and dreaded, biography of Nirvana, had been spotted at a nearby club. Courtney boasted that she was gonna get that girl, and get her good, and clicked off.

Apparently she did. Upon spotting Clarke at a bar, Courtney walked right over and bopped her with a drinking glass.

Outlandish behavior, but at the time, it struck me as amusing.

Until, that is, she more closely surveyed me, the freelance writer whom she had invited to the hotel for a possible interview—and her face turned into one big question mark.

In her ragged beige dress she suddenly looked much taller than the five feet eight she's reported to be, but that may have had everything to do with her aura, a phenomenon I believed in that night. Courtney oozed intensity, her presence swelling through the hotel suite, past the peach couch, and into the back bedroom where the sheets were rumpled. It was as though she couldn't stay put in her physical container. Her spirit ionized a room.

And this power babe, once she'd had time to assess me, seemed unsure that I was the one to tell her story to after all.

I developed a stutter.

Courtney had called me, suggesting we get together, by virtue of the fact that writing was my theoretical career, from which I made hundreds and hundreds of dollars every year. After a decade in the biz, I'd graduated to stringer for *Newsweek* and had called Courtney to interview her for a piece about riot grrrl bands, with which Courtney was, at the time, somewhat affiliated. Back then, in 1992, Courtney had even listed Bikini Kill, the riot grrrl band headed by Kathleen Hanna, as one of her favorites. When Courtney returned my call a few weeks later, the riot grrrl article had already been published, along with the few quotes I'd collected for the story's main writer.

Nevertheless, while she had a *Newsweek* stringer on the line, Courtney took the opportunity to let loose about *Vanity Fair*. She started cannon-shooting verbal fireballs. "[Lynn] did a horrible, horrible thing," she said. "I haven't lived a boring life; she didn't have to lie about it." Her mouth blasted pithy sound bite after pithy sound bite. "I gave her a normal interview," she continued. "I say outrageous things, praise some people, slander others. She made a lot of stuff up, and twisted it. . . . Hole has had bad reviews, but no one raped me before."

Explaining, "I'm just a badly groomed person," Courtney said she was duped into posing for the camera with a lit cigarette. The photo shoot lasted for four hours, she said, and it was her birthday. She was eight months pregnant, and thrilled that she "was doing a fashion shoot with a fashion photographer for *Vanity Fair.*" But they picked that shot—the one Courtney said was taken during a break, when she was having a smoke, just a couple puffs. She said the photographer, inspired, commanded her to "Stay like that!" Courtney herself was appalled at the photo, which she described as "a shocking [image] like 'Here's this bad mother. She deserves to have her baby taken away.'" She added, "Lynn is not my social worker! I have a drug history, but it was not extensive. I told her I did Percodan, and back in Portland I did heroin for a couple of months."

Infuriated by the whole flap, she thought I might be of service. So she invited me to dinner to get acquainted and talk about a potential article she had brewing in her head, a piece that would tell her side, how she felt she was deceived by the reporter, who had been out to get her all along and was just acting sweet to loosen the dirt. The media, after all, had gotten her into this mess; the media could get her out.

She and I planned to meet several days later when Kurt and Courtney—or "Kurtney," as they'd become known to the British press—flew to Seattle with the baby and the baby's nanny in tow.

They checked into the Four Seasons Olympic Hotel under the name Simon Ritchie—Sid Vicious's real name. The name Ritchie seemed a pun; after all, they were the nouveau riche.

And now that Courtney and I were meeting face-to-face, I felt rather uneasy.

The door opened and the nanny, a young brunette

who seemed emotionless in a detached Seattle way, pushed in a black baby carriage.

"Here she is," Courtney deadpanned, gesturing to baby Frances. "My two-headed monster child." The tabloids had gone nuts over the birth of Frances, running pictures of mutants instead of her. Courtney looked away, mockingly averting her eyes to give me ample opportunity to assess her offspring for extra appendages. But Frances was just a normal sleeping baby with a mass of dark hair.

Courtney leaned over the buggy and gave her daughter a kiss. Then she showed me some of the Christmas presents she'd bought—heart-shaped jewelry—and glanced at the TV. Predictably, it was tuned to MTV. Courtney said the people on the music network talked so much about her that it was clear they were obsessed. They even ran news items about the nanny, Jackie.

The Jim Rose Circus Sideshow appeared on the screen. I'd written about the bizarre troupe for *Newsweek.* "I know them," I said, trying to appear mildly in-the-know, when in fact I had just moved back to Seattle two months before and was somewhat clueless about the new and improved scene, which was now the headquarters of grunge.

"They're just a bunch of junkies," she sneered, scarcely taking in the act.

"No, they're not . . ."

Courtney wasn't listening as she headed for the door. I thought it odd for her to put down people for using heroin—especially since, in this case, she was wrong—when she'd reportedly had a bit of a dalliance with it herself. Despite her history, though, that night Courtney appeared entirely straight.

Nevertheless, she was scary, and I decided she was more likable on the phone; she seemed to have come to a similar conclusion about me. It was obvious that I wasn't keeping up with the names she was dropping madly. Courtney could shoot out more names in a minute of conversation than can be heard in an entire episode of *Entertainment Tonight.* Dave, Krist, Shelli, Thurston, Kim, Bruce, Jonathan, Nils, Eric, Everett, Janet, and Robert, would, for example, be tossed around in one sentence, and I had no idea at the time who they all were. It appeared as if that I were being interviewed for the job of interviewing her, and that I was failing her test.

Courtney and I—along with the nanny and baby—soon headed across the street for dinner. The Chinese restaurant was hardly a scene: the only other diners were clearly tourists. They didn't seem to recognize Courtney, having apparently missed the infamous issue of *Vanity Fair,* or perhaps they were thrown off by her hair, which was normally blond, a color that suited her better.

Courtney and I ordered the chicken stir-fry, which was inedibly bland, and Jackie talked about weight, specifically how she wished she could lose some. While I thought to myself that if Jackie had ordered the taste-free chicken stir-fry, overeating would definitely not be a problem, Courtney advised the nanny at great length to cut down on the dairy products. I wished that she'd permitted me to tape the conversation for its amusement factor alone, but at that first meeting Courtney had wanted to talk casually.

Some of Courtney's diet advice was soon captured in an article in *Rollerderby,* a small San Francisco magazine, and later reprinted in *Harper's:* "I have a tip! I lost forty pounds, and I have a real tip. . . . When you're fat like I was—which is five feet eight inches and 150 to 170 pounds—you do not get to fuck the boys you want to fuck. Right? . . . The minute I got skinny and got a nose job and became photogenic . . . every boy I ever wanted wanted me. . . . The thing you gotta do is . . . no cheese. That's it. Period. *No cheese.* . . . It's like sour milk—*lard.* . . . And I lost *forty pounds* by not eating cheese. . . . Don't eat cheese. There are a million things to eat that are not cheese."

That was the essence of the scintillating dinner conversation that night. I started getting twitchy, worried that if I actually introduced a topic it would be uncool or that I'd stutter, or probably both.

Luckily, the conversation turned to Portland, where I'd once lived, as had Courtney. We started talking about the difference between the Northwest's two largest cities. "For me, cities are like boyfriends," I said. "Seattle's a guy who's really good-looking but totally stuck up, doesn't treat you too great, and doesn't care if you leave. Portland's a cute guy who treats you pretty well and wants you to stay."

Courtney looked at me more approvingly after that. In upcoming interviews she began likening cities to boyfriends.

That night she apologized, saying she didn't remember me from the hamlet south of Seattle; I didn't recognize her from Portland, either—at least not at first.

Courtney shot off a list of names of notable Portlanders. She gushed about Katherine Dunn, whose novel *Geek Love*, about the beauty in being different, she adored. "I sent her a long fan letter," Courtney sighed, "but I didn't sign my name."

Courtney rattled off a few more names, including that of director Gus Van Sant, whose movies reminded her of her own childhood. Then she narrowed her eyes and asked, "Did you know Rozz Rezabek?"

"Oh, yeah," I said fondly recalling the Portlander I'd known for over a decade while living there. "Saw Rozz a while back—same old Rozz. He's so charismatic. Even when you know he's feeding you b.s., he still makes you feel special."

Tears sprang from Courtney's spacey blue eyes and ran down her face, smearing her mascara. She looked very upset.

"What's the matter?" I asked, mortified.

"Rezabek is my old boyfriend," she sobbed. "I never got over him."

I suddenly recalled being accosted on occasion by the younger, much fatter Courtney, who'd demanded to know if I, or anyone nearby had seen Rozz. Did we know where he was? Had he mentioned having a fight with her? What did he say about her? Who was he with? Which way did he go? It was as though she were in training for rapid-fire police interrogation. This Courtney looked different all right. I flashed on the former Courtney, recalling that she was the one whose path I had tried never to cross for fear of being grilled yet again.

That Courtney was *this* Courtney? And she still cared about Rozz?

She wiped away her tears, and pulled out a gold Visa card with the name Kurt Cobain on it, a card so new that when the carbon copy was returned, she wasn't sure where to write in the tip; then again, perhaps she had only used it for shopping, and other non-tipping activities.

I was still thinking about her odd reaction to the mention of an old boyfriend. She was married to *Kurt Cobain,* for crying out loud, but she was crying about Rozz Rezabek.

Rozz was by then a white-collar type who lived most of the year in Portland, publishing a newsletter for hospitals and physicians. Formerly a hot-shot local celebrity, he only occasionally played gigs at small clubs and often talked about rereleasing old recordings. He was still funny, and terribly modest, casually acknowledging that he was a fallen star. "I used to draw a crowd just walking down Northwest Twenty-third," he once said. "Now I can't even fill a guest list."

But Kurt Cobain was . . . well, Kurt Cobain. Brilliant, beautiful, talented, sexy, and rich, too—not to mention the father of Frances. Kurt was, to some, the choicest find in the whole music industry, especially since he had allegedly kicked drugs.

Back at the hotel, Courtney sat on the peach couch, chain-smoking, perching her lit cigarettes on the cushions; like a servant, I relocated them to ashtrays. Having witnessed a fire she'd supposedly started in Portland a few years before, I didn't want a repeat performance.

Despite the drama moments before, Courtney was now completely composed, as though the tears-switch had been flipped off. She was looking at me differently since the Rozz incident, as if maybe I was mildly cool after all.

She and Kurt had been talking to Michael Azerrad a lot, she said. They'd suggested that the music-magazine writer pen a book about Nirvana, and now he was around a lot. Courtney seemed a bit jealous of all the attention being thrown at Kurt.

"You should write a biography of me," she said.

The proposition was interesting; it was obvious that the towering inferno of intensity sitting in front of me had a lot more newsmaking on her mind, and that her life goals exceeded merely being Kurt's wife. Her first album was no huge hit, in the United States, at least, but Courtney had star quality. And from little tidbits she tossed into the conversations we'd had a few days before she and Kurt came to Seattle—about dancing in the Orient, something about a sex scandal, a faked drowning, a Birkenstock-riddled upbringing—she seemed to have had a rich past.

"Would you authorize a biography?" I asked.

"I wouldn't have an authorized biography in my house," she said by way of an answer.

But before she'd consider interviews for an unauthorized biography, she wanted me to write an article that told her side of the *Vanity Fair* piece that had made such a travesty of her life, she felt. She wanted the public to know how she felt deceived by a reporter whom she had trustingly let into her house and her life. She also wanted the world to know all about the British biographers who, she said, kept digging up trash—literally.

And so Courtney began telling her story, and it was among the most moving tales I'd ever heard. When she poured her heart out, it could rip up a listener's, and her gaze upon whoever was soaking up her tale was equally as disturbing. It wasn't like talking to a normal person; Courtney, when she wanted, could just strip away the facade and communicate directly with your soul, or so it struck me that night. She was so charismatic, so powerful, so persuasive that she could make even the most seasoned reporters believe that she'd been wronged and that their purpose in life was to become a warrior for her, fighting her battles, portraying her in a positive light. I knew the feeling that night.

By the time she finished describing the stressful day when Frances was born, with reporters prowling the hospital corridors, Kurt kicking drugs, and the social worker flapping a copy of *Vanity Fair* in her face, threatening to yank away her minutes-old child, Courtney was crying again.

So was I.

She admitted to me that she had used heroin in the early weeks of pregnancy, but that she'd stopped after finding out she was with child. She and Kurt were clean now, she told me. They had a nanny. They were good parents. They'd both grown up neglected; they sure weren't going to let that happen to Frances.

She wanted her story told. And she wanted me to place it in *spy* magazine.

Spy? The satirical magazine known for its media potshots, celebrity lampoons, and investigative pieces not unlike the one Lynn Hirschberg had written?

Spy was perfect place for the story, she informed me, though I had my doubts.

Just then the phone rang. It was Nirvana drummer Dave Grohl, her former telephone pal. He had some very bad news: Kurt was messed up. He'd gone to see a movie with some friends and had ended up doing heroin.

The phone rang again a few minutes later. There'd been another sighting; Kurt was really out of it. The phone rang a third time. Courtney was angry and upset, and she begged off the interview for the night. "I lost my husband, tonight," she said tearfully as we walked to the door. "I lost my husband to drugs." She kissed me on the cheek and closed the door.

What a mess. And I felt vaguely responsible. Kurt, still

gun-shy from the experience with Lynn Hirschberg, hadn't wanted to deal with writers the couple didn't know. The first interviews they'd granted since the debacle had all been to proven supporters. "It's just a girl from Portland!" Courtney had loudly told Kurt a few days before when he was yelling at her to get off the phone, something they often did to each other. But he didn't want to meet with me, and it seemed he didn't particularly want her to, either. Doing heroin, when he knew she'd be meeting with someone from the media, struck me as Kurt's way of getting back at her for talking to the press.

The next day when I called the "Simon Ritchie" room, Courtney sounded ticked off. She told me to meet her at the Crocodile Café, then the city's most famous club— the one that all the A&R types smashed into to check out new grunge bands. She would be lunching with Sub Pop's Jonathan Poneman.

"I'm gonna fuck him," she said into the phone, apparently trying to bait Kurt, who was, as usual, telling her to get off the phone. "I'm gonna fuck Jonathan Poneman," she repeated in her I'm-trying-to-get-some-attention voice, the sort one hears after a lovers' quarrel—and it seemed pretty obvious they'd had one.

There was a sudden flurry of background noises. "The second line's ringing," she explained. "My publicist is furious. The baby just puked in Kurt's face—right in his mouth." And she clicked off.

At the appointed time, Courtney was not at the Crocodile. An hour later I walked over to the hotel, but she was not there. Two hours later, at the Crocodile Café, she was having lunch with Jonathan Poneman. He was quiet, blandly handsome, and the epitome of Seattle's frostiness: very polite but giving the feeling that maybe you're not cool enough to share his iceberg.

Walking over to the table, I immediately noticed Courtney's eyes. The night before they had been a stunning shade of blue, but that day they were sea green; they flashed at me with annoyance, as if I was an uninvited intruder. She'd been at least occasionally charming and charismatic the night before; that afternoon, however, she wasn't out to impress me. Courtney was in quite the bad mood.

Especially when she steered the lunchtime conversation to the ebola virus, which made its victims bleed out of every orifice, and ravaged the body like leprosy, though much quicker. She had recently read about the disease, which inspired the book *The Hot Zone,* in *The New Yorker.* She said she had told Kurt that the minute the virus hit the United States, they were going to buy out a grocery store and hole up in their country home hidden in the hills near a tiny Washington dairy town, Carnation; they weren't going to come out until the epidemic was over.

In the meantime, there were other less gruesome annoyances to attend to. For instance, the British fashion magazine *Tattler* had faxed her a list of questions regarding grunge fashion and had asked how Courtney accomplished the barrette-heavy, mascara-smeared, highly tattered look.

"Gosh, I really must be famous!" she said sarcastically, pondering whethering she should give them fake answers. Deceiving the press, after all, was in vogue in Seattle. Caroline Records representative Megan Jasper had recently pulled a media prank: when asked about the Seattle slang, she'd given the reporter for *The New York Times* a list of ridiculous made-up terms such as "swinging on the flippity flop" and "wackslacks," saying they were Seattle vernacular for hanging out on weekends and the ripped jeans that were so popular in the music scene. That the prestigious paper had actually published the "Grungespeak" definitions was a gloat-worthy victory in the scene where the "mainstream media" that were tossing the city so much attention was infinitely unhip.

After lunch, Jonathan walked back to Sub Pop world headquarters, where band posters lined the walls, a bubble-gum machine stood in the lobby—actually just a space shared by several workers—and the background music was the latest in alternative sounds.

After Jonathan departed, I was hoping for an actual interview, which Courtney had promised the previous night—before the calls had come into their hotel room about Kurt being high. But once again, Courtney had another idea: shopping.

We met up with nanny Jackie and Frances. The nanny left for a while, and Courtney wheeled the baby into a pricey store on First Avenue, where she parked the buggy a few feet inside the door and jaunted off to check out clothes. Apparently, I had been appointed assistant nanny in the real one's absence. The baby carriage was blocking the entryway, and people were glaring at me as if to say, "Lady, move your baby." Courtney was busy whipping through the racks in a far corner.

I pushed the buggy to the side, truly afraid to even touch it, lest I flip it over and crash it into a counter. After all, this was the Love-Cobain child. What if something happened to her—what if a kidnapper nabbed her—while I was the temporary attendant?

"Please Frances, don't cry," I silently begged, and she acceded to my pleas, dozing peacefully while I eyed her, nervously looking for any indication of crib death.

Courtney returned, and held up a star ornament. "Cute, huh? But not worth fourteen dollars. I know I'm supposed to be a gold digger, but I don't want to waste my husband's millions."

Bored with that store, she mentioned several others, wanting to know where they were. Having just moved back to Seattle, and with a bank account balance that hovered somewhere in the low double digits, I was clueless. She flashed me a look of disgust.

I suggested we walk through nearby Café Sophie, a former funeral home that had been transformed into a velvet-streamed restaurant and filled with stone sculptures of Egyptian Sphynx-like creatures.

"Why do you want me to go in there?" she demanded.

"Because you'll like it," I said, all but shoving her in. "Isn't it beautiful?" I asked as we walked through the high-ceilinged dining room, where a ghost was said to float over one of the booths.

She didn't respond. But not long after, the bartender mentioned that the Cobains had dined there a few days later.

At the vintage clothing store next door, Courtney made a point of touching every single beaded dress and jacket that bore a Do Not Touch sign. The owner, clearly not recognizing Mrs. Cobain, screamed at her, and Courtney scowled, heading to the back, where she rummaged through hats. "How much is this?" she asked a minute later, tossing a ratty linen dust cap on the counter. It was not marked. I figured it would cost about ten dollars.

"Forty-five dollars," snarled the owner, obviously marking the hat up to a price she was sure was unattainable for the stringy-haired grungester before her.

"I'll take it!" Courtney snarled back. The owner was clearly oblivious to the fact that Courtney could buy out her whole store several times, and Courtney—surprisingly, given her reputation—didn't enlighten her.

We hit the children's store across the street, where Courtney held a blue velvet dress up to Frances and laughed about how it engulfed the child. Besides, it was $150—too expensive, she thought. She mentioned her supposed reputation as a gold digger again, as though this disproved it. She told me that the only things she spent much money on were lingerie and skin-care products.

My mood by then was somewhere between nervous and bored. It was not that exciting to follow Courtney around and watch her shop. Was I supposed to be at her side, taping all her comments about dresses? I hinted around about the actual interview, and Courtney likened me to a dog yapping at her heels. She wanted to return to her hotel—reporterless.

She told me to call her the next day; she was having

some documents faxed to her, and she wanted me to see them. They would show all the trials and tribulations she and Kurt had had to go through to get Frances back. We'd go through them, and I'd get a bona fide interview over high tea in the lovely, heavily ferned Garden Court at the hotel.

The next day, however, the Simon Ritchie room was not taking calls. Two days later the Simon Ritchie party checked into a different hotel; shortly thereafter, they checked into another.

I left a message at their L.A. home that I was not interested in continuing the article, but I would pitch a book about her and let her know what happened.

I didn't see Courtney for months after that, and when I did, she was glaring at me, along with her stoic nanny Jackie, whose face I hadn't imagined could convey such a powerful emotion.

That night in April, when Courtney appeared at the Sub Pop anniversary party at the Crocodile Café, I didn't have the nerve to tell her that when I pitched the Courtney Love biography, the response had been laughter, and the editor had told me she was a gold digger—nobody going nowhere fast. Instead the editor had offered me a different book deal—for an unauthorized biography of Pearl Jam. He suggested I just forget about Courtney Love, because everyone else would.

Courtney and I didn't actually speak that night, except with our eyes—hers seething, mine puzzled and no doubt revealing fear. We wouldn't talk again until a year and a half later, after Kurt died.

But there were always reports of Courtney in the gossip news, starting from that day in late November when we last spoke.

CHAPTER 10

The Anti-King and Queen
(December 1992–February 1993)

THE HOTEL ROOMS WHERE THE COBAINS STAYED—WITH
Frances and the nanny lodging in separate chambers—
were often filthy after a few days, since the couple
requested that their suites not be cleaned; the maids,
Courtney claimed, tended to steal their celebrity underwear and socks. According to someone in room service
at one fancy hotel, the couple mostly lay around on the
bed in pajamas, looking dazed, like grungeabilly rock
stars—though they were very polite and did tip quite
well. Telephone operators, who were typically ordered
about and requested to block certain calls and accept
others, sometimes listened into their conversations. On
at least one occasion a call was made to a drug dealer.
"You've got to come over," one eavesdropping operator
supposedly heard Courtney say. "We're hurting."

The word in the local music scene was that they were
on a binge, that Courtney had given up, given in, and
joined Kurt.

But if they did fall off the wagon, Courtney, at least,
appeared to be back on it soon enough. By the end of the
week she was spotted—looking entirely straight—on
more shopping sprees, using the phone at crowded

stores, announcing she had to call her husband to see how his practice was going with his band.

Meanwhile, they sought out another house in Washington, one that wasn't out in the country. Kurt and Courtney wanted to move back to the Northwest. The encounter with the Los Angeles Child Services had left them feeling very cool toward the balmy state. An invasion of privacy like that probably wouldn't have happened in Seattle, and they wouldn't have been so alone and so friendless. They finally found a place north of downtown, in Sand Point, a middle-brow neighborhood that ran alongside Lake Washington. The house they rented—a modern grayish wood number with a spiral staircase and several balconies—stuck out in the neighborhood of modest homes, many of them tiny bungalows. And Kurt and Courtney would stick out too, when, after taking care of the remaining California legal work, they moved back to Seattle, land o'grunge.

After a brief Nirvana tour to Argentina and Brazil, the couple returned to the Northwest and burrowed into their new home.

No red carpet was rolled out for their arrival. There were no banners, no parades, no welcome wagons from the citizens of Seattle or by the major players in the music community, for the couple whose celebrity, at the time, outshone even that of computer whiz Bill Gates.

Kurt, the media-appointed king of alternative music, whose face smirked from the pages of nearly every national magazine, wasn't widely regarded in Seattle, the town he now called home. He was the antihero. And his wife, early on, was regarded by many as the Antichrist.

In another city, such as Portland, their arrival might have been openly welcomed; it might have even been a source of widespread civic pride. But Seattle suffered from a severe case of cultural elitism mixed with geographical protectionism. In other words, it had serious attitude.

Residents of the stunning metropolis, which was dotted with lakes and wedged between two mountain ranges, were such protectionists and isolationists that with the exception of few city boosters, true Seattleites hated travel articles about their fair residence and despised it when the Emerald City landed atop another "most livable cities" list, lest someone else hear about it, fall in love with its beauty, and move there. People had been furious and on the lookout for newcomers ever since Perry Como took to singing about its "bluest skies and greenest greens" way back in the sixties, when the town was the backdrop for Bobby Sherman's short-lived TV show *Here Come the Brides,* even though the series was filmed elsewhere.

With a haughtiness typically reserved for an Ivy League school, the residents eyed non-natives warily, creating a community that was extremely polite, but was marked by a thick icy reserve; the term "interloper" was bandied about, the adjective "California" was synonymous with "satanic," and the first question was almost always "How long have you lived here?" An answer in the single digits didn't really cut it.

And the frostiness that marked Seattle in general was even chillier in the downtown crowd. Embracing the punk ethic of the decade before, they tended to regard as a traitor anybody who made more money than an espresso-puller. Mudhoney recorded a song for the soundtrack to *Singles,* a movie about relationships with Seattle's coffeehouse-music scene as a backdrop, whose lyrics sarcastically noted, "Everybody loves us. Everybody loves our town." If a band got any bigger than Mudhoney—not exactly a widely known group—it had traded in its street-level credibility and, horror of horrors, gone mainstream.

Nirvana's fame and the attention and people it brought to Seattle did not play well in a city that didn't particularly want the rest of the world to discover it. And by early 1993, when the Cobains set up house on the far edge of town, the damage done by Nirvana and other bands traveling in their wake was obvious: musicians were moving in by the busload, scouts and record label

A&R men were swooping down by the planeload searching for the next Nirvana, and every mention of music in the press referred to the Seattle scene, if it didn't focus entirely upon it.

The ripped jeans and greasy-hair look, born of poverty, was still runway chic. Bands were turning up from far corners, clogging up the cafés, competing for stages, and hoping to be discovered while the A&R men were looking. It was making the denizens sick.

Seattle had become a media sensation. Magazines and newspapers couldn't stop cooing about the beauty of the rain-soaked land, its Starbucks, its cafés, its mountains, its lakes, its scenic vistas, its Pike Place Market salmon-throwers, who even turned up in a jeans ad, and most of all, its bands, bands, bands! Pearl Jam, Soundgarden, Alice in Chains, Screaming Trees, and almost every Sub Pop band in the world were rating national features as well, and their music, along with Nirvana's, was dubbed the "Seattle sound." And all the secrets of the junkie community, which had plenty of musicians within it, were suddenly up for public discussion in *Spin* and *Rolling Stone*.

Nirvana had been plenty popular when they played at small clubs; now that the rest of the country knew who they were, it wasn't particularly hip to admit to liking them anymore. Many people still did, of course, though some felt compelled to listen to the records only at home. It wasn't just that *Nevermind* had gone platinum again and again and again until sales topped seven million. Nirvana had triggered a revolution, marking the first time a band with such an unpolished sound, albeit smoothed in production, had come off so radio-friendly, the first time something that had been kept locked in the underground had appealed so widely to the masses.

The general sentiment among the music cognoscente was that something truly fringe couldn't appeal so widely. And the more radio stations that blared Nirvana's songs, the more videos that were shown, and the less often the band played in the local clubs, the more

Kurt was put down for somehow single-handedly ruining Seattle.

As *Nevermind* stuck, seemingly impaled, on heavy rotation on radio and MTV, and the frantic search for a Kurt clone continued, resentment sullied the feel of the community. Fingers flew at Kurt. Screw the musical boy wonder. Screw Nirvana.

"People are sick of us," Krist Novoselic told the press. "More people probably hate us in Seattle than anywhere else in the country."

He was right. People stared at them as if they'd sold the keys to the town.

Kurt bemoaned his fame in interviews. "It's not that great being on MTV twenty times a day," he told the music mags. And he was sick of the constant media attention and its repercussions. "If I'd known about all this crap, I would've thought twice about putting myself in the public eye. I had no idea people could abuse you so much."

He heaped criticism on Pearl Jam, Seattle's other best-selling band, portraying the band as so contrived, so formularized to sell records, that they might well have been the grunge Monkees.

Between the fame and the attitude, Kurt was becoming isolated. And the feeling would only intensify. If few scenesters greeted Kurt with open arms, even fewer were jumping up and down with joy about the "triumphant" arrival of Courtney.

When he brought his wife to Seattle, he ensured that his social life would never be the same. Courtney stepped in and severed the ties of his friendships as if wielding a machete, though she was typically weaponless in her attacks, save for her mouth and her fists.

At the turn of the year, Courtney was still riled up. About everything. The couple started out 1993 making news with a New Year's Day announcement that they were suing Cedars-Sinai for the medical records that were faxed to the *L.A. Times*. Courtney was still considering taking legal action against *Vanity Fair*, but Lynn

Hirschberg insisted she had tapes of the damning words. Courtney railed about the reporter continually. Lynn was calling up magazines, Courtney claimed, playing tapes of their interviews and giving away bits of information entirely out of context. Take, for instance, the item that Courtney said Lynn was publicizing about Mrs. Cobain's calling her husband the "worst lay in the world," which Courtney admitted she had said, but as a joke: when the *Vanity Fair* reporter had asked for her response to being called the greatest fuck in the world by Kurt on British TV, Courtney had jested that he'd called her the best simply because *he* was the worst.

The *Vanity Fair* incident was an acid burning inside her, although by then the press coverage she'd arranged to denounce Lynn Hirschberg was coming out. *Melody Maker* ran the two-part series on the couple, in which Courtney insisted she'd never done dope at all while with child. "I didn't do heroin during my pregnancy," she told Everett True. "And even if I shot coke every night and took acid every day, it's my own mother-fucking business."

Spin, which ran a photo of the new family on the cover, didn't quite go that far. Sub Pop co-owner Jonathan Poneman, who penned the piece, was a little too worldly-wise to allow complete denial. He just mentioned that "if tales of [their] drug-addled recklessness are taken at face value, then the radiance of Baby Frances can be explained only by divine intervention." His intro was peppered with puns about the Cobains' being hopelessly addicted to their baby. "While gossip merchants trawl for muck," he wrote, "allow me to—pardon the expression—impart the real dope."

Although the articles helped to redeem the couple, Courtney was still furious. And as worried as she always was about having Frances taken away again, she would sometimes perform stunts in public that cast her in an unflattering light. Ticked off at a Nirvana show in Idaho, she simply tossed Frances at the nanny, screaming, "Here, you take her!" and stomped off. When a girl called her "Courtney Whore" in a 7-Eleven, Courtney punched her.

And Courtney's constant anger had a way of showing up whenever she encountered a friend of Kurt's—especially those from Olympia, Kurt's former home.

There were many reasons behind her resentment. Some of Kurt's friends there had derided his fame, and Courtney had by then assumed the role of his protector. She'd had an ongoing feud with one of the record labels, K Records, over the name of one of the bands they recorded called "Courtney Love"—a duo that included a former roommate of Courtney's; the situation hadn't improved when she learned the former roommate had given one of Courtney's diaries to K Records co-owner Calvin Johnson. Early in 1993, Courtney organized a riot grrrl show in London which was such a huge flop that it pretty much killed British interest in the riot grrrl movement. Even though Hole put on an outstanding performance, the grrrls-only show was regarded as so exclusive that not many people came.

Nirvana had a song on a compilation album put out by Kill Rock Stars, another of Olympia's labels, and Kurt was miffed that he'd never received a check; the label's owners maintained they had sent a check, but not knowing Kurt's address, they'd mailed it to Nirvana's bass player, Krist Novoselic. Kill Rock Stars had recorded folk singer Mary Lou Lord, and the label's co-owner, Slim Moon, had invited her to move to Olympia, and when Mary Lou did so, Courtney was furious. And to top it off, despite Courtney's support in the press for the riot grrrl bands, many of the grrrls in the scene didn't much like her. They regarded Mrs. Cobain as an annoying symbol of everything that a grrrl wasn't supposed to be, especially since she'd had cosmetic surgery and, at one show, had pointed out an overweight female in a crowd and put her down.

After months of trying to insinuate herself into the Olympia scene, which was admittedly elitist and smug, Courtney gave up. If she couldn't join them, she'd beat them. Literally. And if she couldn't erase Kurt's past and the friends he'd had in Olympia, well, she'd just make it impossible for him to connect with them. Within a few months, she'd built a thick barrier between Kurt and Olympia, the place she later sang about as a factory churning out riot grrrl robots.

One night, when the Cobains attended a show where one of the original punk bands, Fugazi, performed, Courtney punched K Records co-owner Calvin Johnson. Not much later she punched out another of Kurt's friends, physically and verbally assaulting him, simply because he knew Mary Lou Lord.

And then there was her treatment of Mary Lou herself. When Courtney heard that the folksinger had been written up in the weekly *Boston Phoenix,* with a passing mention that she'd once gone out with Kurt, she went ballistic, faxing the paper two letters, supposedly from Kurt, though the bulk of the letters appeared to be written in Courtney's handwriting. The first letter called Mary Lou "a creepy girl," adding that "I can't remember what happened, but it wasn't much," and that "now my life is plagued by this insane girl." It concluded, "I never took this girl anywhere, except maybe in the backyard to shoot her." The second letter claimed that Kurt didn't "even remember [Mary Lou's] face, her name, nothing," and complained that she had moved to Olympia simply to get chummy with his friends. "This is why I wrote 'Rape Me.'"

The reaction to a passing comment about Mary Lou's once dating Kurt was so absurd that the *Boston Phoenix* published an article about the faxes, thus landing the paper on Courtney's unofficial hate list in a spot not far below Lynn Hirschberg and Mary Lou herself. Courtney made a point of complaining about the *Phoenix* from every stage where the editors might hear about her remarks.

Kurt and Courtney later phoned Mary Lou. Courtney threatened, "I'm gonna cut off your head and shove it up your ass—and Kurt's gonna throw you in the oven." On a roll, they reportedly made threatening phone calls to many others in the Olympia scene.

And they went off on Victoria Clarke and Britt Collins, the unofficial Nirvana biographers, as well, leaving numerous hateful message on their answering machine, including threats to have them snuffed. When the biographers made copies of the many unflattering messages and circulated the tapes through the music scene, Kurt's old friends weren't all that surprised at the contents. Nor was it hard to believe when *Entertainment Weekly* ran a piece about someone breaking into the biographers' apartment. The biographers believed the Cobains were behind the break-in, though their management denied it. Since Courtney had entered Kurt's life, few of his old friends knew who he was anymore.

Besides, Kurt was sinking back into heroin, slinking back to the strip of seedy apartments on Capitol Hill commonly known as "Heroin Alley," where addiction equalized its victims: junkies who were short-order cooks were on the same footing as junkies who were rock stars, all just waiting to score. Kurt quit several times, only to start up again.

That's the nature of heroin. Three is supposed to be the lucky number—the third time a junkie quits, legend has it, is the attempt most likely to be successful. But if it's not, if users don't quit within two years of starting, they typically stay addicted for twenty years, or so goes the junkie lore.

Most of Kurt's former friends from Olympia weren't into heroin, and they had a hard time watching him being sucked in. Many blamed his wife for his habit, although Courtney by then wasn't a daily user—of heroin, at least. When he was using, which was often, he didn't want to see people from his past, and so Kurt's world was shrinking. Other than his wife, his child, and whatever nannies they had that month, one of the few people he saw regularly was his friend Dylan Carlson.

A student of Eastern religion who had known Kurt in Olympia, Dylan headed up an experimental band called

Earth. The band's slow-guitar-heavy sound was so monotonous that they claimed to be surprised when somebody lasted through more than 15 minutes of an Earth show. The one time that happened, it turned out the remaining listener was the club's owner, waiting for the band to quit so he could close up.

Kurt and Dylan began studying the Shiva, Hindu god of destruction.

Kurt didn't go out much anymore. He was typically creeped out whenever he entered a pizza joint or walked down the street. People treated him like a star, assessed the size of his pupils, or snapped his picture. And everywhere hung the unspoken accusation: sellout scum. He took to wearing women's oval sunglasses and hunting caps with the flaps pulled down.

As much as Kurt hated attention, Courtney thrived on it, with or without him. She'd grab the current magazines on a newsstand in a mall, plop down on the floor, and read aloud to the nanny from the current article on Kurt and her. When shopping, she'd demand to use the store phone and then occasionally get into a loud fight with Kurt, saying she was leaving and taking Frances. Courtney never was particularly good at inobtrusively slipping into a scene, although she had fitted in better in Portland, where being an outspoken character was more acceptable.

But in tight-lipped Seattle, land of nods, she was too much—too loud, too dramatic, too attention-grabbing, and too name-droppy. When Courtney walked into a room, few would run over to greet her, and she would often just sit with the nanny and glower, putting down everyone who walked by. She was generally ignored until she walked out of the room, and then the side-of-the mouth muttering would begin: She's no great shakes. What did Kurt see in her? What a bitch.

Courtney wasn't doing herself any public relations favors anywhere, especially not at Nirvana shows. Perhaps not wanting to allow outside access to their at least "occasional" drug use, she routinely made a major to-do about dressing rooms, appointing herself enforcer of the guest list and booting out the other band members' friends. She was said to kick out almost anyone Kurt brought to their home, yelling at him that he was waking up the baby—until her screams did wake Frances up. On one occasion she is said to have come down for a late night snack and grossed out the visitors by eating scrambled eggs with her fingers.

When Kurt and Courtney went to a small record store and found Nirvana bootlegs from which the band wasn't getting royalties, she simply snatched them and took them out of the store. Then she wrote a note to the shop owner, chastising him for selling the CDs and taking food from her baby's mouth. When *The Rocket,* a Seattle rock paper, ran an item about the incident, including the note, it simply made Courtney appear greedy.

The social verdict was quickly reached regarding Courtney: avoid at all costs. Given her antics, her bossy ways, and her sharp tongue, many of Kurt's former pals felt it was not worth dealing with her to get to him, and they simply stopped trying.

Kurt and Courtney just climbed back into bed. For most people bed is simply the place where they pass an unrecalled third of their lives; for the Cobains, the bed was the center of their universe. Piled with periodicals—from British glossies to *People,* the Sunday *New York Times,* and the *National Enquirer*—spiral notebooks filled with scrawled bits of lyrics, novels, a guitar or two, the Yellow Pages, and daily planners, the bed was the site of songwriting and long phones calls at all hours, a place for entertaining visitors and, of course, for sleeping and sex. Not to mention the place for passing out into narcotized oblivion. Nevertheless, whether on the road or at home, with maids or without them, bed was their sanctuary. Whenever they were, they huddled under the covers, where Frances Bean sometimes joined them in the linen cocoon that protected them from the outside world.

Creative and social center of the world though it was,

the bed wasn't the only place they spent time. Courtney sometimes pushed back the covers long enough to fax off letters to reporters who had written about the Cobains, or to go on shopping trips to the vintage clothes store or magazine kiosks and record shops, or to take in a show or show off for a photographer; sometimes she left for a jaunt to the East Coast for more cosmetic surgery. On occasion, Courtney simply flew to another bed in another city, where she could hole up in a hotel for a few weeks writing songs. Kurt occasionally wandered out of the bedroom to score, to get away from her, to lie on the couch watching the PBS series on the Civil War or *Dragnet,* or to stroll a few yards away to compose his music in the closet, where Courtney was known to knock on the door and ask to borrow a riff.

Their home was often a mess, with weeks-old garbage heaped high in the corners, dolls and records and clothes strewn about, art projects spread across the floor, and rotting food and pizza crusts sitting on tables and chairs. Their squalor was so extreme that one newly hired maid walked in and promptly ran back out, screaming "Satan lives here!"

CHAPTER 11

Back to Work
(March–December 1993)

By 1993 both Hole and Nirvana were late in fulfilling their recording contract obligations. And the other band members were waiting for Courtney and Kurt to come to, wake up, and put out.

Hole was not exactly a fiery conversation starter by then, especially in the United States; the band had become more of a concept than a reality simply because they hadn't done much. They'd not only lost momentum in 1992; they'd lost half the band, when Courtney fired the drummer in a huff, and the bass player quit. By 1993, after a year of not touring, Hole mostly meant Courtney's mouth—or whatever was shooting out of it.

A radical rocker who challenged the norm, Courtney wrote her own feminist manifesto, which appeared in *Melody Maker:* "Defy, defy. Use your lifetime of suppression and debunk [men, particularly corporate oppressive ones]. Dupe them. Take them in their sleep when they least expect it. Assassination plots never hurt Hitler. The only way he could have been eliminated was by a woman or a whore who snuck in a knife, who gained his trust and then stabbed him as he drowsed off. Defy, defy. . . ."

But for someone who talked the talk, the walk she walked resembled Betty Crocker more than Susan B. Anthony. Although Courtney had gone on at great length about how she wasn't going to forget her music for Kurt's, she seemed to have done exactly that—sacrificing her career to care for her talented but needy husband, over whom she stood guard like a cross between the great mother goddess and a rabid Doberman.

"Kurt! Kurt!" That was her greeting as she walked in the door, her call from the bed, her call from the phone when she interrupted another band practice. "Kurt! What are you doing? Kurt!" Her attention was sometimes smothering, but he relied on it; it was the one constant (besides stomach pain) in his life. Courtney was the pillar he could lean on when his stomach hurt so bad he could barely walk, when he was overdosing again, or despairing over the exitless cubicle of his fame.

Kurt was still in high fuckup mode; his success had turned into a disaster. It wasn't an ideal situation in which to create *Nevermind the Second.* While DGC, the media, and his fans panted for further evidence of his genius, the follow-up album veered off-track. The plumbing excuse—the one about the tapes and lyrics being ruined when they were left in the tub for safekeeping—only went so far.

Incesticide, a collection of older material mostly owned by Sub Pop, including three cover songs of the Vaselines, had been released in the interim; Kurt's cynicism about it was evident in the album's working titles—*Throwaways* and *Filler.*"

Nevermind had materialized so quickly back in 1991 that it seemed like an unreal inspirational flash. A trip down to the L.A. studio and—bam!—it was done. The strange voyage to stardom had begun.

Nevermind's follow-up, however, materialized in slow motion. Once he'd rewritten the songs, and the rough material was there, the release date wasn't. The label informed him, much to his chagrin, that they couldn't fit in the long-awaited record until fall of 1993. That news no doubt made Kurt feel even more like a commodity, a feeling that was reflected in one of the new album's working titles, *Radio Friendly Unit Shifter*. "It seems like it's taking forever," Kurt lamented to *Spin*. "I feel like I'm stuck in a void."

Courtney knew the feeling. She had many of her songs ready to record, but no bass player. Despite auditioning for over a year, she didn't have a complete band to take on the road or to the studio. She and Eric continued to bug Kristen Pfaff, a talented bassist from Minneapolis, to join, but Kristen wasn't rushing to make a commitment. At least Courtney had found a drummer. Kurt had recommended Patty Schemel, whom he'd once considered hiring for Nirvana.

Finally their careers were starting to get back on track.

By February, Nirvana was ready to set down on tape the album that Kurt had now tentatively titled *I Hate Myself and I Want to Die*. The original plan was to do something more raw and far less radio-friendly than *Nevermind*, something truly alternative in the genre that Nirvana had help to create. One song was almost guaranteed to help his case for anti-commercialism: the album would include "Rape Me," the song that MTV had refused to let him play at the MTV Video Music Awards eighteen months before.

The antithesis of a big-city corporate studio, Pachyderm, Steve Albini's favorite studio, was nestled in the woods of Minnesota. It was the perfect place to create the underproduced sound Kurt was looking for. Two of Kurt's favorite bands, the Breeders and the Pixies, had recorded *Pod* and *Surfer Rosa* there—albums that far undersold their subsequent records, which were mixed by other producers.

But Steve had underground credibility, and Kurt wanted it. If he put out something that the masses didn't fully grasp, no one could accuse him of being a commercial slickster anymore. For the third real album, he wasn't looking to sell multi-millions.

Steve Albini wasn't kissing up to get the job producing

the album, either. He seemed to view Nirvana with as much disdain as the people in Seattle, downplaying the band's importance and denying to the press any personal interest in being involved. And once the album was made, he told the media all about how the record company was sticking its nose in where it didn't belong once too often.

Mixing for Steve usually took only two days, but once Nirvana settled in, the session lasted two weeks. It went slowly, by Albini time, but there were moments. Moments when Kurt shone. Moments when they all kicked back and had their laughs. During downtime, the band and the producer turned to the phone for amusement. In music circles, making and taping prank phone calls was a more popular pastime than using heroin. One night the boys tracked down The Lemonheads' lead singer Evan Dando in Australia and told him Madonna was on the line. While he waited, thinking Madonna's voice would soon greet his ears, Evan was apparently so excited he reportedly said, "I'm going to start beating off." Ba-ha-ha! They couldn't have engineered a more hilarious tape.

However, the session, occasionally tense anyway, grew much more uncomfortable when, a week into it, Courtney flew out to join them. Though Kurt was happy to see her—it was their first wedding anniversary—others felt differently. She had a fight with Dave Grohl, and she butted heads with Steve Albini. Later, when Nirvana biographer Michael Azerrad asked about the source of the problems, Albini said, "I don't feel like embarrassing Kurt by talking about what a psycho hosebeast his wife is, especially when he knows it already."

Courtney countered by telling the biographer, "The only way Steve Albini would think I was a perfect girlfriend would be if I was from the East Coast, played the cello, had big tits and mall hoop earrings, wore black turtlenecks, and never said a word."

Kurt jumped to her defense, telling *Details* magazine, "There was no reason for [Steve Albini] to call her a talentless cunt."

Courtney by then had a new explanation for her unpopularity. She decided that the media portrayal, and common perception, of her as a harpie, arose from the fact that she had married Kurt. "I have no doubt," she told the British press, "that had my husband married Donita Sparks [of L7] or Kim Deal [of the Breeders] they would be stuck with the same archetype as me . . . the witchy woman."

The book *Backlash* was her newest bible, and Courtney bought dozens of copies to distribute to her friends. She even met with the author, Susan Faludi, and discussed how Courtney was getting dissed simply because she was a powerful female. Faludi noted to *US* magazine that Courtney, after reading *Backlash*, understood now "why the media became preoccupied with her only after her name was tied up with Kurt Cobain."

The assertion was interesting but flawed. That explanation overlooked the fact that the Hole singer had been featured in articles of her own long before she became Mrs. Kurt. Throughout her life, Courtney had raised eyebrows by pushing the boundaries of acceptable behavior, whether by bullying, flashing, or verbally attacking people. Certainly Kurt was a conduit for even more attention; but Courtney, with her scenes and her antics and her performing talent, had snagged plenty on her own, without him, and would probably have continued to do so.

Susan Faludi's analysis also failed to mention that in reality Courtney was perceived as an out-of-control maniac because she often acted like one.

And her behavior at a benefit for a murdered Seattle musician was yet another telling example.

When Mia Zapata, a singer for the locally popular band the Gits, was found strangled in the Seattle's International District in early 1993, the police did not immediately turn up any suspects. The feeling that Zapata's murder wasn't getting enough attention prompted friends to put together a benefit to raise funds for a private investigator—and for a women's self-defense group.

Nirvana played the benefit, along with several other Seattle bands. The groups performing that night all shared a small backstage area. It was cramped, but not intolerably so—until a girlfriend of one of the lead singers wanted to get in to the dressing room area. Courtney tried to prevent her entry, and a screaming match broke out between the two feisty women as Mrs. Cobain demanded that the girlfriend leave. To make her point, Courtney snapped a necklace in the girlfriend's face, then slapped her. The girlfriend punched Courtney, and before long the brawlers had dropped to the floor, where they rolled around doing their imitation of mud wrestling, minus the mud. A table and a lamp got knocked over.

While Nirvana was onstage helping to raise money to help stop violence against women, Courtney was backstage engaging in violence against woman. While Nirvana cranked out a hot set for the crowd, backstage grew even hotter—when the dressing room was set ablaze by the fallen lamp. By the time Kurt came back to hear the latest reports of what his wife had done, the fire had been extinguished and the women pried apart.

It was just that sort of hotheaded violence that gave Courtney a reputation for being the Dragon Lady of the Northwest, and that reputation made Kristen Pfaff think more than twice about permanently signing up with Hole.

Though Kristen had filled in for a brief English tour in March, she was committed to the Minneapolis-based Janitor Joe. Hole had continued to audition many other bass players, but kept coming to the conclusion that Kristen was the best.

The advice Kristen got in Minneapolis was almost unanimous: "Don't go." Courtney was dangerous, Kristen was told. Her name was linked to destruction and death and being screwed over. Friends warned

Kristen, who'd already dabbled in drugs, that she would get into them heavily. They pointed out that Seattle seemed to have a lethal effect on its musicians. With the death of Mother Love Bone's Andrew Wood, Seven Year Bitch's Stefanie Sargent, and the Gits' Mia Zapata, few Seattle musicians seemed to be able to make it to thirty.

Kristen's parents, however, saw the opportunity as a great career move and suggested she take Courtney up on the offer. "From a professional point of view, there was no decision," Kristen's father later told *Seattle Weekly*. He counseled his daughter to join up with the band "because they're already on Geffen Records and already have a huge following in England. . . . And with the exposure they've already gotten because of Courtney Love, if you're wanting to move up the ladder, that's the way to go."

Kristen quit Janitor Joe, grabbed her bass, learned Hole's songs, and joined up—at least temporarily. After a summer tour, however, she made a full-time commitment, agreeing to move to Seattle and play on what would become *Live Through This*. What prompted the move apparently wasn't the money: "When I was learning those songs," Kristen said, "it wasn't like there were thousand dollar bills being handed to me. It was like really quality music, and I was really overwhelmed."

Joining Hole was a superior career move, but a questionable social one. Heroin use seemed to be epidemic, and highly contagious.

Before Kristen ever arrived in Seattle, there were signs that the drugs in Kurt and Courtney's life were spinning them out of control; Courtney might not have initiated the heroin binges, but she often joined her husband when he bought some.

There were more efforts to quit. In March, when they returned to Seattle after the *In Utero* recording session, Kurt was pressured into stopping. "Be a good daddy," Courtney begged him again. He performed his last rites with the drug as a steady stream of junkies turned out to climb the winding stairs to the bedroom and shoot up with him one last time.

It wasn't his last time, though. That was obvious to those around him. He'd say he was entirely clean, but then he'd nod off in the middle of a magazine interview or a photo shoot, or he'd leave abruptly to score.

He sobered up long enough to read the press, however. In April the *Chicago Tribune* reported that DGC Records, once they heard *In Utero,* found it "unreleasable." In May, *Newsweek* reported on the matter as well, including a quote from Steve Albini. "The gullibility of these bands will never cease to amaze me," Albini said. "Every one of them thinks the record company is on their side." *Newsweek* added that the band was going to hire a sound engineer to "tinker with the band's tapes and give them a more commercial sheen."

Kurt blew up when the news reached him. Nirvana issued a press release lambasting the *Newsweek* article, saying DGC was not pressuring the band to change the record and that Nirvana had "one hundred percent control of our music." Because of Albini's too-quick working ways, all they did was slightly remix two cuts, and pull the song "I Hate Myself and I Want to Die" from the album. (It reappeared shortly after *In Utero* was released, on the compilation CD *The Beavis and Butt-head Experience.*)

Courtney, in the meantime, was making progress on her career. Having convinced Kristen to join, Hole scheduled a recording session in the fall for the long-awaited album. *Live Through This,* which Courtney hoped would be "a completely accessible punk record," was finally written. And in the meantime Hole put out another recording, albeit an EP, which was released only in Europe on the German label City Slang. The cover bore a picture of Kurt, age six or so, surrounded by gift bows. The back was decorated with candy hearts and pills. "My Beautiful Son," the title song about Kurt looking fetching in Courtney's smocks, came out on April 8, 1993.

That May, Courtney's "beautiful son" came home from a party so messed up he literally turned blue.

She pulled him into the bathroom, tossed him in the tub, and ran cold water over him to no avail. She shot him up with an illegal drug that can counteract the effects of an overdose; she forced pills down his throat to make him puke. And she called 911, then walked him around, slapping him and screaming at him to keep him alive.

An ambulance whisked him away to Seattle's Harborview hospital, where he pulled through. Again.

On another occasion he came home so out of it that Courtney summoned his mother to their Seattle home and literally threw Kurt at her, yelling, "This is your fucking son!"

Kurt, obviously wasted, looked up at his mother and croaked, "I'm not on drugs, Mom. I'm not on drugs. Uhhh."

It had to stop.

She drew the line, at least for herself, and started going to Narcotics Anonymous, so intent on detoxifying that she even bought the best juicer money could buy. Her intent to blend up healthy vegetable mixtures was met with rolled eyes from Kurt.

And then Courtney decided that not only was she going to pull herself out of the black tar hole and get back in the groove; she was going to get Kurt off as well.

In June 1993, Courtney instigated an in-home rehab session. Kurt protested, but she proceeded with her plan, even calling in a psychic.

A few days later the police were called to the Cobain residence. The police report listed the incident as "assault, with intent," and noted that Courtney accused Kurt of pushing, grabbing, and choking her. At least that's what she had said during her 911 call. Once the police arrived, she claimed that the scratches were self-inflicted. The charges against Kurt were dropped when Courtney said that if the matter was legally pursued, she would testify that nothing had happened. The Cobains didn't want any more attention drawn to their domestic situation: as always, in Courtney's mind, any close brush with the law meant that Frances might be once again taken away.

Kurt later explained the incident away saying they were in the garage playing their music too loud. "Courtney and I went running around the house screaming and wrestling," he told the press. "It was a bit Sid and Nancyesque, I have to admit, but we were having a good time. And then we get this knock on the door, and there are five cop cars outside and the cops all have their guns drawn."

The reality was that their fight started when Courtney blocked a drug deal. Unaware of the plans he'd made to score, she was hanging out with a psychic in the bedroom, drinking juice and trying to be healthy, when someone arrived to deliver Kurt's goods; instead of heroin, this time he'd ordered crack. Courtney flipped. When she chased away the dealer, Kurt blew up. He began hitting her. She tossed some fresh-squeezed orange juice in his face, and the fight continued. According to the report, he allegedly pushed her, grabbed her, tried to choke her, and scratched her a few times.

Though they later blamed it on the neighbors, it was actually Courtney who had called the police, and when the authorities arrived to find Kurt in his juice-soaked velvet smoking jacket, they asked a routine question about firearms in the house. Kurt started to deny it, but Courtney told them about the three guns he'd recently purchased, which the cops took for safekeeping. One of them was a semiautomatic weapon. Though she made much ado about the guns' presence in the house, and although they'd be taken from the house by the police again, Courtney was there when he bought them. She wanted the news out via the media too, telling one reporter, "I want people to know we have guns. We're gonna get a rottweiller, too."

The police, as is routine, insisted that one of them come to the station with them. This demand incited another squabble: both Courtney and Kurt wanted to be the chosen one. He won that round and climbed into the squad car to spend three hours in jail.

That summer—a gray, rainy, and miserable season with so few bright days it seemed to be merely a continuation of winter, Hole finally took to the stage again. In early July they were scheduled for the Offramp, a dark, sleazy dive heavy on the black leather and long hair, where the feeling of heroin slime permeated the front room. The small music room off to the side, however, one of the few club rooms that actually had booths and tables, made for intimate performances, and after the shows trays of eggs and potatoes were brought out, lending the place a festive after-hours feel.

The day of the July gig, a month after Kurt's arrest, the *Seattle Times* ran an article about the assault incident, not touching on the real cause. The article only increased the readers' interest in seeing Hole and its troublemaking lead singer. That night the Offramp's music room was jammed, and a sense of anticipation permeated the crowd. The expectation was that big-mouthed, bitchy Courtney and her band Hole were going to suck, and everybody wanted to be there to see it.

Around midnight, when Kurt, after taking in a Leonard Cohen show at another venue, showed up backstage wearing red nail polish, Courtney stumbled out to the stage—in a beige slip. She appeared to be drunk and slurred on incoherently about domestic violence and about their fight being written up in the *Seattle Times* that day. Her intoxication, however, did not prevent her from blazing onstage.

Anyone who expected just another band screaming or a repeat performance of the harsh sniping of *Pretty on the Inside* was shocked: Hole played pretty songs, deftly combining brash guitars and sweetly sung melodies that were an alternative to the music typically heard in town. Those who'd expected Hole to bomb had to eat crow: the band was hot. Well, most people thought so, at least. One faction, a group of hipsters, walked out before the set's end, around the time Eric, Kristen, and Patty walked offstage, leaving Courtney alone to stagger across the stage with her guitar, all but falling into the mike.

"Wait, you guys," she pleaded from the stage, like a woman whose lover was walking out the door. "Don't leave. You're gonna really like this one."

Those remaining in the audience braced themselves, fearing the worst. But then Courtney broke into "Rock Star," her musical flipoff to her grrrl pals in Olympia. It was another display of unharnessed, raw, blinding genius.

She was pathetic. But she was amazing.

After the show, Courtney was approached by a freelance reporter who asked her for an interview to appear in the British music paper *New Musical Express.* First she quizzed him on his musical tastes; luckily he was listening to the current release of the British rockers the Fall. Having passed her test, he was allowed an interview—provided he gave her a ride home. Alas, his car lacked a passenger seat, so Courtney, the star—more likely to be chauffeured about in limos—sat crouched on the dirty vibrating floor of a Volkswagen the entire way back to her house. Just to make sure the writer wasn't a Ted Bundy type (Ted also drove a VW), she brought along members of the opening band Adickdid, generously offering them the actual seat in the back while she hunkered down in front.

Once at the house, it was hard to tell that it had been the site of a dispute not long before. The writer found it nearly Rockwellian in its charm. Kurt came down in his pajamas, warmed a bottle for the baby, and briefly joined the interview, even playing cuts from the upcoming Nirvana record, *In Utero.* They listened to more music and drank tea into the night. Positively dreamy.

But it wasn't dreamy for long.

Later that July, Kurt turned blue again from taking too much heroin before Nirvana's show at New York's Roseland. His first show in six months, and he almost didn't make it to the stage.

By the end of the summer, into the fall, and on into the winter, Kurt and Courtney fought worse than ever. About everything. The mounting bills, including thousands of dollars she owed to psychics, which Kurt balked at paying. The car, a Lexus that Courtney had to persuade him to purchase and that he returned to the dealer within a week, after his friends made fun of him. He preferred driving his beat-up Valiant that was so gross some of his pals called it "the mossmobile."

They fought when together, they fought when separated. When Hole left for a tour of Europe at the end of the summer, a long-distance tiff prompted Kurt to paint on the wall, in large red letters, "None of you will ever know my intentions."

The couple fought about the upcoming Nirvana tour in Europe, which Kurt didn't want to go on; as every junkie knows, being overseas makes it more difficult to score. And there were horrible rows about the 1994 Lollapalooza tour, which was offering Nirvana a cool $9 million to headline. Courtney couldn't believe that Kurt didn't want to do it. Only a few months after *My Beautiful Son* was released—a song clearly written about Kurt—Courtney seemed to have tired of being his mother and his human shield against the rest of the world. Hole's album had been delayed for over a year while she played the role of the devoted missus and was thought of as little more than Kurt's loud, brash, controlling wife and the mother of his child. Courtney was ready to have a career of her own.

Besides, by that time she felt that Kurt was having an affair with a mistress who wasn't human. The competing love of his life was one that Courtney couldn't beat up or tell off or get rid of. Heroin was consuming more and more of his time. By then it was more than just something that dulled the pain in his stomach; it was his life. He'd gotten to the point where he was becoming a heroin-procurement machine, with a habit that he himself estimated was costing $500 a day. Worse, he was using it along with the anti-anxiety drug Klonopin; the combination knocked him out so completely that he often lost his memory.

His habit was getting so bad and his relations with the band were deteriorating so thoroughly that Dave Grohl and Krist Novoselic started touring in a different bus. The new royalty split, when it went into effect, seemed to them to be only a way for him to get more money to waste on drugs.

The Cobains sometimes talked of divorcing, but Kurt hated the thought; his parents' split had shattered him. But, as supportive as he was of Courtney's brilliance, he resented the fact that performing would mean leaving him for weeks and months at a time, especially since she usually took Frances and the nanny with her.

Starting late that summer Hole was on the road almost as much as Nirvana had once been. Whenever Courtney left, Kurt entertained himself by dressing up in her frocks, sometimes answering the door for magazines interviews in her baby-doll garb. Whenever she was out of town, he pulled the garbage can up to the fax machine—assuring all their correspondence went straight in the trash.

And although she'd seemed to be attached to his hip for two years and prone to say "my husband" every two minutes, she now seemed to be shoving him out of the picture, disassociating herself from Kurt and his name. Her efforts weren't confined to their home or the phone. Some of them flew off headlines. When Hole went on tour with the Lemonheads that fall, there were reports of Courtney hanging out through the night with lead Lemonhead Evan Dando. She even admitted to the press that one night she and Evan brought in some prostitutes simply to judge whose songs were better, hers or Evan's; they voted for Evan's.

There were other items that didn't sound as wholesome as singing for streetwalkers. Gossip columns ran headlines such as "Love's Lover Is a Lemon," reporting that "Word out of La-La Land is that Boston bad boy Evan Dando of the Lemonheads is this close with

Courtney Love, wife of Nirvana bad boy Kurt Cobain. Ouch! Courtney reportedly is telling anyone who'll listen that Kurt is not *man* enough for her. Double ouch!"

In November 1993, Nirvana's long-awaited follow-up to *Nevermind* finally came out. *In Utero,* which featured Kurt's artwork throughout the liner—including a uterus-bound fetus, along with several dismembered ones—came out, debuting in the number one spot on the *Billboard* charts. (In six weeks it would drop to number 26.)

Around that time, Kristen's old pals from Minneapolis looked her up in Seattle and were appalled. Kristen appeared to be a hard-core addict, and when she met up with the visitors one night, she attempted to swindle them in order to get money to score dope. Someone searched down her parents' phone number to inform them their daughter had developed a severe heroin problem, but the call was never made. Her parents found out soon enough anyway, when Kristen was hospitalized with an infection, apparently from an unclean needle. Kristen began attending twelve-step drug-addiction sessions shortly thereafter.

In mid-December the Cobains bought a gray-shingled $1.1 million hedge-hidden mansion in Madrona, an upscale lake-hugging neighborhood filled with gorgeous old homes. Built in 1901, the house had appeared in architectural history books, and it was decidedly grand; alas, it also had strange karma. The site of a recent divorce and, before that, another rocky marriage, the house—or so the gardener complained—was haunted. A former resident described it simply as "cursed." Not that its history was pointed out to the Cobains before they bought it. But it still seemed a strange choice for Kurt, who liked his privacy, since the three-story house with a mazelike basement—containing a music studio, playroom, and wine cellar—was right next to a park. Courtney, however, loved the mansion that overlooked Lake Washington and was set in one of Seattle's more

exclusive neighborhoods, fille
including the CEO of Starbucks Co
door. The neighbors, in a move unc
warm for Seattle, threw a welcoming pa
Cobains, but the couple did not attend.

Around the same time, in December, MTV flew t
Seattle to tape a show. The program, to be aired New
Year's Eve, was shot in a quickly converted warehouse so
drafty that people had to wear coats. Nirvana was
scheduled to play, along with the Breeders and Cypress
Hill. But the show's top act was Pearl Jam.

That was a slap.

However, Pearl Jam's headman Eddie Vedder—who
was said to hate MTV and not to want the music
network to have concert footage that they could air into
eternity—never materialized for the taping. So at the
last minute Nirvana was bumped up to the number one
spot—on an MTV show, which wasn't exactly prestigious in the local community, and only seemed to prove
Nirvana was more commercial than Pearl Jam.

Despite the compromised situation, despite the way
the camera panned over a crowd of 200 to make it look
like 2,000, and despite playing for the network that had
ruined his life, Kurt looked happy and almost holy.
Wearing a dark sweater, he raised his arms above his
head and gestured for the fans to climb up onto the stage,
which was adorned with large sculptures of angels. MTV
Security had different ideas, of course, and tried to block
the fans' ascent.

Kurt had added another guitarist to the band—Pat
Smear from the Germs, a long-defunct California punk
band—and a cellist, whose solemn playing added to the
serenity of the performance.

But as composed, content, and peaceful as he appeared for the performance—except for the end, when
he toppled over and smashed the oversized angels—
Kurt confessed unhappiness in the limo on the way to
the Four Seasons Hotel. He was sick of the lifestyle, he

...with well-heeled types, ...tees who lived next ...particularly for the

...ed him en route; ...out, he didn't like ...rity.

...tel, he ordered steak ...nd, though, over Kurt's ...away the friend before ...er proof that he was losing

...friends had drifted away during his ...ney, the most recent being Tad Doyle. ...tly lead singer for his band, "Tad," had toured ...urt during Nirvana's first European tour. Doyle's ...onic gastrointestinal problems, which had made the cramped van they shared seem even smaller, had inspired a Nirvana song.

Although Tad had initially opened on Nirvana's *In Utero* domestic tour that fall, it had been booted by December. The reason: interviews Tad had given to the British press mentioning Courtney. "She's out of control," Tad had told *Melody Maker*. "Wherever trouble is, she'll find it or make it . . . she's disgusting."

Another band, Chokebore, was hired to fill the gap, heading into the new year with a roster that included the Butthole Surfers as well as comedian Bobcat Goldthwait. Kurt could have used a little cheering up by then. It was rumored that Courtney's former beau, Billy Corgan, had been calling their house frequently, much to Kurt's dismay. And, as usual, Kurt was disenchanted with touring. But, even though sales of *In Utero* weren't matching the earlier success of *Nevermind,* the domestic tour was still selling out, including two performances in Seattle.

For the first night in the band's hometown, Bobcat was so drunk that he never made it to the stage. The Butthole Surfers weren't up to form, either.

But Nirvana was, even if Kurt was rather depressed. Playing in the town where he lived, he apologized before playing the biggest hit from *Nevermind,* "Smells like Teen Spirit," jokingly explaining that it was "written

into their contract." And then
"Here's the song that ruined our h
and ruined your lives too."

Meanwhile, *In Utero* was sliding down
Kurt's plan to be less commercially viable wa.
working. And Hole's album was about to enter the wo.
of commercially viable music. Kurt and Courtney were
about to trade places.

the charts...
...he introduced it by saying
and ruined it by saying Seattle
Queen of Noise
cleanly

ER **12**

Up, One Down
(January—March 1994)

THE PHOTO SHOOT FOR *Spin, Melody Maker,* and *Details* was scheduled for 4:00 P.M. that January afternoon. At 10:00 P.M. the subject pulled up to the south Seattle motion picture studio where the lights and the cameras had been set up since the morning and the rest of the band had been sitting around waiting for hours with the crew, amusing themselves by trying to name bit actors from old films. Courtney, almost always tardy, had outdone herself by being six hours late for the multipurpose photo session.

She may have been tired and cranky when she stomped into the warehouse for the photo session, but that didn't stop her from immediately taking charge. The stage manager was sent out to the store for refreshments and a tabloid newspaper. "Pick up a *Globe,*" Courtney demanded. "They have a story about me and my husband."

"So who is your husband?" he asked.

"I don't think that's funny," she hissed. But she didn't boss him around so much after that. For the next several hours, Courtney pranced around in various states of undress, burning holes in the carpet as she tossed lit

cigarettes on it, making calls, an⸱
out the shoot.

And although she may not have felt a⸱
it together to smile for the camera, wide-⸱
surreal in her pale beauty. Between the sur⸱
cations to her face and body and her ability t⸱
camera, Courtney could no longer be dismissed⸱
even pretty." She looked gorgeous. Courtney was a⸱
to make her American debut as a rock star in her o⸱
right in a big way—in tiara and black baby-doll dress—⸱
with cover stories lined up in the music magazines, from
Spin to *Creem,* and features placed in the mainstream
press.

Gold Mountain and her newly hired PMK publicist,
Pat Kingsley—who represented Jodie Foster, Julia Roberts, and other megastars—had choreographed a slew of
articles, and flattering profiles of Courtney and her band
would soon be rolling off of presses everywhere. She had
covers, profiles, and reviews lined up.

And the media response was unanimous. Though she
often lamented that everyone hated her and that the
press speared and rotisseried her, it wasn't true anymore. The critics were raving, all but drooling across the
pages about *Live Through This.* For good reason: the
still-unreleased album, as Courtney had promised, was
accessible, filled with catchy hooks, clever lyrics, whis-
pers, chants, and coos broken up with screams, melodic
attacks, and thundering guitars. Advance word of mouth
was strong.

The *L.A. Times* liked it. *Spin* liked it. *Newsweek* liked
it. *Rolling Stone* liked it. *Creem* liked it. *The Advocate*
liked it. Even *Entertainment Weekly,* always quick to
harpoon her and to report on the latest Courtney scan-
dals, admitted, "It turns out she can carry a tune and
write a decent song." Almost every publication was
ready to rave to the masses about Hole's upcoming
album. *Live Through This* was a remarkable achieve-
ment, and the press seemed ready to nominate it for best

en been released to the

g Mrs. Kurt, she was
s Courtney Love, lead

litz, though. She would
magazine's lead times,
o appear three months
ril when *Live Through*
reviews started pouring
mind was still Nirvana,
yone's mind was Kurt,
not Courtney.

Of course, no one knew that then.

At the start of 1994, Courtney's future promised to be ridiculously happy and bright. At least careerwise.

In January, Kurt, along with Krist and Dave, appeared on the cover of *Rolling Stone* as a parody of themselves, dressed in corporate-looking suits with the headline "Success Doesn't Suck"—although the interview inside sure indicated it did. Kurt hinted at breaking up the band; he mentioned "if Courtney and I got divorced" in passing. He talked about suicide, though he assured the reporter that the original title for *In Utero*—I Hate Myself and I Want to Die—was only a joke. About the only thing Kurt didn't do was pose with a gun in his mouth. He saved that telling pose for a European photo shoot in February. When Nirvana left to tour Europe at the end of January, Courtney stayed to do more publicity for *Live Through This,* which was slated for an April 1994 release. Interviews, photo shoots, interviews, publicity. She'd even been asked to act in an upcoming movie, *Tank Girl.* Whereas Nirvana's rise to fame had been largely unseen, the reaction to *Live through This* was expected; people knew they had a huge hit on their hands.

Hole was about to go gangbusters.

Nirvana, meanwhile, wasn't. *In Utero* kept falling

down the charts. In January,
1994 Music Awards Readers' Picks
public didn't vote for Nirvana or *In*
categories. Pearl Jam was clearly the
Vedder and the band were voted Artist of
Band, Best Songwriter, Best Male Singer—
Even the critics cast their ballots for Pearl Ja
critics' poll, naming them Artist of the Year and c
ing Eddie Vedder Best Male Singer. But at least
critics tossed Nirvana a bone, voting them Best Ban
and giving *In Utero* the title Best Album despite what the
readers thought. Compared to the nine awards tossed at
Pearl Jam, Nirvana's two seemed pretty measly, especially to Kurt.

By February *In Utero,* in the number 21 slot, was
wedged between his enemy Axl Rose's band, Guns n'
Roses, and his enemy Billy Corgan's band, Smashing
Pumpkins.

How the record was faring was only one of Kurt's
concerns, though. He was upset about the long tour
ahead of him; he'd told the record company that he
would tour overseas for a month only, but they'd come
back with two and half months of European tours. He
wasn't at all happy at the prospect.

Once there, though, he found receptive audiences. The
shows in Europe were often favorably reviewed, and they
were selling well. When the band played Spain, teenagers
in the crowd smoked heroin and offered it to him. "Kurt!
Smack!" they yelled, but he turned it down. He felt guilty
and called Courtney, crying about being a poor role
model.

It was winter, his stomach hurt, and he was trying not
to do heroin.

"I know he wasn't doing drugs," Tony Barber of the
Buzzcocks, who opened for Nirvana in Europe, told the
British press. "He was walking around drinking Evian
and looking clean every single time I saw him." The
press called him Kurt "Just Say No" Cobain because he

ns with the opening

ong when they were
urtney. They'd never
han a week. Nirvana
ert Johnson dirgelike
p Last Night?"—and
fictitious. As much as
hour-ordeal when she
e of a mess when she
ving an affair, and her

An issue of the British paper *NME* that appeared mid-February gave a whiff of it too. In her profile Courtney did mention that she worshiped Kurt. But she also went on about how much she liked cute Evan Dando, and how Billy Corgan was really good in bed. And about how jealous Kurt had been of Billy throughout their marriage.

The article also noted her self-proclaimed changes in her persona. "I am so fucking charming," she informed the writer. "I seem to have gathered this reputation as a diva, a screamer, a loud girl who will kick your ass if you so much as look at me. So I am Mrs. Please and Thank You now."

Maybe to everyone who could further her career. But to Kurt she was Mrs. No. No, she wouldn't come out to Europe yet. No, she wouldn't let him pass up Lollapalooza without a fight. No, she didn't want him to do heroin anymore. No, she wasn't sure she wanted to stay married to him. And no, if she left him, he certainly wouldn't get custody of the baby.

Nevertheless, even though his physical and emotional state was shaky, he pulled it together to put on a few memorable performances; the high point of the tour was the show in Rome on February 22. Kurt was fired up, and Nirvana played well. Despite throat problems, he sang with a passion, putting on the most amazing show by far on the tour.

After the show, depression s
there; his only friends were his
relationship with them was very str
rubbed him was that his parents had
wish him a happy birthday two days befo
had just turned twenty-seven, their not call
him greatly; when he later mentioned it to
she said that since Kurt hadn't called them
birthdays, they'd decided to ignore his.

Two days later, when Nirvana played Milan on F
ary 24, it was as if someone had ripped his heart out.
was Kurt and Courtney's anniversary, and he spent it
without her. By March 1, when Nirvana played Munich,
he looked like the walking dead. Midway through the
show his voice gave out, the show ended early, and he
was ordered to Rome to rest.

Kurt's problems bordered on the childish, but they
were quite real: his throat hurt, his stomach hurt, his
back hurt, he was sick, he was depressed, he was reportedly trying to stay clean, and he wanted his wife-mother.

The final descent of his downward-spiraling mood
occurred when Courtney showed up in Europe but did
not come to meet Kurt in Rome. On March 3 she was in
London giving an interview to the British magazine
Select, during which she kept popping a tranquilizer
called Roipnol. Not available in the United States, the
drug is sometimes used to treat heroin withdrawal,
though Courtney likened it to Valium.

In addition to giving insight into her drug habits—she
denied taking Ecstasy, though she admitted she "did a
lot of acid in Liverpool and I never recovered"—
Courtney expounded on her desire to succeed with her
upcoming album. "I really want to sell more albums
than Soundgarden," she said. "I just hate them. And I
really love Roddy [Bottum of Faith No More], but I want
to sell more records than his band too."

Courtney was in a carefree, frivolous mood that day,
seeming rather unconcerned that Kurt was sick in Rome.

Queen of Noise

et in. His wife wasn't
bandmates, and his
...ained. What really
...ot even called to
...e. Although he
...g him upset
...is mother,
on their
bru-
It

...al times through the
...e line.

...in London for more
...ith Billy, who was
... made plans to fly
...arjet to whisk them
...f Majorca. Coinci-
...uld be headlining
...rvana backed out,

...riage was looking

...want to divorce. And when he found out
that his wife was with her ex-boyfriend Billy, whom he hated and called "the pear-shaped box," and whose lovemaking abilities she had recently raved about in the press, he was not at all pleased. Kurt begged for one more chance.

Courtney gave it to him. She changed her mind, leaving Billy behind, and joined Kurt in Rome. (Later, when she got a bill for several thousand dollars for the canceled Learjet, she sent it to Billy, who returned the bill to her.)

Kurt and Courtney hadn't seen each other for forty days, a record. For approximately $700 a night, Kurt rented a deluxe chandeliered two-bedroom suite at the five-star castlelike Hotel Excelsior, with a king-sized bed in the main room and with a living room and an adjoining room for the nanny and Frances. Covered in gold wallpaper, room 542 looked out onto the palm tree–lined Via Veneto, with the U.S. embassy down the way.

Kurt filled the suite with roses. Though he wasn't fond of gems, or of wasting his money on them, she loved them, and he bought her diamond earrings, rosaries, jewels. Knowing she loved Roman history, he broke off a chip of the Colosseum for Courtney and bought statues of saints from Vatican City.

He was song-and-dancing, turning on the charm and

romance, ben~
the marriage go~

When Courtney,
rived late that aftern~
toasted the return of his

Later, after the nanny to
and Courtney climbed into
wanted to consummate their reun~
overtures, she rejected them, saying

When Courtney awoke a few hours ~
morning of March 4, Kurt was on the floo~
of gray, a ribbon of blood curling from one
was wearing his brown corduroy coat, and a wa~
was crumpled in one hand; the other hand clen~
note. On eight pages of hotel stationery, he'd penne~
screw-you letter, writing that it was obvious she didn~
love him, but he'd rather die than get a divorce; if he had
to choose between life and death, he was opting for the
latter.

A frantic call came in to the front desk around 6:30
that morning, and medics arrived at the hotel moments
later. The ambulance took him away to Umberto I
Polyclinic Hospital to pump his stomach of fifty Roip-
nols and conduct other emergency procedures that lasted
five hours. Still unconscious, Kurt was then transferred
to the American Hospital. As he was rolled out, Courtney got in a brawl with a photographer who'd been
tipped off about the overdose, kicking him in the groin.
She later wished she hadn't fought him. She wished Kurt
could have seen himself looking almost dead.

He shot at least one photo, however—of Courtney
looking shaken but lovely in a pale, frightened way; she'd
had time to smear on some makeup.

When the word first went out in Seattle, it was relayed
with a certain smugness. Of course, people said. It was
predictable. Kurt would die of an overdose—heroin, no
doubt. That the ordeal was such a cliché and that it had
happened overseas made it somehow more tolerable in
Seattle.

Melissa Rossi

n't die

and woke

his hands,

s were "Fuck

these fucking

ings: a strawberry

talk to Billy Corgan

But it wasn't a heroin ove

abroad.

Within twenty

from his

up from

and

te to the Italian doctor,

ssued loud, convincing

accidental. He had "suf-

due to fatigue and severe

announced. A combination

nd alcohol had caused "com-

of cash
il. He
ade
hed a
d a

O'Connor, wasn't so clinical in her description. "All I know," she told the press, "is he suffered a massive drug overdose."

Within a few days Kurt was out of the hospital. Courtney called the *Select* writer from the Rome airport and gave context to the overdose: "This was just a tiff between me and Kurt, okay? . . . He was just upset that he was in some awful place and I was away enjoying myself and shopping. It was not a suicide thing." And then, before clicking off, she added, "You know, I wish [the overdose victim] had been Eddie [Vedder of Pearl Jam]. They'd have had a fuckin' candlelight vigil for him."

When Kurt arrived back in Seattle, he couldn't have missed the billboards that had been up for weeks, jeering him from all over town. The ads for a classical music radio station, read in large black letters, "Roll over, Nirvana."

CHAPTER 13

The Promise
(March—April 1994)

THE CLOSE CALL IN ITALY SHOOK HER. DEATH HUNG IN THE air, an unspoken promise, a constant threat.

Their new three-story house in Seattle wasn't exactly Cheery Recuperation Central, although this home was cleaner than usual, as they'd hired several kindly nuns to tidy up. The mansion was barely furnished, since they'd hardly moved in before Kurt had gone overseas, and there was a creepy vibe in the air. The house was filled with cold spots and negative energy that gave some people the willies. The Cobains and some of their entourage, which by then included Pat Smear and a new nanny, quickly became convinced it was haunted, due in part to a chilly gust of wind that swirled down the stairs with such force it seemed spirit-driven.

When they returned several days after the Rome overdose, Courtney became Kurt's shadow, following him from room to room, frantically banging on doors if he shut them.

He was acting irrational, depressed, like both a caged animal and a frantic child. The trauma of their loosely held together marriage smacked of his parents' divorce, which had left him feeling utterly abandoned.

Now it was happening all over again, but this time the stakes were bigger. Courtney—his surrogate mother and co-conspirator, who built up his fortress against the world—was considering leaving him. And if she did, she would take the baby. If she bolted, she would be taking Kurt's entire world with her.

Kurt's response to the increasing likelihood of a breakup was to dull his pain with more heroin; before he left Rome, he'd made arrangements for a dealer to hide some in the bushes near the Seattle house. A few days later he told Courtney he was leaving to practice with the band, but instead he drove back to Heroin Alley on Capitol Hill. When he came home messed up, she was livid, and more hell-bent on keeping him there, under her watchful eye—which only made him all the more eager to escape and head back to the heroin dealers.

He seemed to be on a kamikaze mission, determined to destroy himself with any means available. Sensing the threat, she asked him to freeze his sperm, hoping for future Cobain offspring, with or without him. He retaliated by denying her request and writing a song about a frozen uterus.

And if his concerns were emotional, her focus was increasingly financial—specifically the $9 million that Lollapalooza had waved in his face and that Kurt was waving away. Nine million, and he didn't want it.

Unbelievable. To Courtney at least. And to Gold Mountain and Geffen, when Kurt made good on his threat to cancel. The wind-up grunge toy was konking out.

And meanwhile Courtney was winding up.

Hole had made a great record. The band had the needed buzz, the connections, and the extremely photogenic expressions for the camera. Courtney was ready to soar on every count. Except one. Kurt.

She couldn't leave him just then, in his needy condition. But it appeared hopeless and heartbreaking to stay, especially if Kurt was going to continue on his self-annilhation course.

Sadness and tension filled the house, and the new nanny cried hysterically every night that she stayed there. Between the ghost, the depression in the air, the constant fights about Lollapalooza and drugs, the environment was unnerving. The nanny gave her notice. But according to the police reports, she didn't get away before witnessing more melodrama.

On the night of March 18, 1994, two weeks after Kurt went into the coma in Rome, he had locked himself in their bedroom with a gun and refused to come out. Courtney banged on the door frantically, but he wouldn't unlock it. "Just leave me alone!" he yelled. So Courtney called the police, crying and saying that Kurt was going to kill himself.

While waiting for them to arrive, she attempted to break down the door with a fire extinguisher. Finally he opened it. She grabbed the gun from him and pointed it at her own head. "I am going to pull this right now," she screamed. "I cannot see you die! I can't see you die again!"

He grabbed her hand, yelling, "There's no safety! You don't understand—there's no safety! It's going to go off!"

When the police arrived, Kurt emerged calmly from the room, handed over the gun, and explained that he was just trying to get away from Courtney. The police took three handguns—the same ones that had been confiscated the summer before and later returned—as well as a semiautomatic rifle, twenty-five boxes of ammunition, and a vial of unidentified pills. They offered to drop him off at a friend's house.

"Yes, please," Kurt said wearily, "take me away. Take me anywhere but here."

Shortly thereafter, the new nanny quit. She was at least their fifty nanny since Frances was born.

Not long thereafter, a dealer called from Seattle's Capitol Hill. Kurt was at his place, buying too much heroin, acting like he was trying to overdose; the dealer wanted him out. Courtney told Krist who drove over to pick up Kurt, who willingly got in the car. He sat there like a child while Krist lectured him, saying that he was out of control. Kurt asked to stop at a nearby Jack in the Box, that had a drive-through window. Once there he hopped out of the car and ran.

He didn't go home for several days. He told his junkie pals that he and Courtney were splitting up.

Kurt made a few rare public appearances on Capitol Hill, even stopping in at Linda's Tavern, a new hangout favored by musicians, where the sight of him caused a small to-do, since he hadn't been spotted socializing for months. He seemed, as usual, uncomfortable with the attention.

While walking down Broadway, Capitol Hill's main drag, he ran into an old friend, one of many who'd gotten lost in the shuffle of his marriage and fame. Kurt was in disguise—wearing his plaid hunter's hat pulled low, flaps down, and the large oval sunglasses that made him look like a sanitarium escapee. When he later went out for dinner, he didn't look the waiter in the eye, had a companion order for him, and all but hid under the table at the scene his presence was creating.

He was extremely depressed, an obvious clue that the overdose in Italy wasn't accidental. Anyone who had nearly died accidentally would have been happy to be with the living and to be given a new lease on life. A suicidal person, who awakens after attempting to die, is depressed at having failed at death too.

Kurt told the friend that Courtney had cut off his money, so he was going to pick up $100 that had been wired to him, supposedly by his mother, and he was going to score.

The next night he ran into his Olympia friends again, and he was very anxious. Had they seen Courtney? he asked. If they did, they were to tell her he loved her.

An attempt at reconciliation followed, and Kurt went back to the house. At home, he found a script that director Gus Van Sant, with whom Kurt was acquainted, had sent him. Gus had a movie idea called *Christmas on*

Stark Street. The script was based on a group of transients who sat in the doorway of his downtown studio. The director offered the role of Binky, one of the street people, to Kurt. Even though Kurt loved the script, he never got back to Gus about it.

Kurt was promptly greeted with an intervention. During the third week of March, Courtney brought in a counselor, and they tried to confront him about his heroin use. Kurt denied there was a problem, and went down to the basement to play guitar with Pat Smear, who had been living at the house since the now-canceled *In Utero* tour.

A few days later, on March 25, Courtney had scheduled another intervention that was harder to evade. Kurt's band was there. His management was there. Her management was there. At least three of the people with whom he'd formerly done heroin were also there in his house telling him he had to stop using.

In true intervention style they laid into him, telling him that, yes, he had a problem, and if he didn't do something about it, they were all going to walk out, close the door on him, and not return until he was clean. One by one they recounted the details of how he was screwing up. His bandmates said they'd break up the band. Courtney said she'd divorce him. "You've got to be a good daddy," she begged. His world, already small, was threatening to shrink even further.

Courtney flew out that night without saying good-bye. That's apparently what she was told to do by the interventionists. And apparently, for the first time in her life, Courtney was taking orders.

She checked into the luxe Peninsula Hotel in Beverly Hills, where she later called in a physician and started her own detox program.

Finally, the next day, with Courtney gone, Kurt relented and agreed to go to rehab in California in a few days.

It was unfortunate that Kurt's heroin use had become the focus of people's attention. The real problem was his desire to self-destruct; drugs were just his way of doing it. Almost everyone, however, was in denial about how real his death wish was.

Gold Mountain had hushed his problems up, still maintaining that the Rome overdose was accidental, and they seemed to believe their own lies. The band didn't know it was a suicide attempt; the household help were told it was accidental as well. Even Dylan Carlson, his best man and best friend, apparently didn't know.

So when Kurt showed up at Dylan's apartment on March 30 and mentioned that he and Courtney didn't yet have a burglar-alarm system in the house, he said there'd been trespassers and he needed a gun for protection. When he explained that he was afraid to purchase one under his own name, since the police had taken his other guns, Dylan, a major gun enthusiast, accepted his story. They headed off north of town to Stan's Gun Shop, where with the $300 Kurt gave him, Dylan bought Kurt a Remington 20-gauge rifle and a box of ammunition.

Kurt hid the weapon at the house before he left for the airport with Krist that day. On the way he and the bass player had a screaming fight and Kurt broke up the band.

A block away from the ocean, the Exodus Recovery Center in Marina Del Rey was a well-known stop for celebrities who needed to dry out. The twenty-bed facility was tucked away in a corner of the Daniel Freeman Marina Hospital, a complex of innocuous-looking four-story white buildings.

The rehab center had a steady clientele of musicians whose art form was often intricately tied up in drugs, and that week Kurt was just one of them. Also there was Gibby Haynes, lead singer for the Butthole Surfers, whose band had toured with Nirvana months before. He was one of Kurt's favorite musicians and, for the near future, his rehab roommate as well.

When Kurt walked in through the sliding doors, past

the plush blue chairs in the lobby, and checked in during that last week of March, he was making a commitment for a twenty-eight-day stint. But his desire to quit drugs was not strong. The issue for him was that his marriage was ending and Courtney would take Frances with her; even if he went through rehab, their relationship was so rocky it didn't look like it would last much longer.

He had little incentive to fight his drug problem when he'd just lost his reason to live. And Courtney, who'd had flown out of Seattle without a farewell, and who had arranged his trip to rehab, reportedly called him only once while he was there.

She later said that she tried to call him more often, but couldn't get through via the hallway pay phone that was the patients' only line to the outside world. But Kurt felt betrayed by her insistence that he go there; then, once he was inside and ignored, the message coming through to him was "You're on your own. We're through."

He hid his pain rather well, though, content with the decision he'd reached. "I was ready to see him look like shit and depressed," one of the other rehab patients told the press. "He looked so fucking great. He walked out an hour later."

Kurt was in the well-guarded rehab center for just two days before he escaped. He went out for a smoke and climbed over the six-foot brick wall in the back—but not before calling Courtney.

She told the press that Kurt called at the hotel and said, "Courtney, no matter what happens, I want you to know you made a really good record." She asked what he meant by "no matter what happens."

He said, "Just remember, no matter what, I love you."

Kurt reportedly hooked up with another musician, who drove him around L.A. on the freeway trying to get him back to the rehab center, while Kurt kept demanding to be let out of the car. Finally he made his way to the airport and flew back to Seattle.

When the word got to Courtney that he'd bolted from

rehab, she became hysterical. Figuring he'd gone to score, she tried to head him off at a local dealer's house. But Kurt didn't show up. She was driven around to other dealers; she called musicians all over Los Angeles, asking them to be on the lookout and to notify their drug suppliers. Unable to locate him, she gave him a few hours to score, then canceled his credit cards—a bad move, as it turned out: if he'd used the cards, he would have left a trail. As it was, except for a charge at a hotel in Seattle, where he apparently talked an employee into getting him a $2,000 cash advance off the card, Kurt's movements were hard to follow. It was as if he'd walked into a mist.

According to a private investigator Courtney hired, it was Courtney who filed a missing persons report, claiming for reasons unknown that she was Wendy O'Connor, Kurt's mother. She listed the address of a heroin dealer in Seattle, where he might be found, and mentioned that he might have a gun and was probably suicidal.

The police later admitted they didn't take the report that seriously. Kurt Cobain struck them as the sort of person who would take off by himself for days at a time.

Courtney stayed in Beverly Hills. That was the recommendation of the interventionists who'd overseen the ordeal in Seattle. Once again she was playing by the rules—an unusual thing for her to do. She ignored the warning bells going off in her head, telling her what was likely to come down if she didn't go back to Seattle. "I didn't listen to my gut," she later said.

She seemed to be tired of the charade that their relationship had become. She wanted to go up, and Kurt's only direction seemed to be down. She'd spent the last two years playing his mom, the perpetual seeker in an adult game of hide-and-seek, the perpetual savior in the game of I-hate-myself-and-I-want-to-die. She was angry at Kurt for ditching the rehab effort, for his refusal to play Lollapalooza, for his extreme stunts when she was days away from being crowned a star.

This was supposed to be her hour. The one she'd been waiting for her whole life. *Live Through This* would hit the stores in two weeks; she wanted to be in top form, dried out and ready to go, not frazzled and freaked out. Why was he pulling this now, just before the release of her record, the one that everyone said would go platinum, the one that would transform her reputation from world-class bitch to world-class talent? How was she supposed to give interviews when she was worried about him? When Robert Hilburn of the *L.A. Times* showed up at her hotel, she burst into tears.

But she turned her back on her husband. She stayed in the Beverly Hills Peninsula, continuing her own in-hotel drug rehabilitation and finishing some last-minute business before Hole's record release. To track down Kurt, she called in a pudgy private investigator by the name of Tom Grant, whose number she had found, typically, in the Yellow Pages. She gave him a list of heroin dealers with whom Kurt was likely to be found, and described her husband as being too helpless to so much as hail a cab by himself. Then she sent the investigator to Seattle.

According to Tom Grant, as he left her hotel room, Courtney threw her fists in the air like a cheerleader and yelled, "Save the American icon!"

Grant flew to Washington State on March 6 and, to cover all bases, subcontracted the assignment to yet another private investigator. Courtney would soon rue the day she'd let her fingers do the walking.

One of the PIs on the job also worked for a tabloid, *The Star,* and continually leaked information to the paper, and Tom Grant himself would in time become one of Courtney's greatest detractors. Meanwhile, the word went out, in that side-of-the-mouth way, that Kurt had flown the coop, returned to Seattle, and was missing—a report that ended up on CNN. What *didn't* make the media was the multitude of rumors that trickled up from the junkie world: that Kurt was buying rounds from the drug dealers—putting up the money for everyone present—and that he was horribly depressed; that he was clearly trying to overdose; that while the dealers would sell him as much as he wanted, they didn't want him hanging around and dying on them, leaving a star corpse for them to dispose of; that he said Courtney was having an affair with Billy Corgan and had told him about it in Rome, and that this confession was what had led to the overdose there. "Where are my friends when I need them?" he lamented to one dealer. "Why are my friends against me? Why am I the one who's wrong?"

Even though he was showing up occasionally in Heroin Alley, Kurt was doing a fine job of eluding all who were looking for him. Even Dylan joined in the search, driving around with Tom Grant, scanning the streets, waiting outside a dealer's apartment, searching the Lake Washington abode—though never thinking to check the room over the garage.

Nobody—at least nobody who is talking officially—saw Kurt after Saturday, April 2, when neighbors spotted him in the adjacent park, looking forlorn as he sat on a bench. It was a warm day, but he was dressed in many layers of clothing, as if to blanket himself against the bitter cold of his reality.

All that's left is the whispering of rumors.

Wherever he was, it was a horrible time for Kurt, a cruel cosmic test when everything he had known as a fact the year before turned into a question mark. Before, he'd wanted fame. Now he didn't. He'd wanted enough money to have a sense of security, at least. Now he didn't care. He'd been regarded as brilliant. Now he was regarded as a sellout. And now his wife's record might eclipse his. Maybe he didn't care. But maybe, in some un-punk way, he did.

It was un-punk, of course, to even care how his record was faring, but Kurt, as might be expected, did care. "I don't pay attention to polls and charts," he had told *Details* magazine a few months before, "but I thumb through them once in a while and see, like, Eddie Vedder is nominated number one songwriter in *[Rolling Stone]*, and I'm not even listed."

So, during that week when Kurt was missing, it didn't help matters that the new issue of *Rolling Stone* came out, showing that *In Utero* had fallen off the Top 40 charts. Inside was a rave review of *Live Through This*. And on the cover was a photo of Billy Corgan and his Smashing Pumpkins.

A small group of people, perhaps only a few dozen, had an uneasy feeling that something was going to happen and it wasn't going to be pleasant. That feeling was mixed with denial, but some could see exactly where Kurt was headed. "If he's bummed out after Rome, that means he wanted to die," one friend was told. "He's not long for the world." The friend shuffled uncomfortably and looked down. "I don't want to think about that."

The words of an unnamed music executive quoted in *Vanity Fair* rang true: "She's going to be famous, and he already is, but unless something happens, they're going to self-destruct."

On Wednesday, April 6,* Kurt climbed the stairs to the greenhouse, a storage area over the free-standing garage, and shot himself full of heroin for the last time. Then he picked up the shotgun that Dylan had bought him, pressed it to his temple, and, gazing out over Lake Washington, pulled the trigger.

On April 7, Courtney called the desk clerk at Peninsula Hotel in Beverly Hills to request a nasal decongestant, saying she was having an allergic reaction to a prescribed tranquilizer, Xanax.

The hotel clerk called 911 and reported a possible overdose, and Courtney was rushed to Century City Hospital. The police, upon searching her "vomit and

---

*The coronor's report would list April 5 as Cobain's estimated date of death, but this was refuted by friends who claimed Cobain had placed phone calls to them on April 6.

blood-splattered" room, found a syringe, a prescription pad, and a substance they believed to be heroin. They promptly arrested her for possession of a controlled substance. Her lawyer claimed the substance was actually "Hindu good-luck ashes" and that the prescription pad had been left in her room by a doctor.

Released after posting $10,000 bail, she checked herself into Exodus, the same rehab facility from which Kurt had fled the week before.

Friday, April 8, 1994, began as another gray morning in a series of sunless days in Seattle. The electrician who was installing a burglar-alarm system at the Cobain household thought at first that he saw a mannequin lying on the floor of the greenhouse—until he noticed the blood running out of the right ear.

He alerted his boss, who called a local radio station before dialing 911. The word went out over the airwaves: a male Caucasian had been found dead at the Cobain's house.

Some of Kurt's old friends, when they heard the news, chalked it up to another junkie fatality. Just another one of those addicts Kurt had been hanging out with.

By eleven o'clock that morning, a small crowd had formed outside the sprawling gray house. TV crews pulled up, as did a few carloads of fans and reporters. Neighbors walked by, wondering what all the fuss was about. Teenagers were crying. The reporters seemed stiff and creeped out.

The coroner's office said the dead man was Kurt Cobain. Police near the taped-off driveway were overhead saying that Courtney was with the Los Angeles police. She would fly back to Seattle.

The *Seattle Times* ran a cover photo showing part of Kurt's corpse. Shot through the greenhouse window, it showed only his sneakered foot and one pale hand, next to the cigar box that held his needle and stash. But it was chilling and disturbing in its finality, and that issue of the *Seattle Times* was the only one to sell out in recent history.

Kurt's mother told the press, "I told him not to go

and join that stupid club." She was referring to the one that included Jimi Hendrix, Jim Morrison, and Janis Joplin, all of whom died at age twenty-seven from drug overdoses.

The limo pulled up to the Lake Washington abode that evening. Courtney, eyes swollen, rushed past the crowd with Frances, and into the house. Guards quickly appeared to block entrance.

When she was taken to identify the body, she anointed his corpse with kisses. She snipped a lock of his hair and considered planting his heart under an oak tree. She brought home the clothes in which he'd shot himself, washed them, and wore them for days. She made an altar for his hair and ashes.

Sheets appeared in the windows, makeshift curtains to block out the stares of the hundreds of grief-stricken fans who'd come to pay their respects, and she wandered in the park next door, leaving flowers and poems. The sheets also blocked the view of the persistent reporters, some of whom were climbing trees trying to peer in.

As the news traveled, suicide hot lines lit up around the globe. Thousands of people, devastated by Kurt's decision to end it, considered taking the same path themselves. And the world press corps descended upon Seattle.

That Friday during an opening at a downtown art gallery, the Center on Contemporary Art, the mood was grim. The topic of Kurt's suicide, then just sinking in, was rarely broached, but it hung heavy in the air, its announcement made with every glum nod of the head.

Although druggies tend to consider all overdoses suicides, Kurt's death was the first in the music scene that was so patently self-intentional. His suicide also rattled people in a different way: the cloak that fell upon the city was guilt-infused. Those who had called him a sellout were creeped out. Many people, including the media types who had made him so uncomfortably famous, could sense their fingerprints on the trigger.

The changing attitude of the masses was evident in the graffiti that appeared in Linda's Tavern, the Capitol Hill hot spot that was one of the last public places where Kurt was seen. "It really hurt that it was Kurt," read the message on the bathroom wall. "It would have been better if it was Vedder."

Eddie Vedder appeared to be among the most moved: At a show that night he spoke out against making idols of mortals. Citing Kurt's death as the reason, Pearl Jam canceled its summer concert schedule.

Courtney sought help from people she'd known in Portland, since she had made remarkably few friends in Seattle. Kat Bjelland flew in from Minneapolis; Thor Lindsay, who once owned the coolest record store in Portland, came up to escort her to the funeral service; another Portlander put together the tape of Courtney reading the suicide note that would be broadcast the next day. And before long, Courtney's former Portland pal, Bad Actor Dean Mathieson, would arrive on the scene.

Nirvana's management, Gold Mountain, and other music industry people flew out and checked into the Four Seasons Olympic Hotel; the inn was brimming with media, including MTV's Tabitha Soren, who taped newscasts from the park next door to the Cobain house. Frances was sent to the Four Seasons with a nanny.

Several radio stations organized a candlelight vigil to be held at Seattle Center. DJs everywhere bemoaned Kurt's death and spoke of how beloved he was, how he was the voice of his generation, what a tragedy it was, the death of this person who was the hero of millions.

That Saturday, the day after Kurt's body was found, was the unfortunate date of the anniversary party at the Crocodile Café for Sub Pop. Initially there was talk of canceling the bash or at least banning the media, but ultimately the party went on as scheduled, and certain members of the press, such as Ann Powers from *The Village Voice,* were let in.

Through the windows, the partygoers watched the

television cameras outside, with reporters shoving mikes in people's faces, asking questions that made them cringe: "Kurt Cobain just died. How does that make you feel?" Many of the party attendees didn't comment or said such things as "I hate myself and I want to die"—the original title for *In Utero.*

Inside the club, where the crowd piled into the tiki-decorated band room and squeezed into booths in the back bar, the mood wasn't as morbid as some had feared. But the conversation was not about Kurt. A veil of silence had descended upon the city. Few people wanted to talk, especially to the media.

And the media, the hated media, were all over the place by Sunday, when the vigil was held. MTV, *People, Rolling Stone, Details, Inside Edition, Hard Copy, A Current Affair,* and *Entertainment Weekly*—all of them had sent reporters to cover the tragedy. Tour buses roared down the narrow street past satellite trucks. It was like a final joke on Kurt: bringing the fourth estate to Seattle for his death. He'd ensured it by the way he'd ended his life.

And he'd ensured something else: that *Live Through This*—the album that would launch Courtney as a star, the one she had been trying to make for fifteen years—would be cursed. He had blown the publicity campaign. So there, music machine. So there, Courtney.

Kurt also created an instant myth. Now he would be regarded as a rock martyr. Courtney and Frances would be the closest link to the new god.

On Sunday, April 10, Courtney's picture beamed from the cover of the *L.A. Times Sunday Magazine,* with the prophetic headline "The Trials of Love"—though her trials had scarcely begun when the story was penned. Based on an interview conducted the week before Kurt's death, the article was ostensibly about Hole's new record, which the writer, Robert Hilburn, described as "the boldest in a series of outstanding records . . . by a new wave of gifted female artists." He noted that when he'd interviewed her the week before, she appeared "frightened and fragile" and that she broke down in mid-interview. "I know this should be the happiest time of my life," she said, "and there have been moments when I felt that happiness. But not now. . . . I don't care about Lollapalooza. I just never want to see [Kurt] on the floor . . . again."

By the time the story came out, she had; a postscript tacked on the end of the article explained that the piece had been printed before Kurt died.

That same day, nearly 10,000 fans, most of them under thirty, had gathered in the name of Kurt Cobain on the grounds of Seattle Center, with the Space Needle looming not far away like a giant reminder of the city's heroin problem. A minister said a few words, and then they played the tape of Courtney reading Kurt's suicide note. One might say it was her finest performance.

"I don't really know what to say," she began in a sob-choked voice." He left a note. It's more like a letter to the fucking editor. I don't know what happened. I mean, it was gonna happen. It could have happened when he was forty. He always said he was going to outlive everybody and be a hundred and twenty. . . . He's such an asshole. I want you all to say 'asshole' really loud."

And then she began reading from the letter, describing Kurt's wording as straight out of "Punk 101."

"Kurt says, 'Over the years I haven't felt the excitement of listening to as well as creating music. I feel guilty beyond words about these things. For example, when we're backstage and the lights go out and the manic roar of the crowd goes out, it doesn't affect me the way it did for Freddie Mercury [the deceased lead singer of the band Queen], who seemed to love and relish the love and admiration from the crowd.'"

Courtney stopped reading. "Well, Kurt, so fucking what?" she said. "Then don't be a rock star, you asshole."

She continued reading the letter. " 'The fact is, I can't fool you, any of you. . . . The worst crime I can think of would be to pull people off by faking it and pretending as if I'm having 100 percent fun.'"

Again she stopped and addressed her deceased husband: "No, Kurt, the worst crime I can think of is for you to just continue being a rock star when you fucking hate it, and just fucking stop."

Courtney resumed reading: " 'Sometimes I feel as if I should have a punch-in clock before I walk out onstage. . . . I'm too sensitive. I need to be slightly numbed in order to regain the enthusiasm I had as a child. . . . There's good in all of us, and I simply love people too much.' "

"So why didn't you just fucking stay?" she yelled.

" 'I have it good . . . but since the age of seven I've become hateful towards all humans, only because I love and feel for people so too much, I guess. Thank you from the pit of my burning, nauseous stomach. . . . I'm too much of an erratic, moody person, and I don't have the passion anymore, so remember, it's better to burn out than fade away.' "

"Good, you asshole!" she yelled.

" 'Peace, love, and empathy, Kurt Cobain.' "

There was more, she told the crowd, but it was none of their damn business.

"But," she added, "I want you to know one thing: that eighties tough-love bullshit—it doesn't work. . . . I should have let him, we all should have let him, have his numbness. We should have let him have the thing that made him feel better. We should have let him have it, instead of trying to strip his skin away.

"I'm really sorry, you guys," she said, audibly crying. "I don't know what I could have done. I wish I'd been here, and I wish I had listened to other people, but I didn't. And I have to go now," she concluded. "Just tell him he's a fucker, okay? Just say, 'Fucker, you're a fucker' and that you love him."

The words were moving, especially broken up with her asides, sniffles, and sobs. The crowd was visibly disturbed, introspective, their eyes downcast as they listened to her grief-choked words. But few were crying. Especially when "Serve the Servants" played from the speaker, and hundreds headed for the fountain. They dived in, holding smoldering pictures of Kurt as they moshed in the water while some of his last recorded lyrics floated through the air: "Teenage angst has paid off well. Now I'm bored and old."

The tears were flowing a few blocks away at the Unity Church of Truth, where the small memorial for Kurt's family and friends was held. Atlantic Records vice president Danny Goldberg spoke about how Kurt had lived longer because of Courtney. Bruce Pavitt, co-owner of Sub Pop, spoke about how much he loved Kurt, adding he was just late in telling him. Dylan talked about Buddhism and the Hindu god Shiva, and the spiritual quest he'd shared with Kurt. Courtney read from Job and Illuminations, and from the suicide note.

Kurt's parents, sister, and half sister attended, along with a few other relatives. Most of the several dozen other mourners were music industry people.

"It was shocking," said one who attended, "how few friends were left." Many of the musicians with whom he'd once been close, and with whom he had toured, were curiously absent.

Among those who showed up for the service was folksinger Mary Lou Lord. Upon seeing the singer, Courtney was the epitome of forgiving graciousness: she hugged Mary Lou, thanked her for coming, and invited her to the Cobain house for the wake. However, most of Kurt's few remaining friends attended the other wake for Kurt—at Krist Novoselic's house, not Courtney's.

That division in the post-funeral arrangements bespoke the breach in his life.

Around midnight, Courtney turned up at Seattle Center with Kat Bjelland and reporter Gina Arnold, who'd written a book about modern alternative music entitled *Route 666,* which featured Nirvana among the greats.

Only a few fans remained from that evening's vigil; most of the thousands who'd burned pictures of him, and dived into the fountains had left. Courtney handed out Kurt memorabilia to the startled stragglers who stood holding candles, asking them Nirvana trivia questions and giving them his clothes and pages ripped from his diary. "Does that make you happy, Mr. Rock and Roll Fantasy?" she railed as though at his ghost. "Eddie Vedder's going to live to be ninety-eight!"

A day later, when the twin emotions of shock and grief still hung in the air, *Live Through This* hit the record stores. Tower Records stayed open late to release it at the earliest possible moment—midnight on Tuesday, April 12, just to help promote its release, as had been planned prior to Kurt's death. The store near Seattle Center was hardly a mob scene, though a few dozen lined up to be the first on the block to have Hole's new CD.

By and large, there wasn't much enthusiasm for the release. The timing could not have been more cruel. Between the album title and lines such as "Live through this with me, I swear that I will die for you," Hole's latest CD hit a raw nerve.

"I'm not psychic," Courtney said. "But my lyrics are."

CHAPTER 14

Living Through This
(April-July 1994)

THEY STAYED. COURTNEY AND FRANCES AND THE ENTOU-
rage, which included Kurt's mother and members of
Hole, stayed in the century-old mansion, the site of
many stormy fights and now a suicide. "Kurt wanted me
to stay, or he would not have done it in the greenhouse,"
Courtney said, as though the self-inflicted death were a
punk housewarming present.

Kurt's mother, Wendy O'Connor, who'd taken to
wearing a black T-shirt upon which was written "Grunge
is dead," even slept in the same bed as Courtney, at
Courtney's request, fearing that her daughter-in-law
would do herself in. "She's the sunshine of my life,"
Wendy told the press.

The cars crawled up the windy road, past the hedged
house, where burly guards—new full-time additions to
Courtney's payroll—now stood at the driveway entrance
and the sheets over the windows had been replaced with
white silk. And hundreds of people strolled through the
park, pointing at the greenhouse where Kurt had blown
his brains out. Along the running trail in back, someone
removed a plank from the wood fence, offering a spy's
view of the greenhouse.

Except for a brief session with MTV, during which she read the suicide note, and another with Gene Stout of the *Seattle Post-Intelligencer,* whose reporters had broken most of the news surrounding Kurt's death, the widow Cobain was not giving interviews.

One entertainment magazine reporter who'd gotten through to her had the phone slammed in his ear, with a threat: "I am going to jump out the window!" Many reporters weren't even trying to reach Courtney. A few rock writers who'd flown in from New York dropped their assignments and flew back empty-handed. The media feeding frenzy, which Kurt's manner of death had guaranteed, left them feeling too guilty to write.

Fans turned the park into a cemetery, leaving more flowers, more poems. One day, in a rare moment when the park was empty, Courtney created an altar of Nirvana 45s on a bench.

"Kids," she yelled, running outside. "Kids, where are you?" Sometimes it seemed she liked the uninvited company and made a point of yelling out the window when people were there. Other times she sank into fits of hysterical crying, regardless of how many surrounded her, comforting her.

The widow did grieve, à la Courtney, via the phone, chain-smoking and pill-popping, wearing Kurt's jeans and sweater, praying and chanting. She shrank in size, she couldn't eat, and spent hours locked up in the plant room over the garage where he had killed himself. The feeling that she'd abandoned him, the knowledge that her affairs had contributed to his terminal depression, and the questions that lingered, coupled with the fear that Frances might be taken away again knocked the wind out of her. "I can take anything," she confessed to Gene Stout, "but I can't take this."

She couldn't sleep despite the many tranquilizers that had been prescribed for her. She wondered unceasingly what had happened during that last week, when she was in Los Angeles and Kurt had flown back to Seattle.

Where the hell had he been while people were looking for him? Was he simply hiding in the bushes around their house?

Courtney called psychics across the country, searching for astral information. Few were able to give her concrete facts, save that they felt he was furious with her and that he had probably died on Wednesday, not Tuesday, as the coroner's report said.

The horrible truth was that Courtney had no idea where he'd spent his last week, and nobody was telling her. She'd heard he was hanging out in a ratty Seattle hotel where he could order heroin from room service. She suspected that he'd been with a female dealer, but when Courtney and Kat turned up at the dealer's apartment, screaming and all but knocking down the door, the dealer swore Kurt hadn't been there during that week. "And I believed her," Courtney said.

With the private investigator she drove to Carnation, where the Cobains had bought a country home, hidden in the hills, that they planned to move to if there was an ebola outbreak. There they found pizza boxes, strawberry Quik, cigarette butts that weren't Kurt's brand, indicating perhaps he'd been there—with someone else.

Things were missing: Chim-Chim, his beloved toy monkey; a feather that he kept in the heart-shaped box; the saints he'd bought in Rome. Other things had just as mysteriously appeared between the time she'd last seen him and when she returned to Seattle: among them, a flannel pillowcase on their bed that wasn't theirs. And everywhere she found pills—mostly Klonopin, the drug he liked to take with heroin—stashed under the mattresses and tucked away in drawers.

There were plenty of questions, but few answers. At least the *Post-Intelligencer* solved one mystery for the public: after intense questioning, Kurt's best friend Dylan had admitted to buying the weapon for him.

But few were blaming Dylan, who maintained he had no idea Kurt was suicidal and had bought the weapon merely as protection for Kurt until the alarm system was installed. However, even though she'd saved Kurt's life several times, many blamed Courtney for his death. In the Seattle scene, the feeling of dislike toward Courtney intensified; many people around the world believed that she was the force that had pushed him over the edge.

When Hole's rah-rah, four-star record reviews and interviews with Courtney ran in magazines, and her wide-eyed likeness peered out from the cover of *Spin* on newsstands everywhere, people were filled with sadness; when *Spin* opened, "Courtney has justified our love," it seemed like a mockery. The tiara she wore on the cover of the magazine should have been a widow's veil. Her childish, innocent look didn't play well; the baby-doll dress was a farce, though at least it was the right color: black. And on the covers of other magazines were pictures of Kurt, looking tragic and forlorn. The expression on his face seemed to be saying, "Duh, can't you see what I'm about to do?"

Even though *Live Through This* debuted at number 56 and never hit the Top 40, Courtney wouldn't have to worry about money for a while. Kurt hadn't signed his will, so his wife and his child were the only heirs. The newspapers reported that Kurt had left assets of $1.2 million, but that figure was low. Courtney, it was said by those close to her, was promptly handed a check for approximately $5 million. And that was before the world went on a Nirvana buying spree.

In Utero was quickly back on the charts, at number 11. *Nevermind* was in the Top 30. Even *Bleach* was selling better than ever before. Nirvana was once again outselling Hole. In its first two weeks *Live Through This* sold 19,000 copies.

Once again, even in death, Kurt was outshining Courtney, making her number two.

Society was looking for something from the widow Cobain. A message from the new Yoko, the grunge Jackie. They got drama, declarations, and promises, but many of her messages were mixed. She gave Kurt's suicide gun to Mothers Against Violence. She sent at least one heroin addict to rehab. She talked about starting a foundation to study depression. She talked about working to change state laws that hindered junkies from heading to rehab. She talked about taking Kurt's ashes to a Buddhist monastery, where she eventually did take some of them. She talked about starting a scholarship fund for artistic social rejects in Aberdeen, Kurt's birthplace.

She quickly reversed her opinion about who and what caused Kurt's death. Upset about the failed intervention, Courtney had sobbed at the candlelight vigil. "We should have let him have the thing that made him feel better," she'd said.

But while she had at first absorbed some of the blame for Kurt's suicide, saying she should have come back to be with him, she soon reversed her stance. The problem was heroin, she now insisted. The problem was its accessibility. The problem was the Seattle scene.

Three days after the candlelight vigil, Courtney called the police and turned in heroin dealers. She called the press and gave them sound bites about the Emerald City's heroin problems: "It's like apples in an orchard," she said. "It's falling off the trees." She belittled the local police, saying they weren't doing anything about the drug problems. "I asked them, 'Don't you get embarrassed [knowing] that Seattle is so famous for grunge, cappuccino, and heroin?'"

The heroin community, already uneasy after Kurt's death—which prompted a few junkies to quit, at least temporarily—was now panicked. Heroin dealers fled the city, and some never came back. And with them they took the knowledge of where Kurt had spent his last days.

After she turned in their dealers, few users would even talk to Courtney, much less help her in her search for information.

And Hole's amazing record was lost in a cloud of doom. It hardly moved from its low spot on the *Bill-*

board charts. Merely playing a cut from it could clear a room. Courtney canceled the Hole tour originally scheduled to kick off on May 3. DGC dropped all promotion indefinitely; the celebratory poster of a crowned, bouquet-clutching beauty-pageant contestant just didn't cut it. MTV, fearing a poor reception, delayed release of Hole's video for "Miss World" and instead tossed on loads of Nirvana.

Courtney left Seattle and, with Kat, headed to Canyon Ranch, a spa in the Southwest, where they wrote songs about Kurt. After a few days, Kat took off and Billy Corgan stepped in, consoling her and making her play music every day. But as supportive as he was, Billy had cold feet about resuming his romantic involvement with Courtney. After what had happened to Kurt, Billy's on again, off again affections were in the off position. At least temporarily.

In all the darkness only one ray of light broke through: in early May, Courtney was cleared of the drug allegations. All charges against her were dropped. The paraphernalia was prescribed by a doctor, prosecutors were told; the empty prescription pad was left there by accident. The amulet that supposedly hid heroin, it was believed, merely held Hindu ashes.

"I am delighted this nightmare is over," Love said via her attorney. "I can now concentrate on putting my life back together and mourning the loss of my husband."

When Courtney returned to Seattle somewhat calmer, an avalanche of hatred began. Among the poems to Kurt, the sympathy cards, the drawings, the flowers and gifts, were piles of hate mail.

There were letters condemning her for allowing Kurt to be alone, for letting him get into heroin, for abandoning him in his final hour, for using him. "You killed Kurt!" The messages came scrawled on cards and inside envelopes, from the far corners of the world, sometimes addressed only to "Courtney Love, Seattle, Washington." Some of them were written in blood.

America Online closed down the Hole folder—the

Internet site where subscribers wrote about the band—after someone posted a death threat to Courtney.

The finger-pointing and accusations were horrifying. She was already suffering from survivor's remorse, and she obviously felt guilty enough, without the burn-the-witch mentality back in her face.

Granted, not everyone blamed her. Many pitied the widow. Others demonstrated true concern, among them R.E.M.'s Michael Stipe, who called several times daily. And some, including Nirvana producer Jack Endino, believed Kurt had stayed on the planet longer simply because of Courtney. "I think she kept him around longer than he might have been otherwise," he told *People* magazine.

Knowing that Kurt had been suicidal for years, Wendy O'Connor likewise was one of Courtney's most vocal supporters in the press. "Kurt would've drowned [a lot earlier] without her," she told *Entertainment Weekly*. Her father, however, noted that "Courtney's got a lot of karma to answer for . . . [but] now that Kurt's dead, everybody's ready to forgive her."

To many, who regarded Kurt as a hero, she was to blame. Yoko Ono may have been the scapegoat when the Beatles broke up, but she had never had to put up with accusations of the sort that were flying at Courtney daily.

Equally as disturbing to her were the entrepreneurs trying to make a quick buck off of Kurt. Ads appeared on the back of Seattle's free weekly offering for sale copies of the death certificate. The starkly brutal *Seattle Times* picture of Kurt's body lying on the floor of the plant room ran again, enlarged for *People* magazine. Though the pale clenched fist showed that rigor mortis had set in, at least that picture didn't show his face. The more gruesome Polaroids the police took of Kurt's corpse, showing his bulging eyes and the brains coming out of his ear, had disappeared. According to Courtney, they emerged in the hands of a young Canadian man who hoped to sell T-shirts emblazoned with pictures of the body. Courtney got the pictures back and had her lawyer scrape the image off of each one.

Reporters called nonstop for interviews, sometimes showing up at the house and climb the trees again. Stringers for the tabloids parked outside her home and watched her every move through binoculars. Chrissie Hynde was lined up to approach Courtney about using a photo of Kurt for the animal rights organization PETA. The group wanted to use the picture with the slogan, "You need fur like you need a hole in the head." There was a small flurry in the publishing world as the call went out for books about Kurt. This infuriated Courtney to the point of threatening would-be biographers over the Internet: "Be very, very afraid." Michael Azerrad's Nirvana biography, *Come as You Are,* published before his suicide, and now including a hastily written final chapter on his death, flew off the shelves. And someone was stalking her.

The widow fled to New York and went on a shopping spree. Her first public appearance since Kurt's death was at Manhattan's swanky Bar Six with designer Anna Sui. She checked into the Royalton Hotel, but left in a panic after a late night phone call from a stranger hissing "You killed Kurt Cobain!" The switchboard reported that the call had originated from a room in the hotel.

Courtney escaped to a Buddhist monastery in Ithaca, where she chanted and bought a stupa for Kurt, essentially buying his sainthood. She placed some of Kurt's ashes in the shrine, in addition to a statue of a deity that was holding an oversized diamond so heavy that it nearly toppled the figurine. She left some of Kurt's ashes at the monastery to be made into small, cone-shaped sculptures called *tsatsas,* and offered up the Cobain country house in Carnation, Washington, as a retreat for monks.

She jetted to Los Angeles, where the now very gaunt widow, dressed in black, was escorted to the MTV Movie Awards by R.E.M.'s Michael Stipe.

And then she flew to Atlanta for more cosmetic surgery.

When she came back with lifted and plumped breasts, there was more hell to attend to. The first headache involved Dean Mathiesen. The former manager of Portland's Metropolis, whose house she had once accidentally torched, came to her with disturbing news. He'd been approached by Overlook Press, the small Manhattan publishing firm where soon-to-be *Bongwater* novelist Michael Hornburg worked as a graphic artist, to write a biography of Courtney. She was less than thrilled at the prospect: Dean knew years' worth of her exploits, her romances, the stories of stolen boyfriends, clothes, and drugs, not to mention the fires that seemed to combust spontaneously in her presence.

Courtney made a counteroffer: drop the book, leave Manhattan, and come to work as her assistant.

Mathiesen agreed and flew to Seattle.

It was a good move. Dean was an ideal companion for the grieving widow; his consistent attentiveness and ability to heal with kindness and humor helped pull her through. A take-charge managerial type, he took up some of the many duties that had been heaped upon Hole's guitarist, Eric Erlandson, who at times that spring had looked as if he would collapse from the stress. And Frances adored Dean; though not officially her nanny, he often entertained her, and he was capable of lasting in the household for more than a few months—unlike most other employees.

MTV hesitantly played "Miss World." Courtney made plans to record another video for "Doll Parts," and *Billboard* announced that despite withdrawn promotion sales of *Live Through This* in the first month approached 60,000. Almost twice as many copies as *Pretty on the Inside* had sold in the United States since 1991. But the record couldn't hold a torch to *Nevermind.*

Meanwhile, Courtney's father, Hank Harrison, frustrated that she wasn't calling him, jumped onto the

Internet to save the day. Using the screen name "Bio-Dad," he announced that he was Courtney's real father.

"I got America Online, and it was like three thousand people on there freaking out, so I announced myself on there and I said, 'I am Courtney's dad,'" Hank explained during an appearance on *Geraldo* in May. "Nobody believed me. . . . Then I started shrinking heads, and I did about two hundred interventions on AOL alone."

Courtney did not applaud the move. She wasn't happy about his appearance on *Geraldo*. Nor was she pleased that he was so willing to talk to the press, telling reporters for *People* that he was upset with her and hadn't even seen Frances.

On June 4, Seattle police officer Antonio Terry, who'd been investigating the drug links to the suicide, was killed. His death appeared unrelated to the Cobain case—he was gunned down when he pulled over on an interstate off-ramp to help a stopped car and its driver freaked out and shot him.

But Courtney felt responsible. She believed his death was somehow linked to the investigation into Kurt's drug connections.

With all the death and depression hovering over the Seattle scene, Hole bassist Kristen Pfaff decided to move back to Minneapolis. She had started touring again with her old band, Janitor Joe. In the aftermath of Kurt's death, Hole was taking a break, and their touring future was uncertain. There wasn't much reason for Kristen to stick around. Besides, she told friends in Minneapolis, the Seattle music scene was "polluted and corrupted," and the drug use was out of control. According to one friend, "She said things there were getting crazy, that the drug scene was getting crazy—and it was hard for her not to be crazy when everyone else was." She needed to get out.

By mid-June Kristen was packed up, the U-Haul was filled and ready to go, and a Minnesota friend had come out to accompany her back. On June 15, Eric Erlandson, who'd been romantically involved with Kristen previously, dropped by to bid her adieu, mentioning that he had a date with actress Drew Barrymore. Other friends stopped by to say farewell.

That night, her final one in Seattle, Kristen copped some heroin, shot up, and drew a bath. The 27-year-old bass player died in the bathtub of a heroin overdose. Her death stung all the more, falling, as it did, just two and a half months after Kurt's abrupt demise.

When her death was announced the next day, fingers pointed at Courtney. "It was her fault! It was Courtney's fault!" a woman at Seattle's Capitol Hill bar screamed. She was European, which possibly explained her emotional reaction in the city of restrained responses. But her words reflected the feelings of many. "I'm so sick," she said, "of picking up the phone and hearing someone else is dead."

That woman's sentiments were echoed elsewhere, though not as vehemently. She wasn't alone in blaming Kristen's death on Courtney, who had brought her to Seattle, into the world of glamorized drugs, and provided her with enough money to build up a habit. Whether it was the band, the lifestyle, or peer pressure, people around Courtney just seemed to turn into addicts. She was starting to seem like a walking black hole.

But Kristen's death was just another sign of a sick scene, one in which the bright and the talented were sucked into a world that offered escape from this one, and from everything and everyone in it. An escape from everything except heroin, and the money and maneuvers it took to get more.

When Kristen's family flew to Seattle they were horrified by more than the death of their daughter, a promising musician whose drug habit had only recently emerged. They were equally sickened by the social scene. "There was no sign of the type of remorse you would look for in a person who'd lost someone they care about," her father told the *Seattle Weekly*. "It could have been that Kristen died or somebody missed a bus." The family asked that the remaining members of Hole not attend her funeral.

In the wake of the most recent tragedy, MTV stopped playing the "Miss World" video again. Courtney lined up L7's bass player Jennifer Finch as a potential replacement on the next video, "Doll Parts."

Shortly thereafter, at the end of June, Courtney called me again. She wanted to know what happened to Kurt during his last week.

CHAPTER 15

The Widow Emerges
(June–August 1994)

MY NAME HAD APPEARED IN SMALL LETTERS TRAILING A PIECE about Kurt written for *Esquire* by novelist Stephen Wright. Ironically, I'd been assigned a piece about Kurt several months before—when he was alive. My slant was that the media-appointed King of Grunge was unhappy with the role and that he was self-destructive; one could see it in the way he drove. Though always conscientious when Frances was aboard, without the child Kurt tended to roar through hospital zones at Mach 1 speed, and on interstates he was known to putter so slow that old ladies passed him by. It was said that he sometimes returned rental cars in such a smashed-up state that they were fit only for the junkyard.

I wanted to go for a drive with him and talk about the pressures of fame and the difficulty of living in Seattle as a superstar. Though I'd initially considered a drive to his hometown, Aberdeen, after realizing how much he hated it, I decided instead to take a four-hour drive with Kurt—and Courtney, if she wanted—to Portland. Gossipy though it was, Portland was a family-like community. It was laudable to be an achiever there, especially in the arts. I'd hoped to introduce him to novelist Katherine Dunn, whom he'd thanked in the liner notes of *In Utero*. Katherine was the creative goddess of Portland; in the 1980s when I lived there, she'd helped to establish a feeling of support and sharing in stark contrast to the back-stabbing and competing that existed in Seattle. I'd thought he should meet her.

But Kurt had denied the request for an interview en route to Portland; upon informing my editor of Kurt's decision, I added sarcastically, "But remember to call me when he dies, and at the rate he's going that shouldn't be long." Seven months later the editor called and assigned me a job helping Stephen Wright's report for the piece.

Courtney had been moved by the piece Stephen Wright wrote, and she left a message for me to call her.

When I called her house, Courtney initially sounded so subdued that I asked if I'd wakened her.

"Do you think I sleep?" she asked. "I married a suicidal man."

I knew that, and I wasn't blaming her: she hadn't pulled the trigger, he had. And he'd been showing signs of trying to do himself in for quite a while.

She told me she was shocked at some of the information in the article, including that Kurt believed she was having an affair with Billy Corgan; she denied the affair. She also hadn't believed the article's portrayal of a messed-up Kurt being tossed from drug dealers' homes—until her own sources verified the incidents.

"Where did you find this out?" she wanted to know, perplexed that I was coming up with information before she did.

It was then that I discovered that few in the heroin world were talking to her. She'd become persona non grata since turning in the dealers.

"I deserve to know what was in his head that last week," she said.

I insisted I didn't know where Kurt was for sure. All I'd heard was the tales of him getting so wasted that dealers feared he would die there, and that sometimes he had to be carried out.

While Courtney talked on the phone, she was apparently holding 20-month-old Frances. "Loser," she said to the child. "Can you say 'loser'?"

"When Frances gets old enough to talk," Courtney threatened, "I'm going to have her call you and ask what happened to her daddy."

"And I'll tell her what I'm telling you, C-C-Courtney," I said. "That I don't know." Once again, talking to Courtney had caused me to develop a stutter.

"Are you going to sit there and stutter," she asked, "or are you gonna help me?"

I said I'd try to help. Then I suggested that she ask some of the bands and call Graytop Cab, whose drivers often carted the Cobains around. She thought he'd stayed briefly at a fleabag hotel north of town and suggested I check in and investigate on my own tab. It would be the scoop of the century, she informed me, to find out where Kurt Cobain had spent his last days. She wanted to know more, and she hoped I'd be her information conduit.

We talked about meeting at the Four Seasons Olympic Hotel for high tea. I wanted to introduce her to someone who was more closely linked to the junkies, and he agreed to talk to her. But she didn't call him.

And she didn't call me back for another year.

It was the summer of gloom. Even when the sun finally appeared, it couldn't fully penetrate the darkness that clung to the city. Almost everybody in the downtown scene was still depressed and confused.

Frances Bean had taken to talking to a tapestry of Jesus that hung on the basement wall, telling it all about that day's events and their new puppy. She thought the man in the tapestry was Kurt.

And a twenty-four-year-old Seattle man came forth to proclaim he was the new Kurt. Robert Sceeles drove his

1986 Porsche, decorated with spray-painted graffiti saying "Nirvana," up the driveway of the Cobain home and refused to leave, saying he wanted to be the new lead singer of Nirvana and to marry the widow. When a security guard refused to introduce Courtney to her wanna-be paramour, the man tossed the cars keys into the hedge. He was finally hauled off by the police and slapped with a restraining order preventing him from going within 100 yards of anyone in the entourage.

And then Tom Grant, the private investigator Courtney had hired in California, had a new theory about Kurt's death. He thought Kurt was murdered—*by someone hired by Courtney.* He was open to discussing his theory with the press.

Gold Mountain took out ads in industry mags, threatening to sue anyone who gave credence to Grant's claim, and initially few did. But the claim, the realization that the very investigator she had hired to find Kurt was now calling her a murderer, sent her back into a depression.

And then, that July, carrying a teddy bear back pack filled with Kurt's ashes, she returned to New York, to hang out in hotels with Evan Dando, the handsome lead singer for the Lemonheads, listed among the World's Most Beautiful People by *People* magazine. Courtney even took the stage for the first time since Kurt's death, for the last two songs of the Lemonheads show at Roseland. Courtney's spokeswoman quickly denied the two were involved. But five days later the *New York Post* ran pictures of Courtney making out with Evan while they were in bed with another man and the teddy bear. Courtney maintained their friendship was platonic. "I didn't play hunt-the-sausage with Evan," she told the press.

And then Courtney headed off on the Lollapalooza tour that had been the source of so much fighting in her last days with her husband.

Though she wasn't invited to go on the tour, she

climbed onto the headliners' bus, and occasionally onto the stage with the headliners' lead singer. After all, she knew him rather well: it was Billy Corgan.

As had seemed likely even before Kurt's overdose in Rome, Nirvana had been replaced by Smashing Pumpkins. And Courtney felt entitled not only to the stage but to the money as well. "That $9 million should have been mine!" she lamented to friends.

But her brief appearances during a few of the Pumpkins' sets seemed untainted by financial concern. Courtney tilted her head to the sky and sent a message to her husband, screaming, *"Kurt! Kurt!"* During later performances she added more drama to the show by pointing her hand like a gun and shooting into the crowd, then into her own head.

At the end of July, Courtney took the plunge and dived into the Internet with the same soul-bearing ferocity with which she stage-dived. With the opening words "OK KOOL get me to thee net," she launched her first attack. Predictably, it started with verbal punches—including jabs at *In Utero* producer, Steve Albini, and Pearl Jam's Eddie Vedder—but she quickly branched out into new territory: Courtney asked out writer Jason Cohen, who wrote *Generation Eccch.* She wondered if she should return to college, apologized to Sub Pop's publicist, confessed that she did not do heroin and hardly ever did, announced she was "grossly overfamous," reminded everyone she was a very good lyricist, and notified Billy Corgan, perhaps sarcastically, that she was pregnant with his child. Mockingly apologizing for ruining the public's concept of celebrity by jumping into the Internet ring, she added "I'm accessible! I live in a house! I have a child! I am human!" Her first error-riddled post blasted through cyberspace, ending with a plea to her fans: "And no more fucking mid-suicide E-mail—Call the fucking hot line or write to Vedder—I'm roof borne myself. . . . Stop it, you little alternateen brats."

Often her letters were responses to posts been made at

assorted sites on the Internet where topics such as Courtney's style of dress and onstage antics were routinely discussed.

She answered questions, and expounded on current psychological theories about suicide. She discussed the misogynist roots of such words as "hysterical," and explained why she asked fans trivia questions about her band before giving autographs: "I was getting asked for autographs at, like, malls by people in neon bike shorts they only know me thru a current affair or something— and i started saying 'name a song' wich, of couse they could not." She suggested that Nirvana fans chant the Buddhist prayer "nam-myo-ho-renge-kyo" for Kurt, adding, "When youve had your spouses blood on your fac then youve got something to say."

She asked out someone who had dreams about taking her out, suggesting they go to the celebrity photo–filled Formosa in Hollywood, and promising that "i wil actaully DEMONSTRATE LIVE the utter breakdown of all known laws of physics—and IMPLODE under the signed pic of Doris Day." She slammed Pearl Jam fans, noting, "I want to meet the sheep that purchased the 6th million Pjam record. . . . you cannot like Pearl Jam AND Nirvana."

She mocked people who wanted her dead by running through her remaining methods of suicide since she'd given away Kurt's guns. "Maybe I should ask for them back," she wrote. "I can't tie a noose. . . . I know. One of you can kill me." And she, or at least someone claiming to be her, ripped into Nirvana drummer Dave Grohl, saying that he was signing up with rival band Pearl Jam and that Kurt had despised him for years.

The day after that post however, Courtney sent a cool-headed note to Carol Mariconda, who ran the letters on the Net, explaining that, it wasn't Courtney who wrote that; someone must have accessed her code and sent a false posting.

That was part of the beauty of the Internet. Like anyone using it, Courtney and other rock stars could assume names, like "De10tion" or "Lilacs00," and no one could be sure it was them.

A perfect way to break news about herself! A perfect way to attack people and then deny it! And attack she did—at least admitting most of the time that she was the source of the unkind words.

Her on-line letters and posts inspired an Off-Off Broadway play *Love in the Void,* which portrayed her as a liar for denying the post about Dave Grohl. More significant, though, was the interest she helped to generate in the Internet.

To judge by sites on the Internet, there was more interest in Courtney and her band than UFOs. More than thirty web sites were devoted to Courtney and Hole, running pictures, articles, reviews by fans, and letters about her. The sites were visited by thousands daily, placing them in the top five percent of the Internet's most popular Web pages. And every day hundreds more posted messages in newsgroups, notes about Courtney, which were responded to by subsequent readers.

The messages weren't always kind. While some referred to Courtney as a goddess, many continued to blame her for Kurt's death, and to ponder how she would write her next album now that her singer-songwriter husband was gone.

By the end of the summer, Billy Corgan seemed to be gone as well. Not to worry. Soon enough Courtney had another crush: Trent Reznor, lead singer for the hot and upwardly spiraling industrial band, Nine Inch Nails, who were launching their 1994 The Downward Spiral tour.

CHAPTER 16

The Widow in Love
(August—September 1994)

IT WAS BECAUSE OF THE FREAKS THAT THEY WERE EVER involved to the extent that they were. Well, they did have ten dates together. Their bands did, at least. Beyond that, what really happened between Courtney Love-Cobain and Trent Reznor is a bit of a mystery, except that it didn't end well.

The Jim Rose Circus Sideshow was Trent Reznor's original choice for the middle act of his summer 1994 The Downward Spiral tour, but by the time Nine Inch Nails made the offer, the troupe of freaks was already booked: the performers who hammered nails up their nose and dangled irons from assorted pierced body parts would be playing at the Edinburgh Festival for the first ten days of the Nine Inch Nails tour.

Not a problem. Until the Circus left Scotland and caught up with the tour in progress, NIN would fill the gap with another freak act: Hole. By then Courtney's band had sold almost 200,000 copies without touring and with minimal promotion. They had also lined up a new bassist—the lovely Melissa Auf der Maur, whom Billy Corgan had recommended for the post.

Marketing-wise, media-wise, and Courtney-wise, it

was perfect, an ideal way for Hole to hit the road and pick up where Kurt's death had forced them to leave off—touring with the band that brought industrial sound and psychic pain to the popular stage in the form of dashing Trent Reznor, the ascending music god of 1994.

It was too predictable that Courtney would try to get in and latch on; and it was too predictable that Trent would quickly shake her off. Word had it that he liked his babes a bit younger.

Before she headed off on tour, Courtney went back to Seattle and threw a small party for Frances's second birthday. The party was scheduled to run from around five to eight, but in typical form, Courtney was late and stayed in her room for hours after the guests arrived. They were starting to leave when finally, at a little before eight, Courtney's bedroom door creaked open and she descended the stairs like Cinderella, complete with pink gown and tiara.

"Look, Frances," she said, dramatically entering the backyard, where what was left of the party looked on in shock, "I'm the Queen!" Taking off her tiara, she tried to crown Frances with it, tangling the child's hair in the process. Frances began crying.

Then Courtney sliced the first piece of cake and dug in. Several days later, Hole left to hit the road, for what would be almost a year of nonstop touring.

Their first gig, at the Reading Festival—also the first they played with new bassist Melissa Auf der Maur—was described by the press as "sloppy" and "the weekend's biggest disappointment." Jeff Buckley was the surprise hit of the festival, catching the critics' eyes, and Courtney's as well.

In the meantime, the band flew to Cleveland to meet up with Trent and his Nine Inch Nails.

Ten dates—ten short dates—and Courtney turned herself into a continual scene-making nightmare. It started during the very first show on the tour, in Cleveland, when she staggered onstage and gave such a pitiful performance—musically, at least—that the soundman turned down her audio level and cranked up Eric's to compensate.

At least her between-song banter was livelier than her playing. "I punched out a guy on the plane," she confessed to the audience. She told them she'd been offered the Guess? jeans ad campaign, adding, "That's so retarded, those stupid pants." Seeming to address Kurt's ghost, she said, "I give you a morning blow job, I make your fucking breakfast, so leave me alone." At one point she drunkenly pulled up her shirt, and ripped off her black bra. Flashing her breasts at the crowd, she yelled, "Now you know why I get all the guys, you fucking shitbags." As the set drew to a painful close, the rest of the band walked off, leaving Courtney onstage alone, sobbing as she strummed on her guitar and slur-sang, "Someday you will ache like I ache," over and over. She stumbled across the stage and leaned against a speaker, looking as if she might faint, and was promptly escorted offstage, but not before flashing the crowd again and flipping them the bird.

The crowd was stunned. The writer who reviewed the show for *Spin* called her performance "devastating . . . like watching your sister strip for a stag party."

Perhaps the widow Cobain was not psychologically prepared to return to the stage, but to stay alive, she needed to perform. And she sought romantic diversions as well.

How close she actually got to Trent, how tight they were (and in what way), was never fully known to the press. Trent rarely spoke of it, except to minimize the involvement, and Courtney's take on the subject appeared rather skewed.

But if there was a little hanky-panky, which Courtney insisted that there was (telling friends in December that she was pregnant by Trent, an assertion that many doubt), the Love-Reznor connection sure didn't last long. By the time their tour buses parted ways, Courtney was reportedly having a dalliance with a member of the opening band, Marilyn Manson—a band of guys who performed in drag.

Trent was no doubt mighty relieved when Ms. Courtney packed up and moved out of his life.

Except that she didn't. While Hole toured the country on the "Live Through This" tour, Courtney continued to call Trent, his management, and the management of other acts on the road with NIN, trying to find out where Trent was staying. She wrote to him. She faxed him. She sent comments to him via the press. In Los Angeles she barged into a Nine Inch Nails after-show party; within seconds Trent, who had been notified, hastily snuck out of club without her noticing. But his relief was again short-lived. She found out where he was staying and turned up to pound on his hotel room door while he stared through the peephole, amazed and alarmed, at his relentless pursuer. Minutes later, after suggesting that an emergency situation was brewing in his room, she came back with a maid, who let her in.

But Trent wasn't there; panicked at her return, he'd jumped from his balcony onto the balcony of his manager, in whose room he was hiding.

Courtney rifled through his belongings.

The attention, the surprise appearances, the phone calls, the letters, the chasing and the begging—it was the same technique that had won Kurt's heart. But Trent wasn't biting.

Ticked at his cold response, Courtney retaliated via the Internet, sending juicy letters over the information superhighway, available to any computer owner who knew where to look. She jumped on sites where NIN fans exchanged information about the band, as well as other bands' Internet spots. She railed about Trent. She mocked his love of his silver Porsche and his beer drinking, and she slammed the backstage parade of starstruck gals at Nine Inch Nails' shows, writing about how disgusting it was, and intimating that the band should be thankful she wasn't telling more. (Apparently she'd forgotten that she herself was a former groupie.)

Some of her points were valid. Historically, some women at rock shows—not just those Nine Inch Nails fans—clamored for celebrity attention. And at some bands' rock shows, they did climb through the chain of command, tossing out sexual favors every step of the way.

That Courtney would talk about the link between musicians and groupies at all was actually radical, since that topic is usually hush-hush. But that she implied that Nine Inch Nails' shows were the only ones at which groupies begged for the stars' attention, was laughable; it came off like sour grapes.

Grunge's First Widow was making a fool of herself, but despite being advised to calm down, Courtney would not let go. She slammed Trent via more articles—in which she feigned amazement that he was denying their relationship—and via the stage, where she belittled his manhood. "Nine Inches? I don't think so," she told audiences. "Four inches is more like it."

Trent retaliated via the press, too. "I didn't want to be her boyfriend, and now she harasses me," he said, though he later retracted it.

Between her onstage remarks, her media assertions, and her claims to friends that she was pregnant with his child, Trent was finally said to have threatened to make known the contents of the letters Courtney had sent Trent, which supposedly contained unflattering ments about Kurt.

She toned it down. For a while. But she s turned back to the Net to call him, amon "a dckweed homophobe and mysogist soul." Referring to their suppose "lousylaylousylaylouseylaye wha and dishonour for that lousy

By then there were other was talk that she had c herself fanned the fl confused. "I've, uh, hung out with Courtney only once and talked to her a few times on the phone," he told *US* magazine.

There was talk of her and Scott Weiland, lead singer of Stone Temple Pilots, who was rumored to have left his wife to hang out in hotels, at least for a while, with Courtney. What is certain is that when Scott was later busted for possession of cocaine and heroin, Courtney was there to help him through. He wrote a letter, apologizing for his "disease called drug addiction," and Courtney read it over the air on L.A.'s KROQ.

And at least one of her Internet encounters had led to romance; she flew one stranger she'd met in cyberspace to Europe for a rendezvous.

Billy Corgan by then was pretty much out of her personal picture. Courtney claimed to have put an evil curse on him and, at one show, dedicated "Violet" to him, saying, "This is about a jerk who's losing his hair."

And she was starting to tell people that she had actually given Billy a leading lyric in a Smashing Pumpkins hit called "Disarm." *Request* magazine would later report that "she claims that she gave him 'the killer in me is the killer in you'." Billy didn't deny it in the article.

But according ___ Courtney hadn't told
the ___ to mention that the
___ She told him she had
___ in his San Francisco
___ journals and love
___ said.

___ re getting lots of
___ a *Rolling Stone*
___ she was wearing
___ rry, she'd had it
___ rt had designed
___ 's ashes around
___ attle's Calvary
___ ced she'd have
___ her announce-

ment, however, the cemetery officials balked and demanded payment of $100,000 annually for guards and upkeep. Courtney dropped the plan.

Her antics were getting old, but she didn't stop them. Despite her publicist's post-event dusting, Courtney continued to put on a show that seemed to inform the public that if they thought she was bad, she was worse than that.

When Hole played Portland, Courtney walked onstage before a screaming full house chanting her name as though she were the second coming. By the third song, she'd stomped off. The reason was painfully obvious: someone had yelled out, "You killed Kurt!"

"I'm not playing anymore," she said, dropping her guitar. "You can blame [that] little fucker."

The crowd screamed for the band to return, and a frantic fan ran backstage, begging for the show to continue.

Courtney flipped out, screaming, "Get the fuck away from me!" Then she allegedly punched the girl in the mouth.

Finally the Petulant One returned to the stage, carrying food from backstage. She pelted the crowd with cold cuts, telling them, "We've never had a show as fucked as this." It was a town of losers, she announced to her fans. "No wonder Kathleen Hanna [of Bikini Kill] turned out so lame," she screamed. "Tonya Harding. Look at the women who come out of here."

Courtney neglected to mention that she was one of them.

The pummeled fan filed charges, which were dropped after a settlement of several thousand dollars was paid by the promoters. Courtney didn't put forth a penny.

At other shows, however, her behavior was exemplary, and she came off like an angel. In September, when Hole played the Academy in Manhattan, the press was so tired of her antics and bad shows, that they were ready, in the words of one, "to smash her like a bug." That night's show was swarming with blood-thirsty media. But the band was so tight and she sang so well that the press had to change their plans. "She was astonishing," Barbara O'Dair wrote for *Rolling Stone,* "moving fluidly from plaintive drawl to throat-reeling scream in a red-hot hour of punk rock." The reviews redeemed her. Those who graded gave her an "A."

But when she reached the West Coast, she was back into the action-adventure mode, particularly after her reunion with Mary Lou Lord, to whom she'd been so kind at Kurt's funeral. When Hole had played the Palladium in Los Angeles, where Mary Lou was visiting with bigwig music types, the singer from Boston was invited to the Hole show. Thinking any problems between her and Courtney had been resolved, Mary Lou stepped into an after-hours party for Hole wearing a backstage access wristband given to her by an agent from the William Morris Agency.

Sixty people or so hovered around Courtney including Stephen Dorff and Porno for Pyros leader Perry Farrell, who also organized Lollapalooza each year. When Danny DeVito came to pay his respects, Courtney stretched out on the table, hamming it up for him and sharing his cigar. A few minutes later, surrounded by fans and autograph seekers, Courtney looked up to see Mary Lou.

She immediately dropped the pen, ran over, and tried to push Mary Lou, who took off running with Courtney in hot pursuit. They raced down several flights of stairs, Courtney a few steps behind Mary Lou. "I'm gonna kill you!" she screamed, while her breasts flapped out of her baby-blue slip.

In the parking lot, a bouncer caught hold of Mary Lou; adrenaline-surged by the fury not far behind her, she simply wriggled out of his clutch, and left him standing there holding her wig, jacket, and shirt. Both of the now nearly topless singers headed into the traffic of Sunset Boulevard. Mary Lou flagged down cars and ultimately lost Courtney, whose long dress kept tripping her up, by hiding behind a telephone pole. Courtney later claimed to a Canadian writer that she had found Mary Lou hiding in a Dumpster. But life wasn't all hide-and-seek. Courtney was reportedly getting back into drugs.

Courtney reportedly left a bent, scorched spoon—used for melting down heroin—in the bathroom of an San Francisco eatery and was chastised for it in a gossip column that ran in the underground magazine *The Nose.*

By then she was allegedly using heroin again, at least occasionally, between the pills. Dolls and needles. She even admitted it in the end-of-the-year issue of *Rolling Stone.* "I take Valiums. Percodans. . . . I have used heroin—after Kurt died."

In December, just as she appeared on the cover of *Rolling Stone* with her newly formed breasts, just before Hole was scheduled to appear on *Saturday Night Live,* the band played San Francisco.

At one point during that visit, she hopped on a city bus and gave the stunned occupants an impromptu tour of the neighborhood where she'd once lived, pointing out sites where she used to work, where friends lived, where there had been fires, sometimes crying at the memories.

Early the next morning she turned up at Rozz's apartment. Though he lived in Portland most of the year, he'd kept the run-down studio in San Francisco. And when she stopped by, he was there, celebrating his first wedding anniversary with his baby-faced wife, who was a decade younger than Courtney.

Perfect timing.

"I had a nightmare," Courtney told Rozz as she stepped into the apartment and looked at the lace curtains on the window, the candles, dried flowers, and baby rattles that were just where she'd left them. In the dream, she said, he had published a book of her love letters.

The letters were still there—over a thousand of them, by Rozz's estimation, some still unopened. They were just a few steps behind her, in the closet, along with the costumes she'd stolen from movie sets and that she and Rozz had ripped in sexual frenzy years before, stored among school records, financial statements, photos, and diaries—both hers and his, which she had graded and written comments on.

Courtney didn't take back the things she'd left there. It appeared to Rozz that she didn't care if he wrote the book. She just wanted to make sure that if he did, he said some nice things about her; she even mentioned bankrolling a book, if he wrote one.

Once they sat down at the table and played what Rozz referred to as "international pharmacy"—with Courtney offering him her latest pharmaceutical finds from around the globe—she seemed to be suffering from a bad case of the guilts. She wanted to give him some money—a few grand, maybe, for the months she'd "sublet" his place, sometimes without his permission.

And, oh, yeah, she asked, what did he think of her album?

He hadn't heard it, much to her shock and dismay.

According to Rozz, Courtney brought up the subject of his old notebook. What did he want? she asked. Ten grand? A record deal? Everybody borrows lyrics, you know.

She referred to her riches as "blood money" and seemed to want to get rid of it.

He declined the offer. Rozz claimed that Courtney later offered him a writing credit on her next album. after a stop at the bank machine where she transformed her pile of gold plastic into thick stacks of green, she took Rozz and his wife out shopping.

She bought Rozz a pair of $4 sunglasses. She bought his wife $4,000 worth of clothes. Before they left his place, she had tucked away wads of money throughout their apartment, as if hiding eggs for an Easter hunt.

"Excuse me, I'm a rock star, could I get a little service?" Courtney used the line often on that shopping spree. "I'm going to spend a lot of money!" Once the help recognized the grunge goddess, they often kicked out the rest of the customers, so the girls could turn the store into their own personal dressing room.

"Rozz, do you like this? Rozz, is this too tight? Rozz, do I look fat? Rozz, do I look pretty?" Poor Rozz was hearing it in stereo, from his wife and from Courtney.

Of all the dresses they tried on, there was only one that he really flipped over—a tight purple velvet number, size three. His wife looked incredible in it. Alas, they didn't have the dress in Courtney's size.

A few hours later Rozz and his wife refused the limo that Courtney had sent to transport them from their apartment to that night's Hole show. Rozz and the missus were too busy having a fight—about the purple dress. It was missing. The only dress he'd really liked—and his wife had somehow lost it.

Not to worry, though. The missing garment reappeared the following week. On TV. On Courtney who was wearing it in a promotional spot for *Saturday Night Live*. The dress had undergone a little alteration, however—"if it doesn't fit, rip it" being Courtney's tried-and-true fashion motto.

In December, just about the time the magazines naming *Live Through This* album of the year were hitting the stands, Courtney was said to have checked herself back into rehab.

How could she have continued to do drugs? Easy: they numbed her. And besides, as she loved to point out, "Accessibility is nine-tenths of the law." Drugs existed. Therefore she used them. "I don't think God necessarily put us here to be sober all the time," she told *Rolling Stone*. "But I also don't think he put us here to be junkies."

In times of pain and in certain cities such as New York and L.A., she might fall back into drug use again. But she'd get herself clean, too. No one needed to pull an intervention on Ms. Courtney Love-Cobain.

One thing Courtney excelled at was pulling herself out of a hole. Emotionally, however, she wasn't quite ready to do that. At least not without a major scene, or five hundred.

CHAPTER 17

In the Spotlight Still
(1995)

SINCE THE FIRST OF THE YEAR IT HAD BEEN CLEAR: COURTNEY Love was America's foremost female mediamonger. And her publicity blitz started on a high note: she came off like a goddess in the music-awards department, with Hole's *Live Through This* voted best album of the year by *Spin, Rolling Stone,* and the *Village Voice.* With her new title as leader of 1994's most celebrated band, she emerged as the most talked-about woman celeb, and at least once a week, often more, she rated a gossip item, if not a full-fledged article.

Madonna seemed bland and well-mannered in comparison, scarcely causing a stir even when she put a bullfighter in her new video—in which she appeared with Courtney-esque smeared eyeliner—even when she threw an exclusive MTV pajama party, where all the attendants showed up at the Manhattan venue Webster Hall in sleepwear. Yawn.

Meanwhile the British press was calling Courtney "America's most famous woman," and *Spin* had crowned her "our very best rock star." While Madonna had once been a favorite paradigm in women's studies textbooks, Courtney was pushing the limits further than

readers' polls and critics' polls, and chastising the Grammy Nominations Board for the omission.

She made news for landing a small part in *Feeling Minnesota,* a Keanu Reeves movie produced by Danny DeVito, and for a performance in Orlando, when she jumped into the mosh pit and punched out two fans who she said were grabbing at her.

But later that month, in Los Angeles, she took the most cake. She stirred up such a media storm from late 1994 on that she deserved an Emmy, though the closest she got was when she held an Oscar at an Academy Awards party.

Courtney staggered into the Academy Awards ceremony with her grunge twin, and date, British TV and movie star Amanda de Cadenet. The former host of the UK show, *The Word,* was dressed as a Courtney lookalike, from white gown to gleaming crown. Cracking up throughout the ceremony, the two women were the queens of the scene, and were captured for the camera in mid-smooch as they stumbled toward the after-hours parties, frequently tripping over their dresses and spilling their drinks.

Courtney was likewise the show-stealer at the post-ceremony party held in the barnlike space known as Morton's. While Michael Douglas, Arnold Schwarzenegger, Jane Fonda, and Dolly Parton stood around chatting at the exclusive *Vanity Fair* bash, Ms. Love sprawled out on the terra-cotta floor, chain-smoking and spilling out to a reporter for *People* all the details about how, despite Kurt's wishes, she had tried to freeze his sperm. When the Cobains returned from Rome, Courtney told the reporter, she gave Kurt oral sex, spit his semen into a cup, and rushed it to her freezer, only to discover later that the home freezer wasn't cold enough for genetic preservation.

While waiters leaned down to offer hors d'oeuvres, and as the stars came over to her or sent messengers, she chatted away on the floor, pulling broken cigarette after broken cigarette out of her rhinestone clutch and tossing them around her in the search for an untorn smoke. She never did get over to the waiting Maria Shriver, being sidetracked by *Vanity Fair* photographer Herb Ritts, who pulled out an envelope of black-and-white photos of Frances. She did, however, have a chance to chat up Barbara Walters, who said she wanted an interview, to which Courtney agreed. And when the tiaraed singer walked away from Jessica Lange, who had played the lead in a recent remake of *A Streetcar Named Desire,* the blond actress murmured in Ms. Love's wake, "My God, that was Blanche DuBois."

But it was at the next soirée, hosted by Miramax, that Courtney really spiced up the scene. Held at the soon-to-be-closed Chasen's, a favorite haunt of old Hollywood, the bash for a thousand guests had attracted such stars as Quentin Tarantino, Roger Avary, Dianne Wiest, Jay Leno, Jodie Foster, Timothy Hutton, Holly Hunter, and Madonna. The crowd that poured out of the restaurant's California Room into a tent in the back caused such a scene that fire marshals ultimately arrived to push the partygoers out. They missed the Courtney-style fireworks, however.

Courtney and Amanda sauntered in like visiting royalty. Spying Quentin Tarantino, they headed toward the booth where the director sat with a group of friends, who were anything but welcoming to the crowned and crocked duo. Nevertheless, Courtney invited herself into the booth. She fondled Quentin's Oscar, cooing about how much Kurt had liked his work and how talented he was.

Finally she turned to a red-haired woman in the group and asked to bum a smoke. The woman coldly informed Courtney she didn't smoke.

Several minutes later Courtney addressed the redhead again: "Do I know you?"

"Yes, you know me," the woman answered.

"Do I like you?" Courtney asked.

"No, you don't like me," the woman informed her.

Courtney shrugged. "There's only one person I hate—Lynn Hirschberg. If she were here, I'd kill her with this Oscar." Courtney looked at the statuette in her hand.

At that point, Quentin grabbed Courtney's hand, and the redhead fled. The woman, whom Courtney had sat next to for fifteen minutes without recognizing, was Lynn Hirschberg.

Courtney's retelling of the tale for a Chicago radio station was embellished slightly. "So I'm at the Academy Awards . . . party at Morton's, right?" she told DJs at WKQF, who didn't know she was getting the location of the party wrong. "I sit down, and I'm picking up the Oscar; they're really heavy, 'cause they're lead with gold in them. You could totally brain somebody. I'm, like, who do I hate in this room? All of a sudden this little voice . . . peeps up, and she's like 'You don't like me' . . . she said her name was Lynn Hirschberg and she bolted and she hid under Madonna and Ellen Barkin and Jodie Foster's table, and they were kicking her under the table. Jodie Foster was smoking cigars and putting them out on her and screaming, 'Face the music, you bitch!'" Courtney didn't have to worry about Jodie's publicist making noise about the fabricated scene: after all, Jodie's publicist was also hers.

"Had I killed her," Courtney confessed to the DJs, "they'd just go 'There goes Courtney again.' But I kept my poise."

The incident was just one of many that made Courtney a blotter for for more ink. Getting tired of her dramas du jour, the media was starting to take potshots. A mean, if only slightly exaggerated, *Details* cartoon drawn by a fellow musician who knew her stunts well, illustrated a day in Courtney's life. It showed her shopping for extra-high speakers upon which to prop her foot to optimize crotch viewing. And there was the unflattering—some would say shocking—picture in *Esquire,* showing her crawling, without clothes and looking half dead, with the harsh caption "Next good career move: choke on your own vomit."

Gold Mountain was said to be unhappy with her as well. When the management company's Janet Billig, who'd long been Courtney's friend and adviser, left the company, Gold Mountain all but begged Hole to stay on, hiring lawyers to revamp and add special clauses to the band's contract. Many man-hours later, Courtney shocked them by going to a different management company, Q Prime, out of New York.

While she ingratiated herself with some people—Tom Arnold, for one, described her as "a real sweetheart," R.E.M.'s Michael Stipe was still a confidant, and many reporters had become trustworthy "friends of Courtney"—she'd been trashed by more than a few musicians, including some who'd been close to Kurt in Seattle, where she lived.

Mudhoney slammed what everyone, including Courtney, assumed to be her with their song "Into Yer Shtick," asking musically, "Why don't you blow your brains out, too?" Though the band's leader, Mark Arm, told the British press he didn't write the line with one specific person in mind, he added, "If the shoe fits, wear it." When asked how Courtney was regarded in Seattle, her home of three years, Arm responded in typical Seattle form, "She isn't from Seattle." Nirvana's ex-drummer, Dave Grohl, grabbed Pat Smear (formerly of the Germs) and started a new band, Foo Fighters. Songs on their debut album seemed to be directed at Courtney as well with a reference to "the black widow," and lyrics such as "Why am I the only one to see your rehearsed insanity?" and "I've been around all the pawns you've gagged and bound."

Gossip columns skewered her for her behavior during a performance of *Hamlet* which she attended with musician Jeff Buckley. In between searching for pills, she talked loudly, noting, "This is my favorite line!" throughout the play.

On the way to the theater, she'd asked for directions from a photographer; when Courtney and Jeff left the theater that night, they were swarmed by paparazzi, and gossip items played them as a couple. Embarrassed, Jeff called the press and explained that he'd just accompanied her to the play. Noting that Courtney's escort felt "freaked out" and "used," writer Jason Cohen, who profiled Hole in a cover story for *Rolling Stone,* wrote that Jeff Buckley had called him, saying "I went out for one night, and I'm thrust into this weird rock-star-charade heavy thing."

But so what? Such insults paled in light of her crowning glory: *Vanity Fair,* round two.

Queen Bitch Courtney Love made the magazine eat its own words. She shoved them right down its throat as nobody in the magazine's history had ever done. It took three years to battle it out, but unstoppable, undauntable Courtney the Fighter won.

For three years, she'd been furious about *Vanity Fair*'s portrayal of her as a monstrous gold digger who'd slammed heroin when she was pregnant. Her hatred of Lynn Hirschberg was frightening, fiercer than her hatred of other journalists, some of whom she threatened with physical harm; it was so legendary in media circles that some reporters took bodyguards when reviewing Hole shows.

For the new *Vanity Fair* article, karma and the writer, softballer Kevin Sessums, were in her favor. It was as though Mother Teresa had shown up at her door with pen, paper, and tape recorder.

The June 1995 cover story of the magazine made Courtney look like an angel, literally: the cover showed Courtney with wings, stepping out of a frame, which seemed to be an allusion to the earlier feature story, which she'd frequently described as a frame-up.

Inside, she was shown among child nymphs, with her eyes upturned in a wistful, Kurt-searching expression that would have played better on Frances Bean. This piece was so fluffy it came complete with a fairy tale and even a bubble bath, proving once and for all that the grunge goddess did bathe, even though she extinguished her cigarette in the bathwater.

It was yet another mighty victory for the woman who'd broken all the rules, who said she was involved in a dozen lawsuits around the globe. "Everybody wants to see me dead," she told *Vanity Fair*. "But I'm not going to die. I'm a cockroach." And yet, even while the angelic picture beamed from magazine stands nationwide, Courtney made news again on June 11. After returning to her house from a cross-country flight, she was raced to Harborview Hospital in Seattle, supposedly nearly dead from a drug overdose. She walked out the next day.

It was an accident, she assured the media. She just took too many tranquilizers to combat her fear of flying, during a layover on a flight back from New York. "I took three pills on a plane by mistake, and the next eight hours were black," she told an audience. "There's no afterlife. Just black."

Despite the fall, Courtney was back in the saddle and riding at a high gallop for the rest of the summer, starting with Lollapalooza '95. She had to be carried around from show to show, and sometimes off of the stage as well, but she and the band always put on performances that were memorable and often stellar. At the least, they were fodder for more gossip columns.

By then she had a lot more help—twelve lawyers whom she promptly elevated to religious figures. "I am Jesus," she informed Rozz via his answering machine, when he was planning to write a book about her, "and my lawyers are my twelve disciples. Do not fuck with me!" The message puzzled Rozz, who had read her most of his unfinished manuscript, and was under the impression she had liked it.

And just as helpful was hot-shot publicist Pat Kingsley, whose services Courtney has said were donated to her "as a charity case." Others, though, say she was tossing Kingsley close to $10,000 a month. With Pat as her publicist, she was more than media-savvy. She was the press princess, able to place, kill, or at least tone down stories more effectively than the government or the mob.

Reporters often complain that information ends up missing from their stories about Courtney. Perhaps that's the result of one of Courtney's many editor friends, and there are rumors about stories containing unflattering information about Courtney that were yanked altogether.

But one story, while questionable, kept turning up even after it was silenced by advertisements and bullying. Tom Grant, the private investigator whom Courtney hired in L.A., continued with his assertions that she was part of a murder plot.

While his story was interesting to most people, including the Seattle police who investigated Kurt's death, Tom Grant's conclusions were ludicrous. His theory was commonly regarded as laughable—as laughable as the theory of Richard Lee, the Seattle resident who ran a weekly program on cable TV and who claimed that Kurt was murdered. Courtney wasn't able to get Richard's show off the station; but she continually pushed to have Tom's private-investigator license taken away, and placed an ad in *Publisher's Weekly* threatening to "sue the skin off" any publication that gave him credence.

While conspiracy theorists pondered the mystery hourly, few in the music world or the media gave it much credence. There was no need to murder someone like Kurt, who was extremely suicidal. There were photos of him with the barrel of a gun in his mouth; there was the overdose in Rome and the original name of *In Utero:* "I Hate Myself and I Want to Die". But the more Courtney and her legal forces fought to discredit the story, the more interesting it became. Tom's reports, written like the chapters of a mystery novel, were widely read— especially on-line—and a whole batch of new rumors blossomed.

The rumors swarmed around her like locusts. And even with her twelve lawyers, Courtney couldn't make them go away.

Even if she could get the press to eat its words, she couldn't stop the rumors that kept mucking about in the music world about "Live Through This." While Courtney herself admitted that Kurt performed background vocals on most cuts, and that there was two-way collaboration between them—with her helping on songs such as Nirvana's "Pennyroyal Tea"—there was talk that Kurt wrote her album, or most of it.

And there were even rumors about a tape. Few have apparently heard this tape, unlike those of prank calls to Nirvana's British former biographers, or even previews of "In Utero" that made the underground rounds months before the album's release. I was unable to track down a copy, and some people I talked to even questioned its existence. But others maintained they've heard it: a tape of Kurt singing and playing all the songs from Live Through This, solo.

If true, this would be support to Courtney's detractors that he'd been more involved with the songs than he was given credit for; at the least, it would appear a posthumous way to discredit his wife. Then again, had Courtney released a tape of herself playing everything from "In Utero," few would regard it as proof that she had written Kurt's music.

Courtney attempted to blow off the accusations online by "confessing" that O.J. Simpson actually wrote the album.

When Hole released an EP in the fall of 95, "Ask for it," the cover was of two outthrust wrists, gashed and bloodied by razor. On the back it credited Courtney as the brains behind the cover concept.

The EP contained two live version of songs from "Live Through This" (performed on British radio in November of 1991) and three cover songs—from the Wipers, the Germs and Velvet Underground. The lack of new music did nothing to dispel the rumor that Kurt wrote her music.

She cared, but not that much. Courtney was getting bored with the music world. It was time to return to the stage, in the manner in which she'd dreamed of overtaking it originally.

Around then, Courtney called me.

CHAPTER 18

Another Chance to Have Tea
(September 1995)

"I WANT TO KNOW WHAT YOU KNOW," WAS THE MESSAGE Courtney left on my voice mail that September. She added that she was in a Hollywood hotel, checked in under the name Blanche DuBois.

When I called Courtney back, her questions were the same as they'd been the year before. She wanted to know, once again, all I knew about Kurt's last week.

Immediately, my speech problems emerged, this time coupled with repetition. "I-I-I tried to hook you up with someone who knew more," I said about a dozen times in that conversation.

She wasn't ready to know back then, she told me. But now she was.

Well, I had nothing new to report, I told her. Just more of the same: Kurt was buying too much heroin, being told to leave, sometimes needing to be carried out.

But while she was on the line I told her that a publisher had approached me to write a book about her, and I asked what she thought about that.

She paused briefly. "Go ahead," she finally said. "Everyone else is." She added, however, that she wouldn't authorize it.

Nevertheless, we made plans to meet at Seattle's Four Seasons Olympic Hotel for high tea in the Garden Court the following week. I wasn't surprised, though, when Courtney returned to Seattle and did not call me to set up a specific time.

By the time Courtney returned from Lollapalooza in September, something had changed. The thrill was gone from her music; she was only performing for the money, like any other job. She had a renewed love: acting. She'd taken music as far as she wished to go, and now she wanted to use her impressive visibility and her household name to vault herself up onto the big screen. She wanted to get into acting again. She described it as "a whole new way to kick ass." Courtney had inched her way into the movies bit by bit. Although she'd backed out of *Tank Girl* in the wake of Kurt's death, she'd put together the sound track for the movie, and her compilation had received favorable reviews. She'd successfully played a waitress in *Feeling Minnesota.* But now she needed a big part, something that would make her memorable.

And it so happened that Oliver Stone was putting together a new project for Columbia Pictures, to be directed by Milos Forman, who had won Best Director Oscars for *Amadeus* and *One Flew Over the Cuckoo's Nest.* The new movie was about Larry Flynt's life. Woody Harrelson was already cast as the *Hustler* publisher who'd been paralyzed when shot by an opponent of pornography. They were looking for someone to play Larry's wife, Althea, a junkie-stripper who'd contracted AIDS.

The role was sought after by a host of actresses, from Julia Roberts to Patricia Arquette. But the producers were interested in having Courtney audition for the part as well.

Of course there was a catch—a big one.

To be in the movies, she had to stay clean.

And besides, before she could focus fully on pursuing

her acting career, Courtney had a few legal battles to fight.

Thank God for the I'm-Mrs.-Mature suit. Courtney would soon get her money's worth from the black designer outfit she'd first worn to court in Australia. She brought it out again in early October for the Kathleen Hanna assault charge.

Courtney flew back to Seattle for her court appearance. She was worried. She went for the grown-up look, donning the suit, and did her hair in the same style she'd used for her court appearance in Australia. She took Frances to the trial, which was *the* big news in Ephrata, Washington. The lawn outside the courthouse was littered with press. She flipped the bird to the media as she walked into the courthouse, but apparently the judge was already in chambers and missed it.

Courtney pleaded guilty. She said she was sorry for hitting Kathleen Hanna, her eyes wide-open and her chin propped on her hands like an apologetic child.

And it worked. The judge fined her $285 and sentenced her a year in jail—to be suspended if she took an anger-management class and didn't threaten or become violent with anyone for two years.

Immediately, people in the Seattle music scene began thinking of ways to goad her into making a threat.

In November she flew to Orlando to be tried for a battery charge brought by two fans who'd been punched at a show in March. The charge was bogus: mosh pit injuries seemed redundant.

But Courtney put on a show for the jurors. So heavily sedated that she had to be physically aided into the courtroom, she reportedly tossed back more pills once she got there. And then, in mid-trial, she "pssted" the claimants' lawyers, making such strange hissing noises to get their attention that she seemed to be trying out for the role of the demon in *The Exorcist*. "Hey, are you the prosecutors?" she whispered huskily. "Well, can I be O.J., and you can play Christopher Darden?" She laughed to herself, eyes rolling back in her head.

Although she acted like it was all a farce, she was freaked.

Whenever anything of a legal nature happened, it pushed the Frances button. Courtney became panicked over the thought that the authorities would yank away her child, find her an unfit mother again. That was the wound that had never healed, the scab that was picked off every time Courtney had another scrape with the law. But questions of her ability to be a good parent always reemerged when she appeared in front of the camera slurring and unable to walk on her own.

When she flew back to Seattle during a break in the hearing, she was interviewed by Barbara Walters. She bought new furniture, had the house looking lovely, and dressed in a manner more befitting a corporate type than a rock 'n' roll screamer. But her hysteria showed through. Courtney was entirely upset about her court appearance and was convinced she was going to be crucified, forced to stand trial for all of rock and roll. She cried about it over the phone so much, the makeup artists had to redo her makeup several times, and she kept Barbara Walters waiting for an hour while she sobbed about the trial awaiting her, where she was convinced she would be all but burned at the stake.

Back in Florida, where she'd checked into a hotel under the name Mary Magdalene, her fake name had been publicized by the press. Hundreds of message of support arrived, and even more support was winging her way: after another day in court, during which Courtney pounded the table to make her point, the judge dismissed the case before even hearing the defense. Courtney's behavior, the judge reasoned, was the type expected at rock concerts, especially when one was in the mosh pit.

Courtney was the victor again. She hugged her lawyer, cried, and on her way out signed autographs and kissed fans. The southern state was a violent one, she noted to the press. "Even the state of Florida is shaped like a gun."

Now she could focus more fully on getting the part of Althea Flynt. Courtney fiercely wanted the part opposite Woody Harrelson. She lost twenty pounds in a month. She dropped a bundle to get new Hollywood teeth—like Tom Cruise's, she said. She took her diamonds out of her security box to dazzle Oliver Stone at the screen test. She memorized Althea's lines in three days.

But as much as she wanted the part, to make the leap to movies, she faced the hurdle of a drug test. Prozac, Xanax, Valium—any pills prescribed by her doctor were acceptable if detected in her body. But heroin or cocaine found in the urine would prevent her from being insured, or bonded, while making the film. And without bonding, major studios typically won't hire an actor for a movie.

The film's people refused to waive the pee test requirement. The test was designed to detect traces of any drug that wasn't on the approved list. Even drugs used weeks before could be traced.

And so she hopped a night flight to New York. Worried about the test she'd be required to take in two days, she packed her jewels and her clothes and her script and her cell phone and her laptop and lots of magazines to read in-flight.

But once in New York, she took the screen test and the drug test, and breezed through both. The next week the insurance company asked for a hair sample to analyze for drugs. Drugs stay recorded in the hair for the lifetime of the strand.

Courtney balked. The procedure was rare—often used simply to discourage a film house from using an actor.

She instead agreed to another urine test. She passed again.

Still the insurers were worried. Most of the power players didn't want to deal with the off-screen theatrics of the infamous Courtney Love. Life was looking as if it might take a big U-turn once again.

By the time Thanksgiving rolled around, Courtney was convinced she'd lost the part.

It wasn't easy being a rock star whose reputation was such that even gondoliers in Venice, when they heard of Seattle, had been known to sigh, "Ah, the home of Courtney Love!" One of the more absurd aspects of her fame was the toll it took on relationships. Outside of her band, Frances and Dean, Courtney's relations had sunk to a new low. She was so friendless, and so out of touch with the people who loved her—and some, particularly in Portland, still did—that she wasn't exactly swimming with invitations for Thanksgiving dinner.

She couldn't or wouldn't go to her mother's, where her siblings often spent the holidays. The topic of Courtney was never even broached when family friends were present. A picture of the firstborn didn't hang in the hallway with the rest of the clan.

She wasn't even on speaking terms with her father, Hank Harrison. He'd been an ongoing headache for the previous year and a half, and admitting to *Inside Edition* that he thought Courtney would go the way of Janis Joplin. "She's so intelligent," Hank Harrison said. "All she has to do is snap out of it. If she comes to see me, I'll take care of her." Courtney had no desire to reconnect with "BioDad." The month before he'd said unkind words about her when interviewed by MTV. Hank had had legal trouble when his three unleashed pit bulls attacked a neighbor and her dog. He blamed that problem on his daughter. He would never have had to get the dogs, he explained, if Courtney hadn't broken into his place years before. And worse, he was writing a book. About Kurt. "Courtney was not supportive enough of Kurt," he informed the media, though he'd hardly been in contact with her during their marriage and had been banned from backstage access at Nirvana shows. In fact, he'd never even met Kurt.

Courtney hadn't exactly been kind to him, either. Although he'd written seven books, she continually described him to the press as a mere toady of the Grateful Dead, much to his chagrin.

"I'm very disappointed in her," Hank told me after I

Melissa Rossi

tracked him down in Palo Alto. He didn't believe her album had actually sold over a million copies, maintaining the sales figures were inflated; he thought she had bought Hole's Best Album of the Year award. He said he was self-publishing not only a book about Kurt, which he had written, but also another called *Inside Courtney Love,* in which a psychiatrist analyzes his daughter's behavior. "After Kurt died, she should have talked with me and strategized," he said. "I have a big mouth too." Instead, she shut him out, and he was mad.

Her former best friend Amanda de Cadenet had fallen off the friends list as well. In the spring and into the summer Amanda and Courtney had been so tight that Courtney had interviewed her for *Interview* magazine while they lay in bed watching Keanu Reeves movies and waiting for Gus Van Sant to show up for dinner, even though the house was nearly empty of food. "We could serve Gus a ham sandwich and say 'This is for *Cowgirls'*—a reference to Gus's movie *Even Cowgirls Get the Blues,* Courtney had quipped; in fact, when the director arrived, they brought in Chinese takeout, and the six people present passed around the two plates of food with the two forks.

In another demonstration of how much she liked and admired Amanda, Courtney had helped fix her up with a new lover, since Amanda had recently left her husband, John Taylor of Duran Duran. Courtney the matchmaker brought her together with Billy Corgan in much the same way that, years before, she'd tried to match Kat up with Kurt. And though Kat and Kurt didn't work out, Amanda and Billy did—at least for a night. Predictably, Courtney immediately became jealous; she'd never shown herself to be someone who could share. At one of Lollapalooza's next stops, she introduced "Violet," the number she'd written about Billy, as a song about "the jerk that my friend is fucking." After Amanda came into the picture, Courtney only wanted Billy more, occasionally at least considering marriage to him. And though Amanda had been helpful in introducing Courtney to

Hollywood VIPs—taking Courtney to Jack Nicholson's among other things—Amanda was clearly reaping more from their friendship than Courtney was. Hiring ten publicists could not have yielded more dramatic results than showing up with Ms. Love at a high-profile bash.

By the end of the fall, Amanda was on the nix list.

Courtney was also on the outs with Kat Bjelland. "She should never have broken up with me," Courtney lamented. There were people in Portland from the old days who'd remained true to her, who tried to contact her, but she rarely made time for most of them. Other grrrl bands such as Adickdid, who Courtney had previously asked to open for Hole shows and had even put up at her house, had found in the past year that when they greeted her she acted as though she didn't know them. Courtney had fired one of her aides when some members of the entourage had a bout with drugs; the employee was apparently blamed for the reintroduction of heroin into the group.

Courtney surrounded herself with a coterie of soothsayers, even approaching hipster stargazer Rob Brezsny, who declined to provide his astrological services, but they weren't friends; like Dean Mathiesen, they were her employees.

She hadn't remarried; she occasionally fell into reverie about Trent, but he definitely was not available to her. Though she seriously considered wedding Billy, he still wasn't divorced. And she'd pretty much blown any budding anything with Jeff Buckley after the *Hamlet* disaster.

Her relationship with other bands was still iffy at best: Candlebox, an all-male Seattle band, had appeared that fall on the cover of Seattle's premier rock rag *The Rocket,* in Courtney drag, complete with blond wig and tiara. Inside, the lead singer was shown in a black bra, supposedly one of Courtney's that she had left at a photo shoot. Though she was referred to only as "she-whose-name-we-dare-not-speak," at least they hadn't sniped at her in print. Courtney thought the photos were amusing.

Not so with the slams that flew from Tabitha Soren about the MTV interview where Courtney burst in on Madonna. Tabitha snarled at Courtney via her syndicated column for—of all things—Ms. Love's lack of designer clothes. Madonna dissed Courtney's appearance during her MTV interview as a public service announcement discouraging drug abuse. "I think she's supremely talented," Madonna told Bob Guccione Jr. in a cover story for *Spin.* "But I think that drugs have destroyed her brain, or they are slowly destroying her. I am fascinated by her, but the same way I am by somebody who's got Tourette's syndrome walking in Central Park."

Courtney herself likened the incident to a scene from *Valley of the Dolls*—specifically the part where Neely O'Hara gets in a catfight with a wig-wearing older actress.

For all the unkind words being flung at her, Courtney herself was winning the barb-throwing contest. Through the summer, she'd continued tossing daggers at Mary Lou Lord, calling her "the Stalker," portraying Mary Lou's friendship with Kurt as little more than a blow job in the back of a dark van.

In a piece Courtney wrote for the November *Spin,* describing her fun-filled summer, she shrugged off Bikini Kill, whom she had listed as one of her favorite groups in 1992, as "not really . . . a band. [They] don't really play and they don't really write songs." She gave her version of the clocking ordeal, saying Kathleen Hanna, whom she described as "my husband's worst enemy in the world," had made a comment about Frances Bean being hidden away "in a closet with an I.V."

Her shove-off of former best friend and Academy Awards date Amanda de Cadenet was only hinted at in the *Spin* article, with Courtney writing that she'd had "a horrific incident" with a "perennial extra/wanna-be actress," whom she described as "pathological and sociopathic."

Courtney still had a few friends, some of whom

occupied very high places in the media, from MTV executives to editors and writers at the music mags. Yet, despite her protective pals and power publicist Pat Kingsley, Courtney's relationship with the media was getting rocky again, in part because she couldn't calm down and shut up.

The kid gloves had come off when dealing with the widow, and the boxing gloves put on. Jabs were flying at Courtney, who had set herself up as a stumbling target when she had to be helped into the Orlando courtroom and when she turned up screaming at New York clubs such as Bowery Bar, demanding to be let in after she was kicked out for bothering the other guests.

"Courtney Love has officially overstayed her welcome," wrote *Entertainment Weekly* in fall of '92. "When the perenially unstable Hole frontwoman returned last year, determined to rock even harder despite her husband's suicide, you couldn't help but root for her. What a difference a year makes. . . . [P]erhaps it's time Courtney went back into mourning."

Insight magazine put her on the cover—holding a gun—and ran an interview with the private investigator Tom Grant, whose murder-plot theory was now showing up in the mainstream press.

Request magazine put out an issue with a cover photo of Courtney with a red slash through it, above the headline "Love Free Zone." Although it promised that "Mrs. Cobain's Name Does Not Appear Anywhere in This Issue," the magazine wouldn't have been complete without mentioning her, under the headline "Who's Over," with a long list of why they believed Courtney was a has-been. Instead of using her name they merely substituted the red-slashed picture in their eleven-point list of why Courtney "Is, you know, like, over"—which included the punch, "Now that Kurt's dead, [Courtney] will have to write her own material."

She made Blackburn's 1995 "Worst Dressed List," taking the number-two spot to drag-happy shock jock Howard Stern. *Playboy* approached her to pose for its centerfold, but laughed off the singer's demand to be paid one million dollars for the job. (In a subsequent profile of Courtney, the magazine ran an ugly caricature instead of a photo.)

A skateboard designer emblazoned boards with the image of Courtney—shooting Kurt; when she got wind of it, Courtney reportedly called federal agents to retrieve the designs.

And when there weren't enough headlines to satisfy her hunger for constant attention, Courtney got on the phone and called the local radio stations. The day O.J. Simpson was acquitted, she was on a Seattle station adding her insights, noting among other things that she'd known a few African-American men, and they were all drag queens. She called up another station, crying about what to do with Kurt's ashes, which remained in a "froo-froo bag" in her bedroom, where she often talked to them. "Nobody will take him," she moaned, and she wasn't going to make Kurt's final resting place Aberdeen, the town he hated, or Olympia, where he'd once lived.

"What if Kathleen [Hanna] goes and pees on his grave?" she asked.

Courtney also clarified her interpretation of the court ruling on the Bikini Kill singer. "I can't hit anybody in Grant County [where she'd punched Kathleen at Lollapalooza], but I could clock her again in Seattle."

Rarely her own best PR agent, she often came off as laughable. But those who laughed did so with derision and dismissal. At least she had Barbara Walters on her side. Courtney's interview would be part of the taped program *1995's Ten Most Fascinating People,* to be shown in December.

And Barbara Walters wasn't the only one who was cheering Courtney on. So was Milos Forman, the director of the Larry Flynt film.

CHAPTER 19

A Happy Ending
(December 1995)

"I GOT THE MOVIE! I GOT THE MOVIE! I GOT THE MOVIE!"

Courtney just had to call and tell someone her good news. She'd landed the role of Althea Flynt in the Larry Flynt movie. So she chose a Seattle radio station known as "The End," calling from her limo on the way back from the airport to announce the news on the air.

Milos Forman maintained that of all the actresses who had tried out for the role, Courtney was the only one who had love in her eyes. Oliver Stone wasn't so keen on the choice, but Forman kept pushing, and finally suitable compromises were reached. She would only get $1 million, instead of the figure, almost three times greater, that had been considered initially. Since they were having such a difficult time bonding her, she'd be forced to undergo weekly urine tests for drugs, and her money would be put in escrow, ensuring that if she died or didn't show during the movie's filming, they could afford to hire a replacement.

Oliver Stone, whom she continually addressed as "sir," had her crying within minutes of his first official meeting with her as a costar.

But she got the part, and she immediately called the

radio station KNDD to crow about her victory. Shortly thereafter she had more offers, including potential parts in movies with Brad Pitt and Tom Cruise.

Then the Barbara Walters' "Ten Most Fascinating People of 1995" aired. Wedged between segments with house speaker Newt Gingrich and actor Christopher Reeves, Courtney's interview showed the singer looking absolutely beautiful, as she daintily sipped tea. And she effectively pulled much of America's heartstrings as she cried for the camera.

Courtney denied being on drugs and denied doing them in front of Frances. "My God, what a question," she said to Barbara, seeming shocked. The singer informed the viewing audience that she was a really good poet and that her band Hole did not suck. "You wouldn't be talking to me if we sucked," she said, forcing the interviewer to ask her to clarify that "not sucking" meant the band was really good.

Courtney broke down when asked about Kurt's death, sobbing that she blamed herself and wished she'd done "eight thousand million things" to prevent Kurt from killing himself. She also explained her way of purging her own death wish. "I think that's what the stage-diving was about," she said. "Kill me, crucify me, get me, come on, tear my breasts off, take off my underwear . . . take out my hair, break my arms, break my teeth."

But the most wrenching moment occurred when Barbara asked Courtney if she was all right. Smiling through her tears, Courtney answered, "No, I'm not all right."

The segment closed with Frances sitting on her bed wearing an askew tiara, while Courtney strummed on a toy guitar, singing "Twinkle, twinkle, little star, how I wonder where you are"—an obvious reference to Kurt.

The hipsters may have rolled their eyes and dubbed her "the weeping widow," but much of the viewing audience was intrigued. Calls flooded the show the next day commenting on Courtney. By the time the show was broadcast, Courtney was just fine, having beaten the

Orlando rap that had been troubling her at the time of the taping. A few days after the program aired, she packed up her bags and her band and flew to New Orleans to start and finish work on her next album.

The band rented a mansion across from *Interview with the Vampire* author Anne Rice, and a few blocks from her former crush, Trent Reznor. Despite setting a room on fire (her candles again the cause) and being assaulted by guards while she was signing autographs at a show by punkers Green Day, Courtney and the band finished composing the entire album in two weeks.

On the flight back to Seattle, the bag that contained the newly written songs was lost; but not to worry, she promptly hired a detective to track it down.

Once back in the Northwest, she took Frances to see *The Nutcracker*—a most Mommy thing to do; when they went backstage, the ballerinas swarmed around Courtney, asking for her autograph.

Courtney also came to a truce with Nirvana's Dave Grohl. She gave $100,000 to the private investigator looking into the murder of Seattle musician Mia Zapata (just in time for the donation to count as a tax break). She made plans to show Kurt's work at museums across the country. And she set about tending to her latest romantic possibility: Gavin Rossdale, lead singer for the new rock band, Bush. This romance, rumor had it, could work.

And that's the dance of Love, flipping from Courtney the destroyer who leaves burned-up buildings and frazzled minds in her trail, to Courtney the creator who can fill notebooks with lyrics and movie ideas overnight; from Courtney the contemptible to Courtney the absolutely amazing. She's the picture of resilience; even when she plunges over the edge, she quickly reemerges seeming only slightly dazed by the fall.

Given her life thus far, Courtney Love would have been a more likely candidate to be a prostitute-junkie. She could by now be dead or, at best, a bag lady living under a bridge, hissing at all who come near. Instead she's one of the most compelling studies in human nature to rise out of the twentieth century.

Just as she commands the stage with her band, she commands it in life, which she lives as if she'd been cast in a myth, or a multi-star, multi-million-dollar musical melodrama.

These days Courtney Love isn't just the loud, obnoxious force to contend with that she's been for most of her life. Courtney is an icon.

For good reasons. And not just the obvious ones—that she's a rock star who married a rock star, or a media manipulator or a nonstop bad girl. Not even her talent, brains, looks, or sense of humor alone would rate her this distinction.

Those are all factors in her iconization, granted. But the reason she's so hard to ignore, and lends herself to icon status, is that she embodies so many issues of the late twentieth century.

After all, she studied the roles of the pop-culture plays, movies, and books of the sixties and seventies, from *A Streetcar Named Desire* to *Valley of the Dolls,* and turned their characters into her own. Courtney is a walking compilation piece who mirrors contemporary American life—from the pill-popping to the star worship, from the networking to the simultaneous search for power, money, and meaning in a heroless, spiritually bereft society, where one is judged on looks, possessions, job, and dollars.

Her marriage to Kurt Cobain illustrated the plight of the modern woman torn between the role of wife-mother and a compulsion to find her own identity; Courtney's need for independence was coupled with her chronic need to be coupled. She has trampled over all barriers set before her, fiercely blazing a trail through territory known to few women before, but she played her game by the old rules, bowing to the belief that to be powerful a woman must be pretty, and Courtney modified her looks and molded her body each step of the way. Her own brand of feminism included battling other women with her fists and her words. She creates and subtracts, she gives and she steals, she's the epitome of candor, yet she often lies about little things, such as her age—by one year.

Almost anything that can be said of Courtney, the opposite is also true. She's the suicidal cockroach who could survive a world war while battling the war in her own head. She's the will to create locked arm-in-arm with the will to destroy. Her fifteen minutes have been up for the last ten years.

For all her flaws, Courtney above all is an inspirational story. She wriggled free from the grip of addiction, she wrestled with alienation, she transformed anger—often directed at her—and proved that if people keep trying they can get what they want. It may not come when it's desired, or exactly how it's desired, and the goals, once reached, may not bring happiness. But they can be attained; despite what the naysayers scream from the sidelines, wishes can come true.

And with all lights ahead of her shining very green, Courtney has once again emerged as one of this era's most remarkable people, a woman who trips over herself, who's crashed many times, but who continues to pick herself up, smear on some lipstick, and carry on with her dreams. Powered by insecurity, relentless drive, and considerable genius, Courtney Love is, and will continue to be, a star. A star who keeps shooting out of the ashes.